Photograph Credits

Page 2:

These French cotton and silk furnishing samples from 1914 are roller-printed in the same pattern but in different colors. The expense of designing and printing a pattern is an investment from which the textile manufacturer demands as large a return as possible, and one way to increase sales is to print a design in a range of color combinations. In the nineteenth century and early twentieth century, a mill might run the same pattern in a dozen or more color ways. If more than one type of cloth was used—sometimes the same pattern was printed on six different fabrications—a customer would be able to choose from over seventy variations. Some would appear only slightly different from the rest; others would look so dissimilar as to seem like completely different designs. The practice continues today in the textile industry, though usually only three colorings are produced.

Preface

THIS BOOK IS the catalogue for the largest picture show in the world: the images on printed cloth. The authors have been fascinated throughout their lives by patterns like these—Susan Meller within the textile industry, Joost Elffers as a conceptual thinker about design. Patterns appear in all kinds of places throughout the history of visual art. It is on printed cloth, however, that they are most ubiquitous and, at the same time, least noticed, for here they are so common as to be commonplace. In part, *Textile Designs* is intended to redress the injustice of that invisibility, for it is a testament to the creativity of the anonymous artists of the textile industry.

Most of the designs shown here come from the collection of the Design Library, New York. This collection was begun in 1972 as a collaboration between Susan Meller and her late husband, Herbert Meller. They began with gleanings from attics, barns, and country antique shops near their home in Vermont, finding mainly American printed cottons of the nineteenth-century and early-twentieth-century patchwork-quilt variety. But soon their interest took them to Europe, where they were able to acquire collections of pattern books from nineteenth-century textile mills. These swatch books, as they are called, made possible the creation of *Textile Designs*—itself a swatch book of sorts.

The Design Library serves as a resource for designers in the textile industry. Since those designers need to be able to find specific patterns easily, Susan Meller evolved a categorizing system based primarily on motifs. To date, approximately five hundred thousand patterns—the total collection numbers several million—have been filed. This system provided the organizing structure for *Textile Designs*. The book is intended not only as a remarkable collection of images but as a memory bank for designers.

Joost Elffers' interest in recurring patterns was initially formed by modern art and by the rigorous systems of mathematics and logic. These concerns led him to the creation of a book about snowflake patterns, which show that the same basic structure can be infinitely various. But eventually he came to feel that though the patterns he had been investigating had an austere, pure beauty, that kind of beauty was finally bound up with an ideal, and ideals are always unattainable. The repeat patterns of fabric designs, on the other hand, are real and impure, constantly cannibalizing each other, borrowing from anywhere and everywhere. And they exist not only in the mind but in reality, proving their popularity with every new product of the textile industry. In the end, Elffers found that what is real is more beautiful than what is imagined and out of reach.

Elffers began to explore the textile designs of different periods for a series of books in which the patterns are reproduced as collections of gift-wrap papers. The project put him in touch with textile museums in America and Europe and eventually brought him into collaboration with Susan Meller. This book is an iconography of textile motifs, a vocabulary of pattern. Some of the motifs here can be found in the images left to us from prehistory; many go back to classical times or to ancient Egypt. But they are also literally in the fabric of everyday life. What is demonstrated here, in fact, is the extraordinariness of the ordinary. Despite their long experience with repeat patterns, the authors have found that working on this book has changed the way they see—that everyday sights that once barely registered in their consciousness now have a way of suddenly popping into focus.

It was a great luxury for the authors to live with these designs every day for the four years it took to make *Textile Designs*. They consider themselves extremely fortunate to have had the pleasure of playing with two hundred years of textile designs while creating this book.

TEXTILE DESIGNS

Two Hundred Years of European and American Patterns

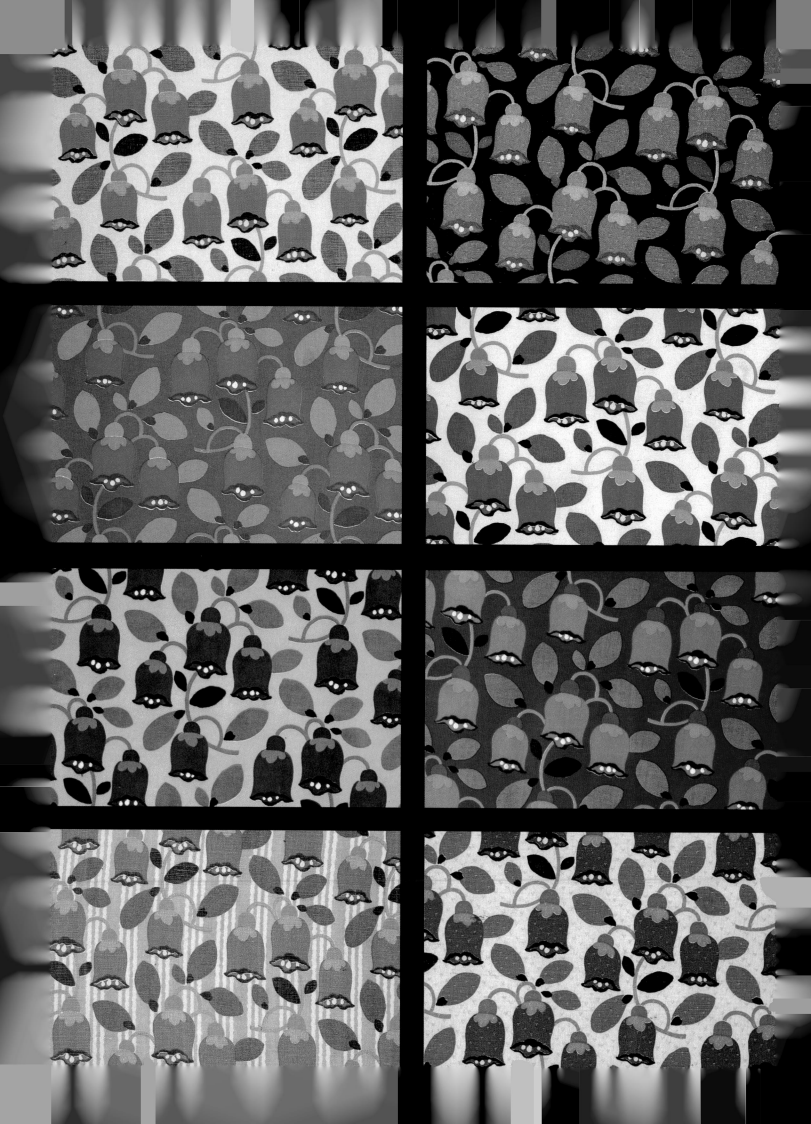

TEXTILE DESIGNS

Two Hundred Years of European and American
Patterns for Printed Fabrics Organized by
Motif, Style, Color, Layout, and Period
1,823 Illustrations in Color

SUSAN MELLER   JOOST ELFFERS

David Frankel, editorial consultant
Photographs by Ted Croner

Harry N. Abrams, Inc., Publishers

PROJECT DIRECTOR: Darlene Geis
EDITOR: Ellyn Childs Allison
DESIGNERS: Joost Elffers, Susan Meller, Darilyn Lowe Carnes, Michael J. Walsh (paperback cover)

LIBRARY OF CONGRESS CATALOGING-IN-PUBLICATION DATA
Meller, Susan.
   Textile Designs: 200 years of European and American patterns for printed fabrics organized by motif, style, color, layout, and period / by Susan Meller and Joost Elffers: photography by Ted Croner.
   p. cm.
   ISBN 0–8109–3853–7 (clothbound) / ISBN 0–8109–2508–7 (pbk.)
   1. Textile design – Themes, motifs. 2. Textile printing.
I. Elffers, Joost. II. Croner, Ted. III. Title.
NK9500.M45 1991
746.6'2041 – dc20   90–48073

Textile Designs Digital, the royalty-free CD-ROM version of this book, is available from The Design Library.
No textile designs may be reproduced without written permission from The Design Library, P.O. Box 31, Cold Spring, N.Y. 10516.
E-mail: info@design-library.com

Paperback edition published in 2002 by Harry N. Abrams, Incorporated, New York.

Clothbound edition published in 1991 by Harry N. Abrams, Inc.

Printed and bound in Japan
10 9 8 7 6 5 4 3 2 1

Harry N. Abrams, Inc.
100 Fifth Avenue
New York, N.Y. 10011
www.abramsbooks.com

Abrams is a subsidiary of
LA MARTINIÈRE GROUPE

Acknowledgments

We would like to give our very special thanks to the following people:

David Frankel, whose way with words was invaluable in helping us write the text

Ted Croner, who managed to keep his sense of humor and keen focus while shooting more than 2,000 photos

Susan Birnbaum, who gallantly typed enough revisions to stuff a mattress

Andreas Landshoff, whose belief in the book and personal efforts helped make it into an international publication

Darilyn Lowe, Ellyn Allison, and all the other people at Harry N. Abrams, Inc., who contributed to the publication of this book

Nicoletta Lanati and Osvaldo Santi, Agnes Prevot, and Angelica Rösner, who so generously and conscientiously translated the short texts into Italian, French, and German, respectively

All our friends, family, and colleagues who gave us the benefit of their enthusiasm, advice, and knowledge

And last, but not least, our project director, Darlene Geis, who "discovered" the Design Library/Loft in an article in *Women's Wear Daily,* suggested a book, introduced the coauthors, and stood firmly behind *Textile Designs* all the way

Contents

KEY TO CAPTIONS

c.	circa
C	century
BP	block-printed
CP	copperplate-printed
PP	perrotine-printed
RP	roller-printed
SP	screen-printed
A	apparel
AYG	apparel yard goods
YG	yard goods
HF	home furnishings
HFYG	home-furnishing yard goods

scale: The designs are reproduced
    at percentages of their
    original size. For example:
    100% = same size
    110% = enlarged 10%
     90% = reduced 10%

Whenever some of the information
is missing from a caption, the
reader should assume that those
details are unknown.

Explanation of Terms

The specialized terms and their abbreviations used in the picture captions are explained below. A key to all the abbreviations in the captions is printed on the contents page.

BLOCK-PRINTED (BP). Block printing is among the earliest forms of textile printing. Among the oldest existing examples is a child's tunic of the fourth century A.D. from a burial site in Upper Egypt; however, it is known that printing blocks were used in India during the fourth century B.C. By the late Middle Ages, block printing was an established trade in Europe, particularly in Italy and Germany, and during the eighteenth century and early nineteenth century, the craft became a very prosperous industry. The United States saw little commercial block printing through most of the eighteenth century, but by 1774 the John Hewson and Bedwell & Walters printworks were both operating near Philadelphia. The blocks were made in different woods for different purposes: boxwood and holly for small-scale, finely detailed patterns; pear for borders; walnut and lime for large-scale prints. The design stood out in relief on the carved wood. Since the different colors occupy different shapes in a design, separate blocks had to be carved for each color. Then the cloth was stretched tight on a long padded table. The block face was pressed against a dye-saturated woolen sieve, then applied to the cloth. A hefty blow with a wooden mallet to the back of the block transferred the design. Pins called pitch pins were nailed into each corner of the block. After every stroke of the mallet, the printer moved the block to the next undyed space on the cloth. The pitch pins helped him to line up the successive impressions. In addition, in a technique called pinning in England and picotage in France, small brass pins were hammered into the block to create dots of various sizes for fine detailing. These pins could withstand the printer's repeated blows with the mallet better than finely carved wood. Block printing is largely obsolete today. But it is still used on a very limited scale for expensive home-furnishing fabrics and silk foulards, particularly in England.

COPPERPLATE-PRINTED (CP). By 1765 Robert Jones of Old Ford and the firm of Bromley Hall in Middlesex, England, and Francis Nixon of Nixon and Company, in Drumcondra, Ireland, were all producing copperplate-printed textiles on a regular basis. In France, Christophe-Philippe Oberkampf was probably the first to install a copperplate press, in 1770. The procedure was as follows. The design was engraved on a flat copper plate, which was then well rubbed with printing dye. Next the dye was wiped off the surface, remaining only in the incised lines of the engraving. Cloth was then laid over it and extreme pressure was applied by means of a mechanical press, in order to transfer the design to the cloth. The first copperplates were quite large (those used at the Oberkampf factory were 45 inches long by 27½ inches wide), allowing a designer to work with large-scale patterns. (The blocks used in block printing, on the other hand, could be no bigger than the printer could comfortably manage by hand.) This new technique gave rise to a new style of print, the scenic toile, which depicted finely engraved images designed by master artists.

ROLLER-PRINTED (RP). The first mechanized fabric-printing machine to use engraved metal rollers was patented by Thomas Bell, a Scotsman, in 1783. Two years later, when it was put into service at the English printworks of Livesay, Hargreaves, Hall, and Company, near Preston, the six-color roller printer did the daily work of about forty hand-block printers. A similar machine installed in the Oberkampf mill at Jouy-en-Josas in 1797 could print more than 5,000 yards of cloth a day, compared to the hand-blocked output of between 30 and 100 yards a day per printer. (Production varied according to the number of hours worked, the printer's skill, the number of colors in the design, and the width of the cloth. Oberkampf considered that a good hand-block printer would produce 25 ells—1 ell = 1.18 meters or about 3 feet 10¾ inches—of four-color cloth a day, about 32½ yards.) By the 1820s, most Western mills were using roller printers. And by 1836, American mills alone were turning out about 120,000,000 yards of printed cloth a year. The design was transferred to a copper cylinder by means of a pantograph, whose diamond point cut through the acid-resistant varnish with which the cylinder was coated. When the cylinder was rotated in an acid bath, the exposed lines of the pattern were etched into the copper roller. The printing press ran cloth under the engraved rollers in one long continuous ribbon. Since the late 1950s, most rollers have been engraved by a photographic process that eliminates the need for a skilled engraver. Modern machines may be able to print up to eighteen different colors at a time, but to avoid the expense of engraving so many rollers, and of running the machinery with so complex a setup, most prints use no more than eight colors. The roller printer made textile printing the first fully mechanized industry and put it at the forefront of the industrial revolution. Modern roller printers can turn out around 1,200 yards of cloth an hour. But the method is more expensive than screen printing, which has largely superseded it.

PERROTINE-PRINTED (PP). The perrotine press, invented by Louis-Jérôme Perrot of Rouen in 1834, mechanized everything about block printing except the blocks themselves, which still had to be carved by hand. Besides printing several colors at once, the machines soaked the sieves with color, transferred the color to the wood, stamped the blocks on the cloth, and moved the cloth forward to take the next impression. The method was faster and more accurate than block printing by hand: covering the entire width of the cloth in one operation, it increased the rate of production by 250 percent. But it restricted the size of the vertical repeat to 5½ inches and the number of colors to four. A perrotine-printed pattern has the precision of machine-made goods, but the carving of the blocks introduces a handcrafted look. A perrotine-printed design can be difficult to distinguish from either a block-printed or a roller-printed one.

SCREEN-PRINTED (SP). Screen printing resembles the ancient device of the stencil. In hand-screening, a fine-mesh silk cloth tightly stretched on a frame receives the design. The pattern is defined by painting out the background with a protective varnish. The color is then applied with a squeegee, which presses it through the screen onto the cloth below. Each color requires a separate screen. Most screen printing now uses a photographic process to "engrave" the design on the screen. Commercial silk-screen printing by hand began in the 1920s. Most popular in France, it was a useful technique for short runs of high-fashion fabrics because it was faster than wood-block printing and cheaper than roller printing. (The economies of scale made a roller printer more practical for longer pattern runs.) The bright colors and freely drawn patterns of the "art silks" then in style were also better suited to screen printing than to other means. By the 1930s, screen printing by hand had spread to a number of European countries and to the United States. By the 1950s, many Western mills were capable of fully automated screen printing with flatbed machines. This method was fast—producing 350 yards an hour—and could deliver up to twenty colors. It was particularly accurate in capturing free, painterly brushstrokes from an artist's rendering. Furthermore, the machinery was relatively inexpensive to set up and operate. Yet during the mid-1960s, flatbed screen printing in its turn was challenged by the rotary-screen printer, which essentially transferred the screen from silk to fine metal mesh shaped into cylinders. The new technology combined the roller printer's continuous high-speed registration and the clean, uncrushed color of the pressureless flatbed screen.

PAPER IMPRESSION. A paper impression is a form of printer's proof. After the block, plate, or screen is engraved, but before the cloth is printed, a copy of the design is run on paper to check for any irregularities. The results of this long-standing practice are often preserved in the mills' pattern books and are an invaluable source of documentation. They are the first visual record of a pattern and may be marked with the pattern number, the name of the engraver, and the date. The ultimate thrill for a textile scholar is to find an original painting, a paper impression, and a sample of printed cloth all in the same pattern.

GOUACHE ON PAPER. Gouache, an opaque, water-soluble paint, is the textile designer's traditional medium. Of all the pigments on paper, its flat, saturated color most closely resembles the look of textile dyes. Gouache is easy to work with, flows smoothly from the brush, dries quickly, and allows fine shading and blending of color. Preparing the painted design is the first step in the production of printed textiles. This pattern, painted in repeat to the manufacturer's specifications, is sent to the mill to be engraved.

DYES. The fabric designer's dyes are not the printer's: they are thin, translucent, water-soluble inks for use on paper. Their colors are intense, luminescent, and vibrant, but often seductively deceptive, for it is hard to capture them on cloth. They began to be used by designers in the 1950s, when bright-colored prints were in vogue.

APPAREL YARD GOODS (AYG). These textiles are printed in continuous lengths and marketed by the yard to be sewn up into clothing. They may be sold directly to the public in retail (over-the-counter) fabric stores, or they may go to apparel manufacturers, or to jobbers—the textile industry's wholesale, "to-the-trade-only" middlemen. In the eighteenth and nineteenth centuries, printed cloth was sold by the piece rather than the bolt. A piece varied in length according to the region and the year. For example, in France around 1800, a piece averaged between 13 and 22 yards. The term "piece goods" is still used interchangeably with "yard goods" within the industry.

APPAREL (A). Not all apparel patterns are sold by the yard. Scarves and handkerchiefs, for example, though they may be printed on a continuous length of cloth, are eventually finished and marketed as individual squares.

HOME-FURNISHING YARD GOODS (HFYG). Designers conceive these patterns not as clothing but as interior decor—upholstery and drapery fabric, bed and table linen, and toweling, for example. In general, home-furnishing prints tend to be larger in scale and repeat than apparel designs, and, in order to accommodate the needs of the furniture manufacturers, the cloth is wider than apparel textiles. Home-furnishing fabrics are usually more expensive than apparel goods. They often employ more colors, requiring an average of twelve screens rather than the five or six for ready-to-wear, and use a more costly base cloth. One-directional patterns appear more frequently on furnishings yard goods than on apparel. Traditional patterns are easier to sell than adventurous ones, particularly because the buyer is likely to live with the purchase for quite a long time. Home-furnishing prints often strive to suggest not that they are in style but that they have never been out of it.

Introduction

The art that is frankly decorative is the art to live with. It is, of all visible arts, the one art that creates in us both mood and temperament. . . . The harmony that resides in the delicate proportions of lines and masses becomes mirrored in the mind. The repetitions of patterns give us rest. The marvels of designs stir the imagination.

OSCAR WILDE,
"The Critic as Artist"

The Ghost Artist

EVERY YEAR, THE modern textile industry spins out printed cloth by the hundreds of thousands of yards a day. The countless images that wrap our bodies and decorate our homes are in fact seen so often that they take special attention to be seen at all. And the artists who make the patterns for these designs are for the most part anonymous. They are ghost artists. Theirs is the kind of art in which the personality and the ideas of the maker recede so far into the background as to disappear.

A modern painter might resent being compared to the designer of a pink polka dot—even though fine artists and textile designers often arrive at quite similar shapes and forms, and though art has precedents in design at least as often as design follows art. But the painter's canvases are intended to stand up to the long and exacting gaze of the connoisseur. It is the nature of a textile pattern, on the other hand, to duplicate itself endlessly, so that the basic image is lost in a sea of repeats. It is also generally assumed that the fine artist works at a level of ambition and in an emotional and intellectual range that most commercial art just doesn't need. The commercial artist, too, must always aim to please the market (a temptation to which fine artists are, of course, immune). And the textile designer is a link in an industrial production line. What finally appears on cloth has passed through many hands and many machines; it is the rare designer who has much control over the final outcome.

Our purpose in this book is not to argue that the ghost artists of fabric design are the neglected equals of art's innovators. We wouldn't even claim that the patterns collected in this book are "great" in the way museum artworks or, for that matter, rare historical fabrics, are said to be (though some of them impress on any terms). But it needs to be said that in the long history of image making, the value of originality is a fairly recent idea, and a Western one at that. It is only for some few hundred years now that we in the West have valued originality and novelty above all things in art. In fact, we have equated it with freedom. Fabric patterns go back to humanity's earliest times and belong to a much older tradition of symbols, where originality is not an issue.

The Weave of Words

IN SELECTING THE swatches for *Textile Designs*, we tended toward the typical rather than the exceptional. Most of them could easily have been replaced with others; any one design, in fact, may seem trivial, too bright, too bold—having any of the ordinary flaws of the everyday, for we're dealing, after all, with cloth to be worn around the house and to work, cloth to hang in the window and to upholster the couch, as much as about that peacock type of cloth for special occasions that is the everyday's disguise. Yet what an extraordinary collection of images this common cloth turns out to be. Together, cumulatively, these patterns become individual words in a gigantic language of the visual imagination. This book is a kind of dictionary of that language.

Any vocabulary constantly expands and contracts. Words are added by coinage or by import from elsewhere and words are dropped as they become obsolete. But every new word falls into a recognizable category: they are all familiar parts of speech. The pattern vocabulary is likewise vast and illimitable, but the basic grammar, the structure, is finite. In Western fabric design, the parts of speech are florals, geometrics, conversationals, ethnics, and art movements and period styles—the subjects of chapters in this book. And each of these large categories has subcategories, such as roses and sprigs among the florals, or circles and squares among the geometrics. The successful textile designer seeks not to devise something never before imagined but to create a variation on one of these preexisting themes. (Or perhaps not even to do that—a quantity of any season's print fashions are frank borrowings from earlier designs. If a period look has returned to style, its patterns may need a little updating.) It's hard to find a printed cloth that doesn't belong to one of the time-honored genres. The textile designer, in any case, doesn't usually try to expand the basic repertory. It is the tool of the trade, the language that makes speech possible—why try to transcend it? So much can be said with a rose.

It always has been standard procedure in the textile industry to look to existing cloth for ideas. In the ebb and flow of fashion, there is a progression, a dance, that the designer must somehow be able to follow. Too soon is as dangerous as too late. After a couple of seasons of large-scale prints, say, there may be a swing to a "no-print" look of small, unobtrusive geometrics, or of faux-wovens such as printed plaids and textures. The designer must sense the timing of the incoming trend. The next step is often to consult the swatches of earlier days, looking for something that can be modified for the arriving moment—something old that can be recast as new.

The Recycling Wheel

THE PATTERNS OF printed cloth suggest a larger pattern that contains them—what we may call the recycling wheel, which sets the motifs of textile designs on a circular road of eternal return. Nothing disappears, and nothing appears out of nowhere. Just as the individual pattern repeats incessantly over the course of a print run, its motifs are in repeat over the course of the decades. Prints can be thought of as having a temporal dimension: in the family of cloth, every era coexists. So we may also imagine the recycling wheel as a clock face, where all time's hours are visible simultaneously, though the clock's hands only point to one moment in the round. Just as those hands move at different speeds, the motifs come and go in different rhythms. Some are seasonal—every spring brings its flowers, every Christmas its snowmen. Some motifs follow the tides of politics, or of wealth and recession. Some appear rarely, some are always being printed somewhere. None vanishes.

Though any number of styles have come and gone in the two hundred years of mechanical fabric printing, the motifs translated through those styles are continuous. They also predate the modern textile industry, often by millennia. Many of the images in this book have appeared on prehistoric cave walls, in Egyptian hieroglyphs, on Greek pottery, and in pre-Columbian textiles, Islamic mosaics, medieval European tarot cards, Chinese robes, Indian temples, Persian carpets, Celtic manuscripts, Tibetan thankas, as well as on factory-printed cloth. The context changes but the symbol endures, altered only superficially by each artist who handles it—who gives it the characteristics of the new place and time.

A Clash of Symbols

AS THEY PASS through the ages, symbols gather and lose meanings. What was powerful to one culture becomes decorative to another, and what was once decorative may become powerful again, even frightening. The swastika, for example, is found in almost every ancient culture. Its symbolism varied, but it was always mystical and positive. It remained that way for thousands of years until its appropriation by the Nazis. It now conjures up such disturbing associations that we have deliberately chosen to exclude it from this book, even though we had many nineteenth-century examples to choose from. But is it possible to make a neat distinction between what is meaningful and what is decorative? With the turning of the recycling wheel, symbols move in and out of their ability to affect us deeply. Some "strong" symbols we grant special significance, and we may reserve them for special uses. A Christian, for example, is careful with the cross. But crosses appear in every culture, their importance and their content varying. And even as motifs lose their overt power, we make sure to keep them in sight—by making them decorative.

Then we surround ourselves with them. The clothes we wear and dress our children in, the sheets we sleep under, the carpets we walk on, our wall coverings, curtains, furniture—symbols grow over these things like ivy. It's as if textile patterns were an immense library of images waiting for us to attach meaning to them, or as if Jung's idea of the collective unconscious were made literal in this storehouse of shapes. We love to see these motifs, love to see them so much that we cover everything with them, to the point where they become commonplace and disappear—they hide in the light, waiting for the turning of the wheel.

The Swatch Book

THE SWATCH OR pattern book is the annual or seasonal record of a textile mill's production. It contains samples of the mill's designs—perhaps portions of the artists' original painting ("croquis"), perhaps impressions of the designs printed on paper before being printed on cloth, perhaps actual "swatches" (random cuttings of fabric), or perhaps some of all these things. Swatch books are an invaluable record of design history and source of inspiration. Each pattern, repeated perhaps hundreds of thousands of times on the thousands of yards of the print run, goes out into the world to endure history's rough justice. Since only a tiny minority of printed fabrics are considered worth preserving, the cloth eventually wears out and disappears. But the swatch book stays in the shop. Usually, the cutter has made no attempt to preserve the pattern entire or to show how it repeats; yet from this fragment a designer can re-

This pattern book of about 1810–20 from the studio of an
Alsatian textile mill contains mostly Turkey-red designs
painted in gouache. The designs have been pasted in at
random with no consideration as to direction. It is
impossible to determine whether these patterns were ever
actually printed on cloth, but if they were we know that
they would have been block-printed on cotton to be
fashioned into women's clothing. This was a popular look
of the period and a specialty of several Alsatian printworks.

Around the middle of the nineteenth century, mainly in
Paris, businesses were formed to meet a rapidly expanding
international demand for swatches of the latest European
fabrics. Since travel was very time-consuming and
expensive, these firms played a vital role in disseminating
fashion intelligence. They operated as subscription
services, mailing envelopes of swatches (at first loose, later
in booklets) that had been chosen to meet the needs of
particular markets. The subscribers often pasted the pieces
of fabric into large ledgers for ease of retrieval. This
illustration shows one such book. Dating from 1898, it
contains printed cottons and silks that have sometimes
been labeled by the service with the names of the original
manufacturers. One of the first swatch services was
J. Claude Frères of Paris, which supplied the designs in
this example.

create the whole or, rather, can grow an "original" pattern out of a cell of the old. It's as if the swatch were a gene: its offspring have their own individuality, but they also show their ancestry.

A swatch book is a kind of running commentary on its social era, readable in the same way that the layered earth is readable to the archaeologist: each has taken a sensitive impression of historical shifts in climate. But the swatch book is also a tool for recycling textile motifs, which lie in it dormant, waiting for reuse. And since each swatch is not only the pregnant parent of some future design but also a descendant of a design in the past, the swatch book is a kind of family tree of the motifs in the pattern vocabulary—a family tree of the world's symbology. The swatch book often jumbles images from every time and place, exposing the family it describes as quite incestuous. But the promiscuity it so unblushingly records predates the modern mechanical-printing industry. The fleur-de-lis was part of a god's hat in ancient Nineveh before it became the coat of arms of the French monarchy. To study fabric designs is to grow hesitant about assigning any style or motif to a particular region or culture. Clearly it is quite rare to be able to speak of a "pure" style—that isolation is unusual among the aesthetic traditions of the world, which tend to like to talk with one another.

Pattern Politics

THE CONVERSATION HAS continued for thousands of years. The Romans traded with China, and when in the thirteenth century Marco Polo traveled the Silk Road, he was reestablishing an ancient mercantile practice. (It was not by chance that this much-used route between the West and the Orient was named after a fabric.) Cultural exchange, of course, is not always positive or fair. It is impossible, in fact, to discuss printed cloth without talking about the ability of the West, over the last several centuries, to set most of the terms of its dealings with the rest of the world. The plentiful raw materials and large captive markets in the countries that eventually became the colonies played their part in the growth of large-scale industrial textile manufacture in Europe. "Ethnic" images—that is, for the most part, non-Western images (as if Westerners were somehow less ethnic than everyone else)—have made their way abundantly into European and American cloth, and they customarily enter by one of two processes: either the designers are copying an ethnic style in order to mass-produce it and sell it back to its own people more cheaply than they could make it themselves, or they are adapting it for the tastes of the home market. In either case, the design that results is a Western design. If in one sense the symbols in *Textile Designs* live in a kind of intercultural memory, recognizable virtually everywhere, though everywhere interpreted differently, in another sense many of them are products of the particular history of colonialism.

India has a special place in that history, for India is the cradle of the Western textile industry. Indian craftsmen developed sophisticated methods of printing and painting cloth many centuries before Europeans followed their lead. Until the early 1700s, when the French and English uncovered the secret of India's mordant-dye technique, cloth that would stay colorfast in sun and water was imported into Europe from India. This is why so many English words for fabrics and garments are Indian in origin: *bandanna, calico, cashmere, chintz, dungaree, khaki, pajama, seersucker, shawl*. A whole class of prints, the indiennes—an eighteenth-century European craze— was named, understandably, after the source of the fabrics it imitated. Yet who today thinks of chintz's lush florals or a pair of print pajamas as Indian in any way? The recycling wheel is voracious: it spins up images from every country and every age, revolves them in time, and brings them back transformed to the top of the cycle, only to pull them under again and start the process over.

Now this may seem like a description of the workings of twentieth-century commerce. And it's surely true that the efficiency of modern machinery, modern factories, and modern marketing—all once largely localized in the West but now scattered over the globe—has greatly sped up the turning of the recycling wheel. But is a circle Western, or a stripe, or the idea of reproducing a flower or an animal on cloth? Mechanical printing may have altered these traditions, altered them drastically, just by simplifying the making of them, but it did not invent them. The patterns in *Textile Designs* are European and American, but they take their symbols from everywhere, giving them European and American shape.

The Superfluous Necessity

PRACTICALLY, WHAT WE need from cloth is limited. It wraps us from sun, wind, wet, and other people's eyes; it softens furniture, floors, windows. But cloth could do all this and never take a dye. We have a need for the colors and shapes of design, a need for visual richness. All printed textile patterns are an illusion—a surface decoration laid over cloth's weave and structurally unnecessary to it. It was a tenet of modern art that form should follow function and that, as the Austrian architect Adolf Loos wrote in his essay "Ornament and Crime," of 1908, "The evolution of civilization is measured by the removal of ornament from objects of use." In these terms, printed patterns are superfluous. Yet once it was discovered how to make them affordable to everyone, they became a fixture of any day's, any place's, visual scene. (One New Hampshire firm, Cocheco

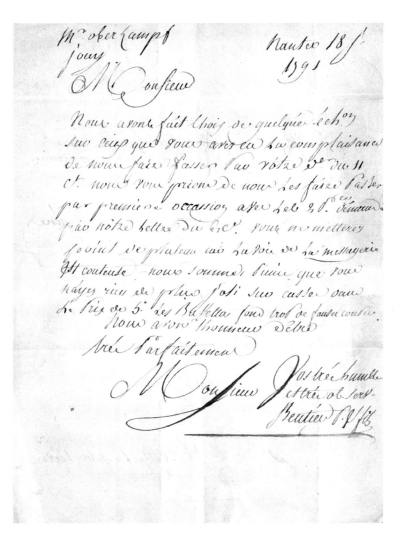

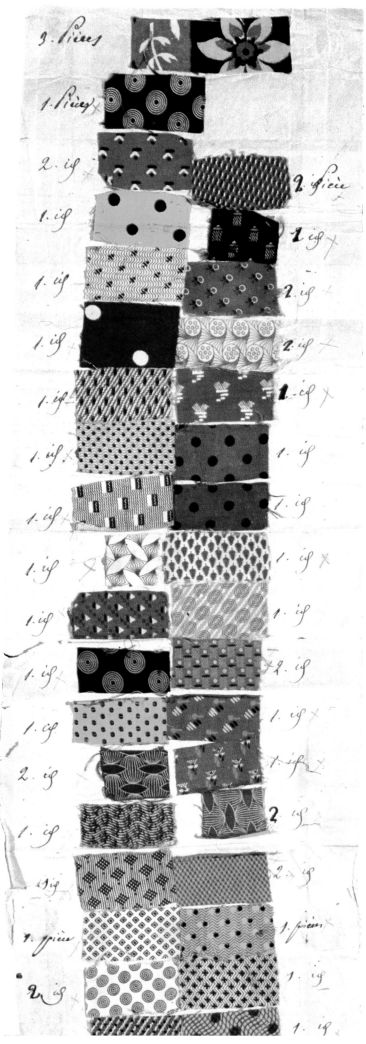

On June 18, 1791, a Nantes textile firm dispatched a rather petulant letter (reproduced above) to the great textile printer Christophe-Philippe Oberkampf. Translated into English, it reads: "We have made a selection of several patterns from those you kindly sent us. In accordance with your letter of the 11th, we would appreciate your sending them to us as soon as possible, along with those we requested in our letter of the 6th. Do not use a pallet, since the postal coach remains very expensive. We are sorry that you have nothing better or prettier to offer us right now at the price of five sols. The taffetas have too many errors. Your very humble and obedient servants, Beutier Père et Fils." Along with their order, to be sure they received the right patterns, the Beutiers returned to Oberkampf snips of the swatches he had sent them (seen at right). Similar letters are still sent today (or faxed, perhaps) and surely were written centuries earlier.

Opposite:
This illustration shows one page from a book containing several thousand small paintings in gouache of patterns in the French provincial style. Dated 1821, it was either from the Oberkampf printworks in Jouy-en-Josas, outside Paris, or from an Alsatian textile mill. This was a particularly popular look in France, where such patterns were called *mignonettes*.

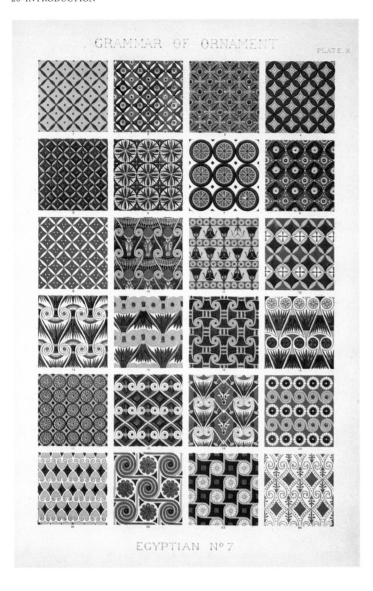

Seen above is a page from Owen Jones's *Grammar of Ornament* (1856); and opposite, a page from Auguste Racinet's *L'Ornement Polychrome* (1869). These two volumes are the outstanding examples of a genre of pattern book produced in Europe in the second half of the nineteenth century. Intended as reference works, particularly for designers, they aimed to establish the principles of good design. Though they presented their knowledge rather didactically, both Jones and Racinet knew how to produce beautiful books, and their work has been an inspiration to the authors of *Textile Designs*.

Manufacturing Company, founded in the 1820s, was producing 50 million yards of printed cloth a year by 1892.) Superfluity has turned out to be on some level a necessity, or, at the very least, something so deeply desired that to speak of it as superfluous seems absurd.

All fashion arises at a particular point in history and can be read as a guide to history. People demonstrate how they belong where they are in place and time by shaping the lines and colors of clothes and home furnishings. But there is nothing to be shaped except what is already there. This is the irony of fashion: always to be up to date yet always to be dated, always to follow behind the turning of the recycling wheel, the hands of the design clock. To be original in fabric design is to make the best use of the old vocabulary. In terms of the last few centuries of art, with their ever-higher estimate of the value of originality, this is a peculiar idea about invention. But as the far older visual tradition of fabric design shows, the pressure to innovate is really a cumbersome burden: the new is so deeply involved with the old that with the right treatment from the artist the old is always new.

Families

FABRIC DESIGNERS ACKNOWLEDGE four families of patterns: floral; geometric; conversational; and ethnic. To these we have added in this book a fifth, art movements and period styles. This last category is really not a family, for it has no motifs of its own. An Arts and Crafts lily pattern, for example, is a version of a floral, and a Constructivist tractor pattern is a conversational. But art movements and period styles provide such distinctive and recognized "looks" that we have given them a chapter to themselves.

Textile Designs breaks down the families into categories based on one or more of the following criteria. *Motif:* the most important factor in any design, determines the family to which the pattern belongs. This is its basic image—a rose, a square, a clown, a paisley. *Layout:* describes the arrangement of the motif—whether it is spaced widely or closely on the ground, in neat order or apparently at random, or in rows that form stripes. (Most of the characteristics of the different layouts are described in our chapter on florals). *Color:* designs are so classified when a particular dye—indigo, madder, or Turkey red, say—is the strongest element of their look. *Printing techniques:* for example, ombré or warp printing, never reproduce a pattern without imposing a certain visual style on it. *Fabrication:* the cloth that takes the pattern also affects the way it looks, and some have become associated with particular kinds of design. Chintz is, strictly speaking, a cloth, but a designer thinking about chintz has a quite specific pattern genre in mind.

Countries

THE UNITED STATES and most of the countries of Western Europe have histories of industrial fabric printing, but France, England, and the United States have turned out printed cloth in the greatest volume. Though it was the British who pioneered not only the copperplate-printing process but roller printing, which revolutionized the textile industry, it was the French who were recognized early on as the leaders in design, and they have preserved their reputation up until today. Christophe-Philippe Oberkampf, who operated a mill in Jouy-en-Josas, near Versailles, from 1760 until his death, in 1815, is considered the father of French textile printing, and his cloth was renowned throughout Europe. He set an unsurpassed standard for design quality. Since the early nineteenth century, textile buyers from all over the world have made regular visits to France in search of the best and most fashionable patterns on paper or cloth.

In 1836 the British government, concerned about lagging behind the French in textile design, established a number of schools to train students to produce acceptable patterns. Twelve years later, a committee evaluated the program and in 1849 the results were published in *The Journal of Design and Manufacturers*. The members must have been disappointed by the testimony of the manufacturers they called on: "The French lead the taste, we follow them," remarked one textile producer. "I go to Paris three or four times a year for no other purpose than to buy designs and see what the French are doing." A calico printer agreed: "All the best designs are adaptations of French designs." Most of the other manufacturers who testified echoed these sentiments. The English schools were accused of poor management, but manufacturers like these probably contributed to the failure of the British effort through their firm belief in the superiority of the French work. (The English government, however, did found a museum, the Victoria and Albert, in 1857, to provide visual inspiration for British designers.) American printers also based a large part of their output on French designs. The great majority of the swatches in this book, in fact, were designed and printed in France, and some that were printed elsewhere may have been originally designed in France (or, for that matter, in another country entirely). In the absence of firm documentation for the source of the design, we have given credit in our captions to the place where the cloth was printed.

Dates

THE DATES OF the patterns in *Textile Designs* are illuminating, for they help to show how motifs and styles repeat themselves. Often a pattern seems typical of a far later time than that of its actual

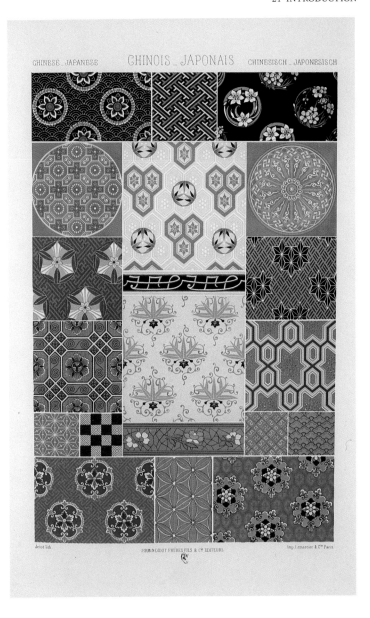

The *mezzaro* was an Italian block-printed imitation of the Indian palampore, but square, whereas the palampore was rectangular. The production of these textiles was centered around the city of Genoa. This example, like most surviving pieces, is from the second quarter of the nineteenth century. It appears that the designer was so intent on faithfully copying an actual palampore that he failed to adapt the flowering tree to the proportions of a *mezzaro*, thereby cutting off the topmost branches. *Mezzari* were worn draped over head and body. Since hair oil was used at that time, most show a worn and stained patch in the center, where the cloth rested on the head. In the twentieth century, Indian manufacturers have made block-printed copies of the *mezzaro*.

Opposite:
This rather small palampore is one of a set of four flowering-tree designs made around 1760 in India for export to Europe. The white background and the delicate, airy feel of the pattern suggest that this hand-painted cotton hanging was intended for France or England. The Dutch, for example, preferred dark fields of red or blue, and the Indian merchants, like their Western counterparts, catered to their customers' tastes.

making. Few examples of Western printed cloth survive from before the eighteenth century. (The rich fabrics we associate with those earlier years are mainly woven or embroidered.) European printers before the mid-eighteenth century were hampered by fugitive dyes and the slowness of the printing process, which involved cumbersome wooden blocks and the application of a fair amount of muscle. With copperplate printing and, far more dramatically, with the invention of roller printing, production grew at an ever-increasing pace. By the early 1800s, European mills were turning out tens of thousands of patterns a year. This was the beginning of mass-produced printed textiles, and it is from this period—about 1790 to the present—that we have chosen the material for this book.

Printing Techniques

TEXTILE PRINTING HAS evolved from block printing by hand, to copperplate printing, to roller printing, to perrotine printing (a mechanized form of the block print), to screen printing by hand, to flatbed-screen printing, to the current system of choice, rotary-screen printing. All these methods have in common their effort to translate the artist's work faithfully from paper to cloth. Each technique has its own look: printing with steel or copper rollers, for example, allowed a fineness of detail that designers have used to advantage. Screen printing, today a more efficient, less expensive process than roller printing, can be used to create a more painterly look.

The technical processes behind these methods can be extremely complex, and even the simplest of them—old-fashioned wood-block printing—required precise coordination among many highly skilled workers: the original designers, the engravers, the color mixers, the printers, the finishers, not to speak of the marketers and distributors of the final product. And before any of this could begin, a firm had to secure the gray goods, the undyed, unfinished cloth. On this front, battles were and still are fought over sums as tiny as fractions of a cent

per yard. (Such figures add up over the printing of thousands of yards.) When we consider what even the most insignificant print has demanded in artistry and in technical and business skill, it becomes an object much more deserving of our appreciation.

Usage

ALMOST ALL THE cloth shown in this book was produced as either apparel or home-furnishing goods. Within each of these markets, textile companies define smaller, more precise arenas. Cloth may be designed specifically for men's, women's, or children's wear, for example, some of it formal, some of it casual, some of it intended only for sleeping in. Categories like these are further broken down by considerations of price, fashion trends, regional tastes, consumer age, and so on. Most of the companies specialize in a particular market. Of course customers in a yard-goods store can buy whatever they want—can make a dress out of an upholstery chintz, or curtains from a menswear wool tartan. But as most designers aim their line toward a specific kind of customer, and as most customers gravitate more to the familiar than to the exotic, a certain order and tradition tend to sort out into recognizable niches the hundreds of thousands of new patterns produced annually. In the examples that follow, we have always identified the fabric as either apparel or home-furnishing yard goods. When a more specialized use is clear—for example, scarves, handkerchiefs, ties, and ribbons—we note that as well.

Family, country, date, printing technique, and use: these are the fundamental facts that identify a textile design. But even such rudimentary information is often unavailable. These anonymous swatches are part of a history of the commonplace that still waits to be told. We have tried to provide the reader with a vocabulary to describe and a means of approaching them; but in the end, each swatch speaks for itself, and often what it says is that it wants a book of its own.

Like the palampore, this length of eighteenth-century cotton from India was hand-painted by the mordant-dye technique. The hand-woven cloth is extremely fine in quality, and the small-scale motifs and allover repeating pattern suggest it was imported into Europe for use as wearing apparel.

1. Floral

IN THE TEXTILE industry, patterns of richly colored, delicately petaled roses and patterns of roses' sharp thorns are both referred to as florals. The floral category includes all the gatherings of the flower garden, in fact, including grasses, but agricultural produce like fruit and vegetables is considered a conversational subject, as are nuts and pinecones. Trees, too, are conversationals, but their leaves are classified as florals, and so is wheat—sneaking in as a grass. All the flowers in the floral family are to some degree abstracted from nature, for if they appear in a scenic print—an actual picture—they are considered conversational.

We doubt that a culture has existed that has not cherished flowers, and certainly in Western history they are scattered thickly through art back to the classical era. But flowers mechanically printed on fabrics have an ironic place in this iconography, for printing, of course, is an industrial technique, and it was the industrial revolution that turned the West urban in the modern sense. The point at which it became possible to mass-produce floral printed fabric was also the point at which the farm and the garden began to disappear from the mainstream of people's lives. More and more, the fruitful earth became something to visit over the weekend, or to keep in a small but prominent pot in a city apartment.

From this perspective, the flowers captured on cloth have a certain poignance: flat blossoms without fragrance, blooming forever to remind a largely urban society of nature's infinitely various and sensual pleasures. On the other hand, they also signify that flowers are far too deeply embedded in our imaginative life to be uprooted from it. Florals, in fact, are easily the most popular genre of fabric patterns. Part of the explanation for this may be sociological: though men of the eighteenth century and earlier wore richly ornamented clothes, for the last two centuries most male apparel has been relatively sober and undecorated. That has meant that women buy considerably more printed cloth than men do, and though one hesitates to say that any motif is implicitly masculine or feminine, it is certainly more common to see women than men wearing florals and choosing them for home furnishings. Both women and men, however, buy far more "basic" cloth than they do fabric with pattern. A solid color, or a straightforward pinstripe, say, never goes out of style and can be worn as long as the garment lasts. A fashionable floral "look" may have no more than a season's life before it retires to the back of the closet. And in a sense, that's what fashion is— an illusion, an illusory impression that catches our eye.

The artificiality of modern living may produce a subliminal pressure to bring images of flowers into one's home, or to decorate oneself with them through one's clothes. But the symbolism of flowers is ancient. Their blooming—which can last as briefly as morning to dusk—is an enactment on a small scale of the cycle of life, a theater of the passage from youth to maturity to age. And since flowers at their lushest are both so beautiful and so fragile, they are a particularly poetic image of life's simultaneous richness and transience. But flowers' twofold symbolism also tells us that they will always be back next year. In this way, floral prints and real flowers are alike: both are perennials.

AIRBRUSH

1. France, 1920s–30s, gouache on paper, AYG, 70%
2. France, 1920s–30s, gouache on paper, AYG, 125%

THE USE OF the airbrush, a painter's spray gun, was popularized by Man Ray's Aerograph paintings, begun in 1917, which introduced a slick, stylized, modern look that influenced Art Deco textile patterns of the 1920s and 1930s. To create this look, textile designers often combined the airbrush technique with stenciling, laying patterns cut out of zinc or copper plates flat on the cloth, then spraying them with color from the airbrush. Finely shaded hues could be achieved this way. The designs shown here were created with an airbrush for use on cotton flannel.

1.

2.

ALLOVER NONDIRECTIONAL

1. **France, 1949, paper impression, AYG, 80%**
2. **USA, 1920s, gouache on paper, AYG, 100%**
3. **USA, 1920s, RP cotton, AYG, 100%**
4. **USA, 1930s, gouache on paper, AYG, 25%**

AN ALLOVER LAYOUT contains more figure than ground: the motifs of the pattern cover more than 50 percent of the field. Such layouts are popular with textile and fashion designers because they tend to disguise a pattern's repeats. Nondirectional designs, which have no implicit top or bottom, left or right, are also commercial favorites; it makes no difference which way they go when the cloth is sewn into a garment, and this eases the work of the cutter, who can make more economical use of a bolt of cloth when shapes can be cut from it in any direction.

1.

2.

3.

4.

ALLOVER ONE-DIRECTIONAL

1. USA, 1930s, gouache on paper, AYG, 100%
2. France, 1900, RP cotton velvet, HFYG, 50%
3. France, c. 1900, gouache on paper, HFYG, 57%

ONE-DIRECTIONAL DESIGNS have a distinct top and bottom. The patterns cut from these fabrics must all be oriented in the same direction, which limits the cutter's freedom of maneuver and leaves more wasted fabric in each bolt. Since World War I, the garment industry's economical designers have tried to reduce such waste by eliminating one-directional designs, which in fact appear less often in twentieth-century cloth. Earlier designers were just as thrifty, but they embraced these patterns, perhaps because labor was cheaper and more skilled or perhaps simply because they had a different sense of propriety. One-directionals, after all, are natural layouts for a floral pattern, showing the flowers' vertical growth toward the light.

1.

2.

3.

ALLOVER PACKED

1. France, 1880, gouache on paper, HFYG, 25%
2. France, 1882, RP cotton, AYG, 125%
3. France, 1950s–60s, dyes and gouache on paper, AYG, 100%
4. France, c. 1900, paper impression, AYG, 82%

PACKING FLOWERS SO closely together that the background largely or totally disappears gives a print a rich, sumptuous feel. Consumers have always responded with enthusiasm to the generosity of this kind of design.

1.

2.

3.

4.

ALLOVER SET

ALLOVER SET is a formal layout of grids and diagonals. It tends to be a static design, seeming antithetical to the delicate organic lines of petals and leaves—though when the motif is sufficiently stylized and simplified, orderly repetition becomes more active in the image than the form of the flower itself.

1. France, c. 1810–20, gouache on paper, AYG, 52%
2. France, c. 1795–1800, BP paper impression, AYG, 100%
3. France, c. 1810–20, gouache on paper, AYG, 155%
4. France or USA, 1930s–40s, gouache on paper, AYG, 115%
5. France, 1930s, gouache on paper, AYG, 115%

1.

2.

3.

4.

5.

ALLOVER TOSSED

1 (left). France, 1930s, gouache on paper, AYG, 39%
2 (left). France or USA, 1930s–40s, SP rayon, AYG, 64%

ALLOVER TWO-DIRECTIONAL

1 (right). France, c. 1945, paper impression, AYG, 60%
2 (right). USA, 1940s–50s, dyes on paper, AYG, 80%
3 (right). USA or France, 1930s, gouache on paper, AYG, 105%

IN TOSSED LAYOUTS, the flowers look as if they had been freshly picked and scattered at random. The stems all point in different directions, giving the print movement and an informal air.

IN TWO-DIRECTIONAL layouts, top and bottom are reversible, giving the fabric cutter more freedom than the one-directional design allows. But where the nondirectional design works equally well sideways as vertically, patterns cut from two-directional prints must conform to the vertical.

1.

2.

1.

2.

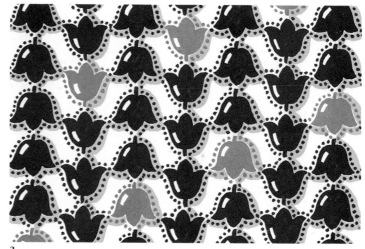

3.

ARBORESCENT

1. USA, 2d quarter 20th C, RP cotton, HFYG, 22%
2. France, 1799, BP cotton, HFYG, 11%
3. France, c. 1880, gouache on paper, HFYG, 28%

THE HEAVY, SINUOUS branches of these designs, usually found in home-furnishing fabrics, may support large exotic birds and flowers, many of them unknown in any country but the mind. The images are the product of a back-and-forth kind of cultural exchange. Through what is known as the mordant-dye technique, textile producers in seventeenth-century India could create colors that would not fade or run in sun or laundry, and they used this method for large-scale, hand-painted cotton panels called palampores, which depicted a fanciful flowering tree. Europeans admired these fabrics but wanted them modified before they would buy them, so the Indian craftsmen were sent European patterns to copy—which they did, altering them to their own tastes. One of the results was the arborescent print—an Indian adaptation of a European substitution for a traditional Indian design. Actually, the prints shown here are European and American imitations of the Indian adaptation, for arborescents have been produced continuously in the West since the eighteenth century.

1.

2.

3.

BAMBOO

1. c. 1950–70, SP cotton, AYG, 50%
2. France, c. 1900, gouache on paper, AYG, 72%
3. France, 1888, RP cotton, AYG, 50%
4. France, 1879, RP cotton, HFYG, 50%

THE THIN POLES of the bamboo design are upright, straight, and almost abstract, but their natural geometry is modified and softened by their leaves and joints. Bamboo is a frequent go-between in the Western love affair with the East, appearing in both japonisme and the earlier tradition of chinoiserie, which by the mid-seventeenth century was fashionable in Europe. During the eighteenth century, Europe imported large quantities of hand-painted, scenic silk and paper wall panels from China. Bamboo motifs showed up in the "Japanese Court" display at the International Exhibition in South Kensington, London, in 1862, providing inspiration for Western textile designers. Today bamboo is still associated with the Orient and the pleasures of the exotic, whether in furnishings for the sun porch or on Hawaiian shirts.

1.

2.

3.

4.

BASKETS, FLOWER-POTS, AND VASES

1. France, 2d half 19th C, gouache on paper, AYG, 50%
2. England, 2d half 19th C, paper impression, HFYG, 25%
3. France, c. 1840, gouache on paper, AYG, 80%
4. France, c. 1940, RP silk, AYG, 100%

THESE MOTIFS HELP to organize a floral pattern, providing a visual focus or a base on which to center a cluster of blossoms. Flowers spilling out of baskets can have a romantic, uplifting effect, hinting that nature's emblems of spring and regeneration cannot be contained by an object of merely human making. Also, of course, flowerpots and vases resolve the issue of how to deal with a plant's untidy roots and stems. Number 2 is exactly the same design as a wallpaper pattern printed by the Parisian firm of Defosse et Karth in 1861.

2.

1.

3.

4.

BLOCK PRINTS

1. **France, c. 1800, BP cotton, HFYG, 75%**
2. **England, c. 1805, BP cotton, AYG, 50%**
3. **France, c. 1800, BP cotton, HFYG, 43%**

IN THE TECHNIQUE of block printing, a carved fruitwood block—small enough to be manipulated by hand—is coated with pigment, set on a length of cloth, and given a hefty blow with a mallet to impress the carved image on the fabric. Then it is moved over, carefully aligned with the preceding print, and struck again. A range of colors can be achieved by repeating the process with different blocks. In 1834 Louis-Jérôme Perrot of Rouen invented a block-printing machine that could print three different colors at once. Called the perrotine, it increased the rate of production two-hundred-fifty-fold. By the mid-nineteenth century, the engraved metal roller printer, invented in 1783 by the Scotsman Thomas Bell, had mechanized the fabric-printing industry. But a few hand-blocked fabrics are still made in Europe, and they are cherished for the traces of the human hand that have inevitably crept in.

1.

2.

3.

BLUE RESISTS

1. Probably England, 2d half 18th C, BP cotton, HFYG, 19%
2. France, late 18th C, BP cotton, HFYG, 50%

MOST PRINTING METHODS are designed to apply a dye to a fabric wherever the figures of the pattern fall. Resist printing does exactly the opposite: what is printed will in the end be left bare. In this technique, a resist—a paste or wax resistant to dye—is printed on the cloth. Next the cloth is dyed; finally the resist is removed. The image appears as the white areas of the cloth—wherever the dye has not penetrated. Blue resist is resist-printed cloth dyed with indigo, and it was popular in Europe and America until it became less costly to discharge the design chemically. The resist method can, of course, be used with other colors, and it can be repeated to achieve a range of colors in the same cloth. In number 1, the resist has been applied to form the ground of the print, leaving the figures standing out in blue. Such reverse resists were used in America during the second half of the eighteenth century. But as they were probably beyond the skill of colonial textile manufacturers, they are believed to have been made in England, probably specifically for export to America and to the taste of the Dutch settlers in the Hudson River Valley, where they were mainly found. There is a hint of both Indonesian batiks and Indian painted cottons in the exoticism and treatment of many of the motifs.

1.   2.

BONNES HERBES

1. France, c. 1800, gouache on paper, AYG, 100%
2. France, c. 1800, gouache on paper, AYG, 100%
3. France, c. 1800, BP paper impression, AYG, 78%
4. France, late 18th C, gouache on paper, AYG, 115%

THIS FRENCH PROVINCIAL style—the name means fine grasses—first appeared around 1800 and was associated with the renowned mill of Christophe-Philippe Oberkampf in Jouy-en-Josas, near Versailles. The look was extremely successful and much imitated by textile printers throughout France, especially in Alsace. Well drawn, at once naturalistic and stylized, bonnes herbes designs won French hearts for their unshowy presentation of familiar regional field flowers, gaily colored against their dark green or black grounds. Numbers 1–3 are Oberkampf designs.

1.

2.

3.

4.

BORDERS

1. France, c. 1900, gouache on paper, HFYG, 40%
2. France, c. 1880, gouache on paper, HFYG, 40%
3. France, c. 1910, gouache on paper, AYG, 125%
4. France, c. 1910–20, paper impression, AYG, 50%

THESE LINEAR PATTERNS are intended to decorate the hem of a dress or the edging of drapery and bedspreads. As such, they are powerful design elements that tend to call attention to themselves; the coordinating print that usually accompanies them is likely to be simpler so as not to compete. Border prints make strong, memorable statements, but manufacturers tend to dislike the limits they set on the cutting of the cloth. And, if a dress is too long, it is often difficult to shorten without compromising the border.

1.

2.

3.

4.

BOTANICAL

1. France, c. 1880, gouache on paper, HFYG, 22%
2. France, c. 1880, gouache on paper, HFYG, 23%
3. France, c. 1880, RP wool challis, AYG, 42%
4. France, c. 1880, gouache on paper, HFYG, 50%

NATURALISTIC REPRESENTATIONS OF flowers on both clothing and furnishing fabrics were very popular during the second half of the nineteenth century. They reflect the reverence for nature advocated by the influential English art critic John Ruskin as well as the Victorian fascination with empirical science (many of these designs were inspired by botanical engravings). Yet there have always been artists who are happy in the minute observation of flowers, and botanical designs allow them to show off their masterful techniques and to let bloom on cloth varieties otherwise seldom seen outside reference books.

1.

2.

3.

4.

BOUQUETS AND NOSEGAYS

1. **France, c. 1870–80, gouache on paper, AYG, 115%**
2. **France, c. 1920s, RP cotton chintz, HFYG, 25%**
3. **France, 1930s, RP silk satin, AYG, 50%**
4. **France, c. 1890–1910, RP cotton, AYG, 100%**
5. **France, 1882, RP cotton, AYG, 50%**
6. **France, c. 1850–60, paper impression, AYG, 50%**
7. **France, c. 1890, gouache on paper, AYG, 50%**
8. **USA, c. 1860, RP wool challis, 100%**
9. **France, c. 1870–80, RP cotton damask, AYG, 110%**

BOUQUETS AND NOSEGAYS are popular with designers because they offer a way to combine a variety of flowers in one motif. They evoke images of romance, gift-giving, and the sentiments of spring. Nosegays of lily of the valley (*muguet*) and violets (numbers 7 and 9) are traditional French favorites.

1.

2.

3.

4.

5.

6.

7.

8.

9.

BOWS AND RIBBONS

1. France, c. 1875, gouache on paper, AYG, 50%
2. France, c. 1860, gouache on paper, AYG, 100%
3. France, c. 1880–90, gouache on paper, HFYG, 50%

Bows and ribbons have been widely used to tie up romantic floral designs since the beginning of textile printing. A softly draped ribbon, as in number 1, is a way to make a floral pattern into a stripe layout without actually lining up the flowers. The folds of ribbons and bows create highlights and shadows that add movement and a three-dimensional effect.

1.

2. 3.

BOX LAYOUT

1. France, c. 1820–40, gouache on paper, AYG, 50%
2. USA, c. 1950s, RP or SP cotton, AYG, 50%
3. France, c. 1920, gouache on paper, HFYG, 25%
4. France, c. 1830–40, gouache on paper, AYG, 70%
5. France, c. 1880, RP cotton, AYG, 85%
6. France, c. 1810–20, gouache on paper, AYG, 85%

THE GRID IS one of the most basic methods of ordering, as city-street plans since classical Greek times attest. The incorporation of flowers softens the grid somewhat, but unless its squares are small or subtle it is considered unflattering nowadays to a woman's body—literally "boxy." This type of layout was more acceptable to nineteenth-century taste.

1.

2.

3.

4.

5.

6.

BREAD-AND-BUTTER, DITSIES, AND DUMB-DUMBS

1. USA, 1920s–30s, RP cotton, AYG, 100%
2. USA, 1920s–30s, RP cotton, AYG, 90%
3. USA, 1920s–30s, RP cotton, AYG, 100%
4. France, c. 1940, paper impression, AYG, 100%
5. USA, 1920s–30s, RP cotton, AYG, 100%
6. USA, 1930s–40s, RP silk satin, AYG, 100%
7. USA, 1920s–30s, RP cotton, AYG, 90%
8. USA, 1940s–50s, RP cotton, AYG, 90%
9. USA, 1920s–30s, RP cotton, AYG, 90%

DUMB-DUMBS (numbers 7–9) because the motifs are so inoffensive as to make no statement at all; ditsies (numbers 4–6) because they're funny little things; and bread-and-butter prints (numbers 1–3) because they always sell. These are the terms used in the twentieth-century American textile industry, but each era and country has its equivalents. Though never considered high style, inexpensive mass-market prints have always been relied upon by textile converters as solid staples.

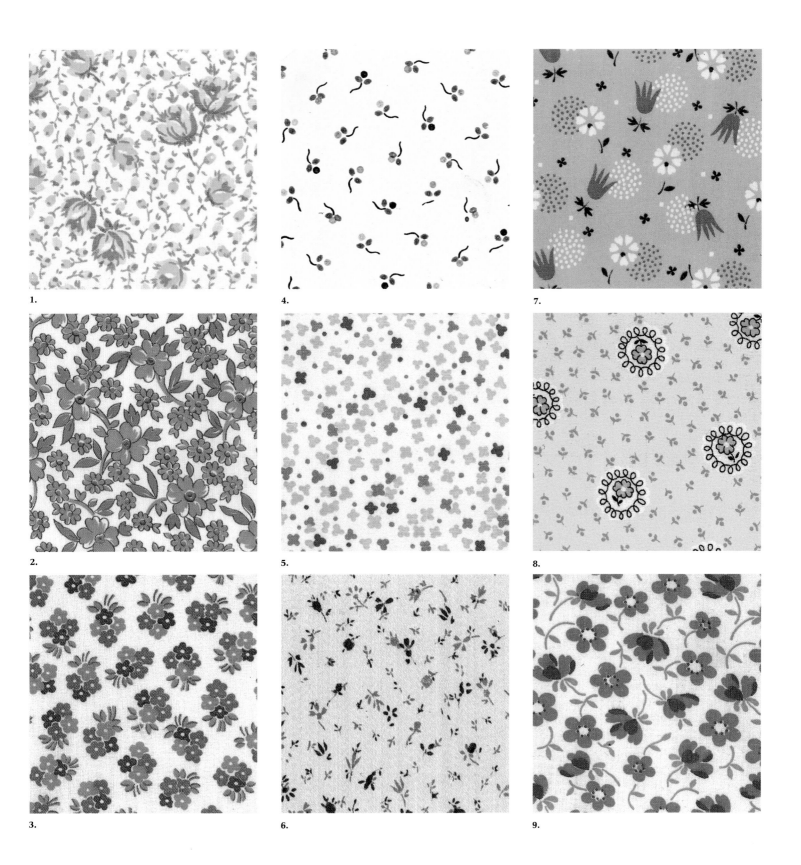

1.

2.

3.

4.

5.

6.

7.

8.

9.

BROCADED LOOK

1. France, 1892, RP cotton damask, HFYG, 44%
2. France, 1874, RP cotton, HFYG, 36%

PRINTED TEXTILES ARE often considered the poor cousins of ornamental weaves, those expensive products of labor-intensive craft that have always found their audience among the wealthy. And the poor cousin often tries to emulate the rich cousin's style, sometimes reproducing it quite closely, if in more affordable materials. These prints are late-nineteenth-century imitations of handwoven silk brocades dating from a century earlier. The brocaded look is still done today, one of a family of mock fabrics that traffic in the semblance of luxury.

1.

2.

BRUSHSTROKE LOOK

1. **France, 1930s, gouache on paper, AYG, 90%**
2. **France, 1930s, RP silk crepe, AYG, 200%**
3. **USA or France, 1930s, gouache on paper, AYG, 50%**
4. **USA or France, 1930s, gouache on paper, AYG, 50%**

TEXTILE PATTERNS GENERALLY begin as a painting that is transferred in one way or another to the wooden block, copperplate, roller, or silk screen from which it is printed. Usually the painterliness of the sketch is incidental and disappears in the transfer. But the images here are designed to preserve the appearance of the painting's basic constituent—the brushstroke. Why? It was the mechanical reproduction of images that made painting an antique art and made the products of handwork a minority in the marketplace. Consequently, of course, their prestige and their value went up. On one level the brushstroke look is another example of a print imitating a more expensive artifact; but perhaps one can also see in it a bow from a victorious technology to a vanquished one. The motif began to appear often on fabrics in the 1920s and 1930s and continues to be popular today.

1.

2.

3.

4.

BUDS

1. France, c. 1820–30, gouache on paper, AYG, 100%
2. France, c. 1830–40, gouache on paper, AYG, 100%
3. France, c. 1860–70, gouache on paper, AYG, 100%
4. France, 1835–40, RP cotton, AYG, 110%
5. France, 1861, RP cotton dobby, AYG, 100%
6. England, 1872, RP cotton, AYG, 100%
7. France, mid-19th C, gouache on paper, AYG, 100%

BUDS ARE ONE of the most popular floral motifs after the rose, and most printed buds are rosebuds. Flowers in general suggest youth, freshness, new beginnings; buds double that symbolism by being baby flowers.

1.

2.

3.

4.

5.

6.

7.

CALICO

1. USA, mid-19th C, RP cotton, AYG, 100%
2. USA, 1920s–30s, RP cotton, AYG, 100%
3. USA, c. 1920s, RP cotton, AYG, 100%
4. USA, 1920s–30s, RP cotton, AYG, 100%
5. France, c. 1860–80, RP cotton, AYG, 100%
6. USA, c. 1920s, RP cotton, AYG, 100%
7. USA, c. 1870–80, RP cotton, AYG, 100%
8. France, 1895, RP cotton, AYG, 100%
9. USA, c. 1920s, RP cotton, AYG, 100%

CALICO BEGAN NOT as a print but as a cotton cloth, taking its name from the Indian city of Calicut, its port of origin. Tightly woven, the fabric took printing well, and by the seventeenth century the English East India Company was importing it into Europe. The Anglicized name "calico" eventually came to refer to a gaily colored, small-scale floral of the bread-and-butter variety. By the mid-nineteenth century, every dry-goods store in America carried bolts of calico cloth, ready to be sewn up into everyday dresses, aprons, and patchwork quilts. It has always been inexpensive—at ten cents a yard, it was the cheapest fabric offered in the 1926 Sears, Roebuck catalog. Calico has remained a fairly steady over-the-counter seller, although the number of converters printing it has declined greatly since the 1950s.

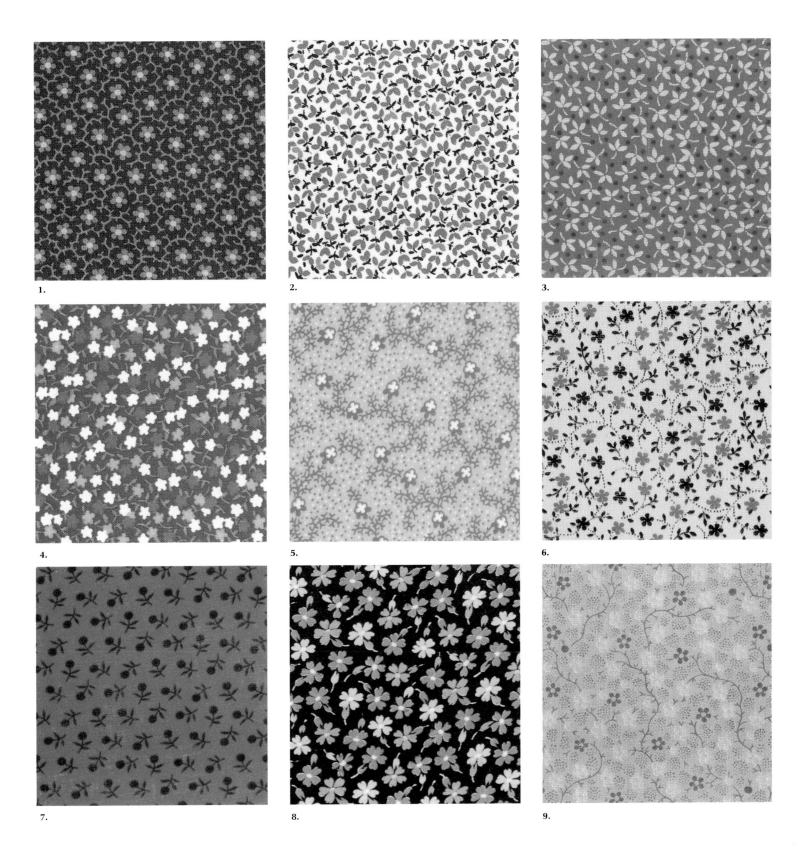

1.

2.

3.

4.

5.

6.

7.

8.

9.

CAMEO LAYOUT

1. France, c. 1880, gouache on paper, AYG, 100%
2. England, c. 1840, RP cotton chintz, HFYG, 50%
3. France, c. 1850, RP cotton, HFYG, 38%

IN THE NINETEENTH century, a frame in the oval shape of the cameo, enclosing flowers instead of a human portrait, was a popular motif in printed fabrics used for both home furnishings and apparel. Today these rather formal designs are largely restricted to home-furnishing patterns.

1.

2.

3.

CARTOUCHES

1. France, c. 1840, gouache on paper, AYG, 60%
2. France, c. 1840, gouache on paper, AYG, 60%
3. France, c. 1840, gouache on paper, AYG, 60%

To the architect, a cartouche can be a variety of different ornaments; what they have in common is a scrollwork effect, like curling paper. The volutes of the Greek Ionic column are also called cartouches. Since the eighteenth century, the word has referred to decorative panels, either painted on wall or ceiling or raised in relief like a tablet, that frame an inscription or some ornamental device or image. The edges of the panel are shaped into rolls and curves to suggest a scroll. Transferred to cloth, in a family of patterns seen most frequently in the 1830s and 1840s, the outlines of the cartouche are freely abstracted into floating arabesques. In these examples, the cartouche has been filled in or surrounded with flowers.

1.

2.

3.

CHALLIS

1. France, mid-19th C, BP wool challis, AYG, 41%
2. France, mid-19th C, RP wool challis, AYG, 40%
3. France, mid-19th C, BP wool challis, AYG, 35%
4. France, 1857–60, BP and RP wool challis, AYG, 75%
5. France, c. 1880, RP wool challis, A (scarf corner), 100%

THE NAME "CHALLIS" is derived from the Anglo-Indian word *shalee* (soft). Challis was originally a lightweight wool-and-silk cloth first produced in Norwich, England, in 1832. Its popularity increased with the invention, by William Henry Perkin in 1856, of coal-tar–based aniline dyes, which created deep and brilliant colors new to the fashion palette of the time— bright magentas, violets, blues. As wool and silk take dye well, tightly woven challis was perfectly suited to printing with aniline and came into vogue as the stuff of rich scarves and rather boldly patterned dresses. Today, challis is expensive in wool and is usually made of rayon, but the typical patterns and colors retain their rich, deep look.

1.

2.

3.

4.

5.

CHINTZ

1. **France, c. 1855, BP cotton chintz, HFYG, 70%**
2. **France, c. 1850, BP cotton chintz, HFYG, 24%**

INDIA IS THE source of many words in our textile vocabulary, since cloth was a major import of Europe's various East India trading companies, beginning with the Portuguese, quickly followed by the Dutch in 1597, the English in 1600, the Danes in 1616, and the French in 1664. The word "chintz" is an anglicized plural of the Hindi word *chint,* meaning variegated or spotted. "Spotted," of course, could apply to virtually any print with a small-scale allover motif; what distinguishes chintz is a glaze of wax, starch, or resin, originally rubbed in by hand—in India with a shell or rounded stone, in eighteenth-century England with large flat flints—and today applied with mechanical calenders. The shiny glazed finish, which was thought to repel dust and dirt, made chintz a popular choice for curtains, upholstery, and bed covers. Unfortunately the glaze disappeared after repeated washings. The print on chintz is often, but not invariably, a floral. The British, incidentally, were not alone in their garbling of other tongues; this material was called *chittes* by the French, *sits* by the Dutch, *Zitz* by the Germans, and *zitiez* by the Russians.

1.

2.

CHINTZ BORDERS

1. France or England, 1st quarter 19th C, BP cotton, HFYG, 55%

2. England, 1st quarter 19th C, BP cotton, HFYG, 75%

3. England, 2d quarter 19th C, BP cotton, HFYG, 100%

THESE DESIGNS WERE printed in long linear runs that repeated the same border pattern as many times as possible from selvage to selvage. From this cloth, individual strips were cut and used singly as the trimmings for quilts, bed curtains, and drapery.

1.

2.

3.

CINNAMON PINKS

1. USA, 1900–1920s, RP cotton, AYG, 100%
2. USA, c. 1860–80, RP cotton, AYG, 100%
3. France, c. 1860–80, RP cotton, AYG, 100%
4. USA, c. 1860–80, RP cotton, AYG, 100%
5. France, c. 1860–80, RP cotton, AYG, 100%
6. USA, c. 1860–80, RP cotton, AYG, 100%
7. France, c. 1860–80, RP cotton, AYG, 100%
8. USA, c. 1860–80, RP cotton, AYG, 100%
9. USA, c. 1860–80, RP cotton, AYG, 100%

SMALL-SCALE FLORALS in pink on pink were a distinct look from the 1860s through the 1920s. Prints like these were not considered modish, but they were a staple in the local dry-goods stores of small towns all over the United States as well as in Europe. Rural in feeling and rather sweet, they often ended up in patchwork quilts and children's garments. While "cinnamon pink" is a provincial American term, people in the industry called these color combinations "double pinks," for obvious reasons.

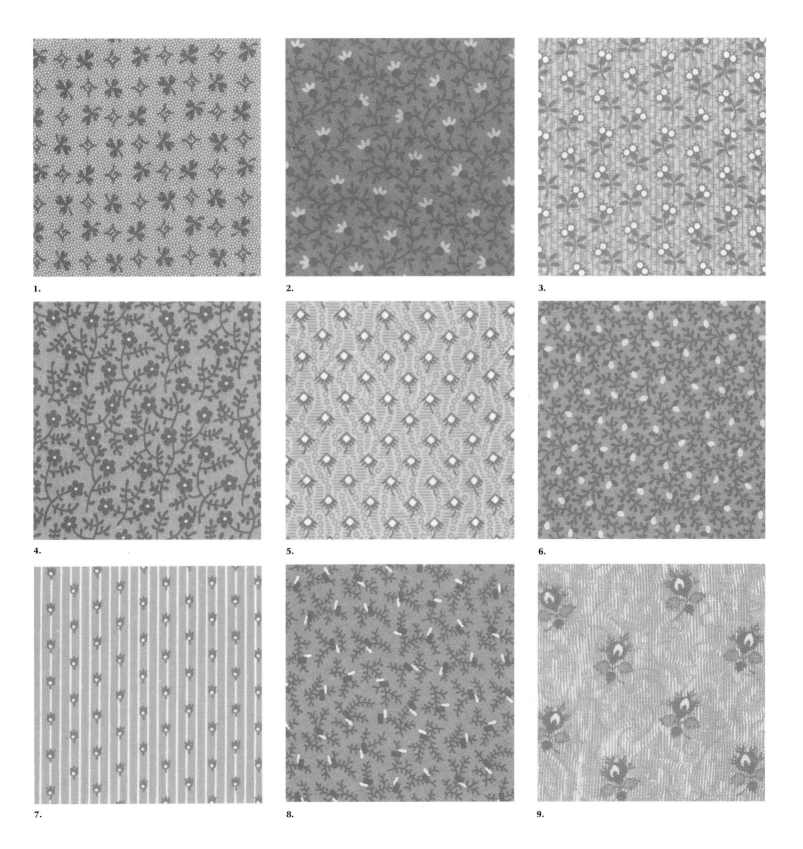

1.

2.

3.

4.

5.

6.

7.

8.

9.

CRETONNE

1. England or France, 1920s, RP cotton, HFYG, 32%
2. England, 1920s, RP cotton, HFYG, 65%
3. England, 1920s, RP cotton, HFYG, 70%

ORIGINALLY A HEMP-AND-LINEN weave from the Normandy town of Creton, by the 1920s cretonne had become a stout, medium-weight cotton popular for home furnishings because of its durability and its price (then as low as nineteen cents a yard in America). A combination of factors gave cretonne prints a look of their own. As an inexpensive fabric with a rather stiff hand and an unappealing texture, the cloth was often disguised with eye-catching colors and patterns. It came into widespread use in the 1920s, an extremely vital period for design; the Ballets Russes were still an important influence and Art Moderne was at its most influential. By using these bold, vibrant designs on affordable cloth, manufacturers succeeded in bringing a fashionable and "arty" look to the mass market.

1.

2.

3.

DAMASK LOOK

1. France, 1920s–40s, gouache on paper, HFYG, 35%
2. France, 1940s–50s, gouache on paper, HFYG, 50%

AN ORNAMENTAL REVERSIBLE weave usually in one color and originally produced in silk and wool, damask reached Europe from Damascus, then a center of the land trade, when Marco Polo returned to Venice in 1295 with robes of crimson damask in the shabby bundles he carried with him. These printed mimics are the vastly lower-priced version. Both printed and woven damasks are traditionally used in draperies and hangings; the genuine article was once the wallpaper of the wealthy. The usual designs are in an established Renaissance style of large-scale formal patterns featuring highly stylized floral motifs.

1.

2.

EMBROIDERED LOOK

1. France, 1882, RP cotton, HFYG, 80%
2. France, c. 1920s, gouache on paper, HFYG, 25%
3. France, 1880, gouache on paper, AYG, 100%
4. France, 1914, gouache on paper, HFYG, 50%

THE EMBROIDERED LOOK is another machine-produced pretender to the status of handworked cloth—a flat print with the three-dimensional look of embroidery, available at a fraction of the cost. These examples simulate crewelwork (number 1), Berlin work (number 2), couching (number 3), and a more formal style (number 4) using satin stitch and the illusion of laid silver thread to outline the motifs.

1.

2.

3.

4.

FLOWER BEDS

1. France, c. 1940s, gouache on paper, HFYG, 25%
2. France, 1st quarter 19th C, gouache on paper,
HF (carpet pattern), 100%
3. France, 1st quarter 19th C, gouache on paper,
HF (carpet pattern), 100%

THE FORMAL GARDEN combines geometry, which always suggests the capacity for order in human thinking, with the softening influence of nature. Flower-bed designs are unusual in textile prints, perhaps because they imply the undesirable presence of earth and dirt on supposedly clean cloth, or perhaps because they dizzyingly raise to eye level what is usually underfoot. On the other hand, flower beds are a felicitous choice for carpet designs such as numbers 2 and 3.

1.

2.

3.

GARLANDS

1. France, mid-19th C, BP silk, A (scarf border), 50%
2. France, 1910–20, gouache on paper, AYG, 62%

ON ANCIENT FEAST days garlands, also known as festoons, were draped over the entrances of temples as a sign of welcome and fellowship. These examples are border patterns; garlands are also used in allover designs to tie the motifs together and to create a feeling of movement. Despite their fresh foliage, they are a rather formal device.

1.

2.

GRASSES AND WHEAT

1. France, c. 1820, gouache on paper, A (scarf border), 66%
2. France, 1888, RP cotton, AYG, 64%
3. France, mid-19th C, RP cotton chintz, HFYG, 50%
4. France, 2d half 19th C, RP cotton, AYG, 68%
5. France, c. 1860, RP cotton voile, AYG, 70%
6. France, 2d half 19th C, gouache on paper, A (ribbon pattern), 64%
7. France, 1810–20, gouache on paper, AYG, 110%

WHEAT IS THE ancient symbol of harvest, of prosperity, and of fertility. But it has been little used by twentieth-century designers, who perhaps have associated the motif too much with a "down on the farm" look or with the bundled sheaves of wheat of Communist imagery. Merchant buyers also tend to shy away from anything the public might read as prickly, itchy, or scratchy. On the other hand, wild grasses, with no particular symbolism, are a graceful frame for a bouquet of flowers, in textile patterns as in real life.

1.

2.

3.

4.

5.

6.

7.

HALF-MOURNING: CHOCOLATES, PURPLES, AND SHAKER GRAYS

1, 4, 8, 9, 19, 21, 25–27, 30–33. USA c. 1880–1900, RP cotton, AYG, 100%
2, 6. France, 1879, RP cotton, AYG, 100%
3. France, c. 1860, RP cotton, AYG, 100%
5. England or France, c. 1870, RP cotton, AYG, 100%
7. USA, c. 1800–1900, RP cotton, AYG, 120%
10–18, 22–24, 28, 29, 34–39. France, c. 1900, gouache on paper, AYG, 100%
20. USA, c. 1900–20, RP cotton, AYG, 100%

"CHOCOLATES" (numbers 1, 4, 7), "purples" (numbers 2, 3, 5, 6, 8, 9), and "Shaker grays" (numbers 10–39, also referred to as "silver grays") were terms used in the nineteenth-century textile industry for dark-hued calicos like these, which were worn by widows who had passed out of the stage of mourning proper, when they were expected to wear black. The sad sisters of cheerier cloths such as the cinnamon pinks, these prints were also favored by practical rural working women, not necessarily bereaved, because their speckled textures and dark colors required less frequent laundering.

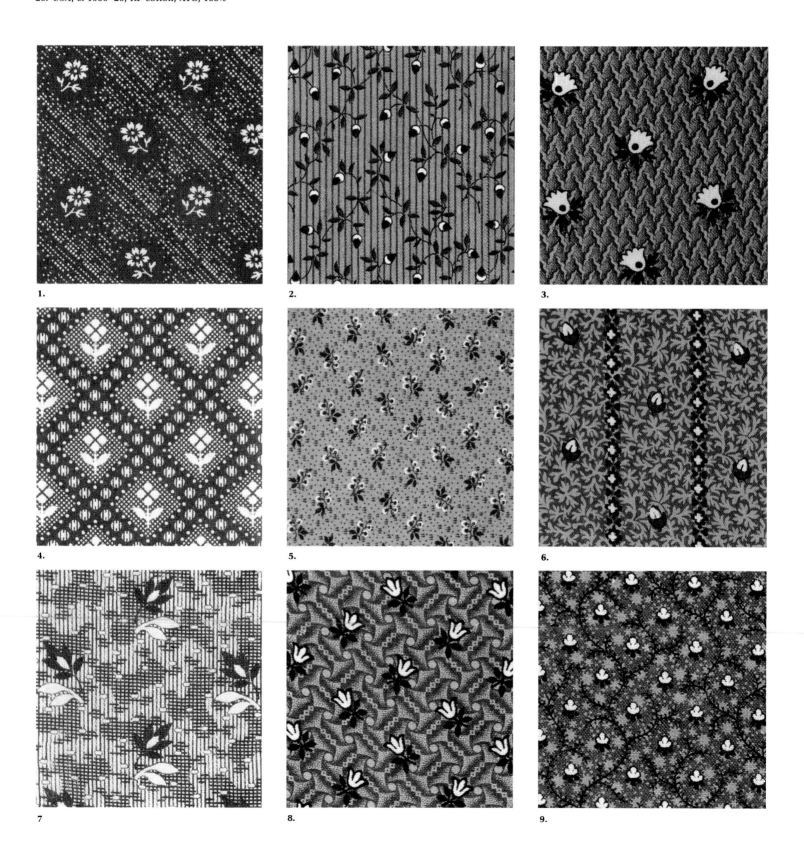

1.

2.

3.

4.

5.

6.

7

8.

9.

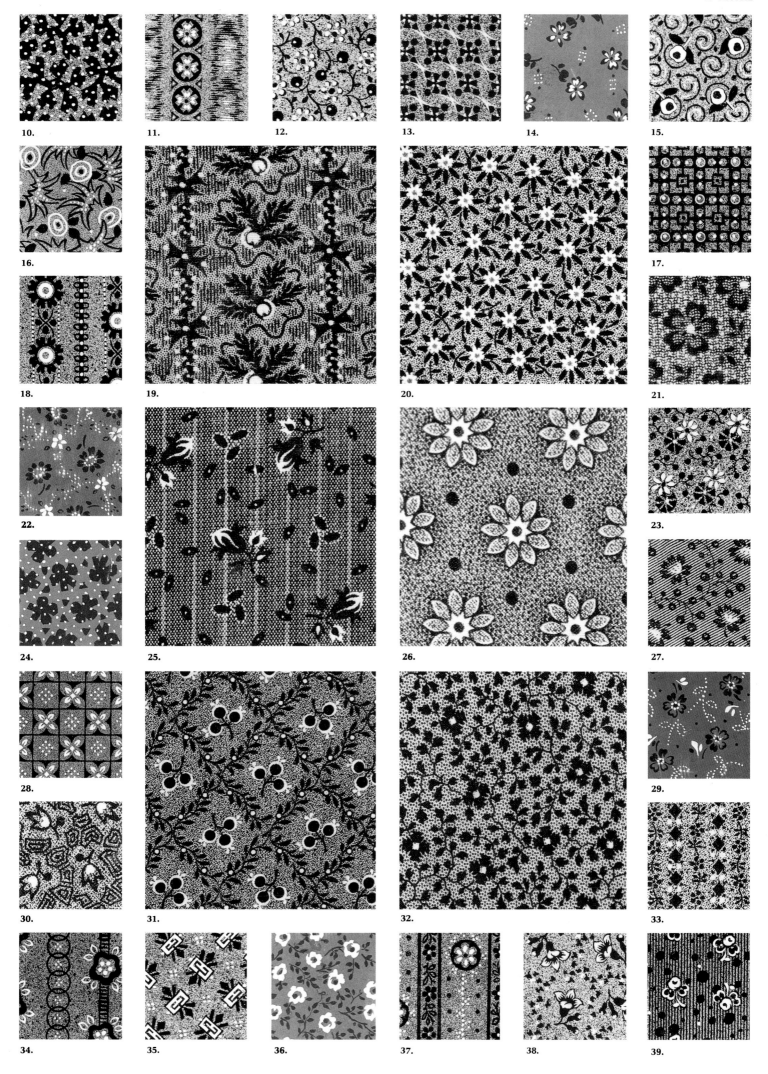

10.

11.

12.

13.

14.

15.

16.

17.

18.

19.

20.

21.

22.

23.

24.

25.

26.

27.

28.

29.

30.

31.

32.

33.

34.

35.

36.

37.

38.

39.

HANDKERCHIEFS

1. USA, c. 1940s–50s, SP cotton, A, 68%
2. USA, c. 1940s–50s, SP cotton, A, 40%
3. USA, c. 1940s–50s, SP cotton, A, 58%
4. USA, c. 1940s–50s, SP cotton, A, 37%
5. USA, c. 1940s–50s, SP cotton, A, 64%

PRINTED COTTON HANDKERCHIEFS were extremely popular in the United States in the 1940s and 1950s, especially with young girls, who were attracted by the sweetness of their designs. They are indeed appealing, though more decorative than useful. They tended to accumulate in a girl's dresser drawer, tucked neatly away in their padded satin hankie case, in the same way that a man's neckties tended to gather in his closet—at a rate of several every birthday and Christmas.

1.

2.

3.

4.

5.

IMPRESSIONISTIC

1. France, c. 1950s, SP cotton, AYG, 50%
2. France, c. 1930s–40s, SP silk, AYG, 74%

EXCHANGES BETWEEN DESIGNERS and fine artists go in many directions. Fine artists are not always as innovative as they would like to think—the pulsating patterns of 1960s Op Art, for example, have precedents in textile patterns of the early nineteenth century. These impressionistic prints, on the other hand, with their blurred, semiabstract outlines and melting colors, are a style that emerged in the 1930s, more than fifty years after the moment of true Impressionism. Applied to silks and other fabrics with a soft fluid feel, the look remains popular to this day.

1.

2.

INDIENNES

1. **France, late 18th–early 19th C, BP cotton, AYG, 50%**
2. **France, 1790–91, gouache on paper, AYG, 100%**
3. **France, c. 1880, gouache on paper, HFYG, 50%**
4. **France, c. 1880, RP cotton, HFYG, 50%**

IT IS A rare print that can claim a history of persecution. Indiennes are French interpretations of Indian hand-painted cottons. Introduced to Europe by the East India trading companies in the seventeenth century, the foreign cottons grew to be in such demand that they threatened local weaving industries and were banned. In France from 1686 to 1759 and in England from 1700 until about 1764, they could be neither imported nor worn. Accordingly, they became immensely popular, even though in France the punishment for breaking the laws included the death penalty. In the French free port of Marseilles, which was protected from the import laws, Indian cottons were both traded and copied, and then smuggled throughout the country. Since they could not be worn publicly they were worn in private, lending domesticity the pleasure of the illicit. Even after they were legalized they remained in great demand. Indiennes became a specialty of the Christophe-Philippe Oberkampf mill in Jouy (number 2 is an Oberkampf design) and survived the French Revolution to endear themselves to Napoleon and Josephine—and to the public ever since.

1.

2.

3.

4.

INDIGOS

1. **England or France, c. 1800–1820, BP cotton, AYG, 110%**
2. **France, late 19th C, RP cotton, AYG, 80%**
3. **France, late 19th C, RP cotton, AYG, 80%**
4. **England or France, c. 1810–20, BP cotton, AYG, 100%**
5. **France, 4th quarter 19th C, RP cotton, AYG, 68%**
6. **England or France, c. 1800–1820, BP cotton, AYG, 110%**
7. **USA, c. 1860–80, RP cotton, AYG, 100%**
8. **France, c. 1810–20, BP cotton, AYG, 100%**
9. **France, late 19th C, RP cotton, AYG, 100%**
10. **England or France, c. 1810–20, BP cotton, AYG, 110%**

INDIGO IS A dye rather than a design, but the patterns printed in indigo—most commonly with resist and discharge techniques—have a distinctive look. As early as 3000 B.C., plants of the genus *Indigofera* were harvested in India for the deep, permanent blue they imparted to cloth. Introduced to Europe in the mid-sixteenth century, dyeing with indigo replaced the earlier and more difficult blue-dye technique based on woad (though not without much protest from the woad growers and dealers). It was and still is one of the most widely used vegetable dyes. The climate of the Caribbean and southern United States is favorable for the cultivation of indigo; established there in 1740, the crop became one of the first profitable colonial exports—only thirty years later, a million pounds of indigo a year were sent to England from Georgia and the Carolinas alone, harvested by slave labor. Many early American homes had an indigo dye pot sitting by the hearth. In this century it has largely been replaced in commercial usage by a synthetic look-alike, but for centuries indigo was a staple of men's and women's apparel, particularly work clothes. To this dye we owe today's ubiquitous blue jeans. (See also *Floral: Blue Resists,* page 42.)

1.

2.

3.

4.

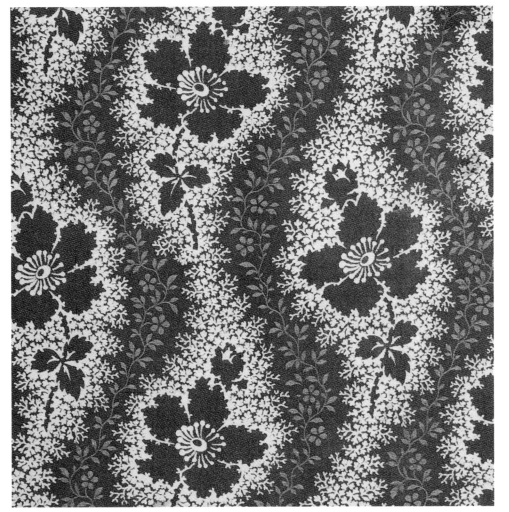

5.

6.

7.

8.

9.

10.

LATTICE AND TRELLIS

1. France, 1876, RP cotton, HFYG, 100%
2. France, 2d half 20th C, gouache on paper, HFYG, 38%
3. France, 2d half 20th C, gouache on paper, HFYG, 50%
4. France, c. 1880, RP cotton, HFYG, 50%

THESE OBJECTS BORROWED from the garden allow a designer to use a grid while giving the illusion of three-dimensionality. Latticework can serve as a background or can be made a motif in itself, wrapped in climbing vines and flowers. But it usually appears in home-furnishing fabrics rather than in apparel. Flowers are worn to decorate the human body, after all; to reduce the body to a support for flowers is to defeat the purpose.

1.

2.

3.

4.

LEAVES

PEOPLE HAVE WORN leaves since Adam and Eve. A floral motif without flowers, they can impart a verdant lushness or a stark abstractness to a fabric while still being organic.

1. **France, 1880–84, gouache on paper, AYG, 100%**
2. **France, 1848, RP wool challis, AYG, 100%**
3. **France, c. 1820, gouache on paper, A (scarf border), 60%**
4. **France, 2d half 19th C, RP cotton, AYG, 70%**
5. **France, c. 1890, RP cotton, AYG, 84%**
6. **France, c. 1820, gouache on paper, AYG, 66%**
7. **France, c. 1890, gouache on paper, AYG, 100%**
8. **France, 19th C, RP cotton, AYG, 80%**
9. **France, c. 1810–20, gouache on paper, AYG, 100%**

1.

2.

3.

4.

5.

6.

7.

8.

9.

LIBERTY LOOK

1. England, 1970s, SP cotton, AYG, 70%
2. Probably France, 1920s–30s, RP silk, AYG, 100%
3. USA, 1920–30s, RP cotton, AYG, 100%
4. England, 1970s, SP cotton, AYG, 100%
5. USA, 1920s–30s, RP cotton, AYG, 100%
6. USA, 1920s–30s, RP cotton, AYG, 115%

LIBERTY'S OF LONDON has been a Regent Street landmark since 1875, when the shop was founded by Arthur Lazenby Liberty. It is synonymous with Art Nouveau—so much so that the name the Italians gave this late-nineteenth-century movement, which expressed itself in everything from apparel to architecture, is *stile Liberty*. E. W. Godwin, Lindsay Butterfield, Harry Napper, C. F. A. Voysey, Arthur Silver, and other well-known English designers of the time created prints for Liberty's. Today, however, the term "Liberty look" refers not so much to Art Nouveau as to the allover prints that Liberty's popularized in the 1920s—lightweight cottons in a distinctively sweet and carefree floral style. This look is still much imitated. Examples 1 and 4 are genuine Liberty designs.

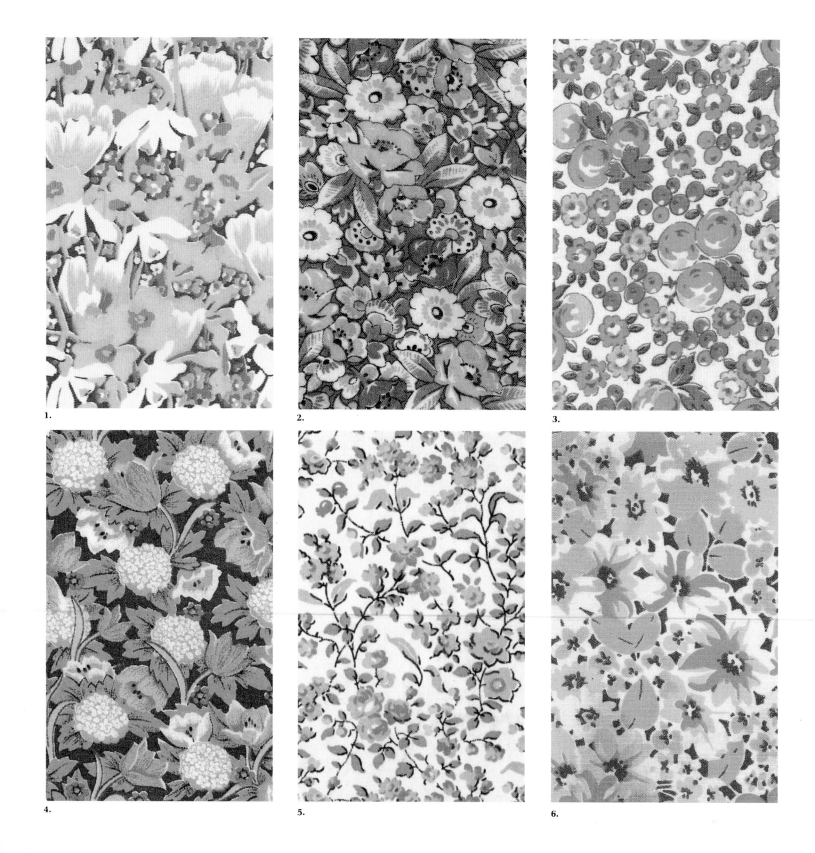

1.

2.

3.

4.

5.

6.

LINEWORK

1. France, 1940s, gouache on paper, AYG, 50%
2. France, c. 1950s, pen and ink on paper, HFYG, 50%
3. France, 1877, RP cotton, HFYG, 38%

TRANSFERRED TO CLOTH, the shadings and delicate line work of pen-and-ink drawings are a way to give texture and interest to a monochromatic design—a useful technique, since one-color printing cuts expenses.

1.

2.

3.

MADDERS

1, 18. France, 1861, RP cotton, AYG, 100%
2, 4, 10, 15. USA, c. 1870–80s, RP cotton, AYG, 100%
3, 9, 19, 20. France, c. 1850–60, RP cotton, AYG, 80%
5, 7, 13, 14. France, c. 1850, RP cotton, AYG, 100%
6, 12. USA, c. 1870s–80s, RP cotton, AYG, 80%
8. France, 1851, RP cotton, AYG, 80%
11. France, 1848, RP cotton, AYG, 80%
16. France, c. 1860, RP cotton, AYG, 100%
17. France, c. 1860, gouache on paper, AYG, 100%
21. France, c. 1870s–80s, RP cotton, AYG, 100%

THE ROOT OF the madder plant, *Rubia tinctorum,* produces a vegetable dye that has been in use since the ancient Egyptians. It is extremely colorfast and can produce a wide range of hues—reds, rusts, oranges, blacks, browns, purples—depending on the mordant used. Also, the dyeing process is relatively simple. Though genuine madders are rarely used today, because their active ingredient, alizarin, has been made chemically since 1869 from the coal-tar product anthracene, madder was the most commonly used dye in eighteenth- and nineteenth-century textile printing. It was especially popular in the second half of the nineteenth century for everyday clothing. Bolts of madder prints, like indigos, calicos, and neats, were a stock item, and they inevitably ended up as pieces in nineteenth-century American patchwork quilts.

1.

2.

3.

4.

5.

6.

7.

8.

9.

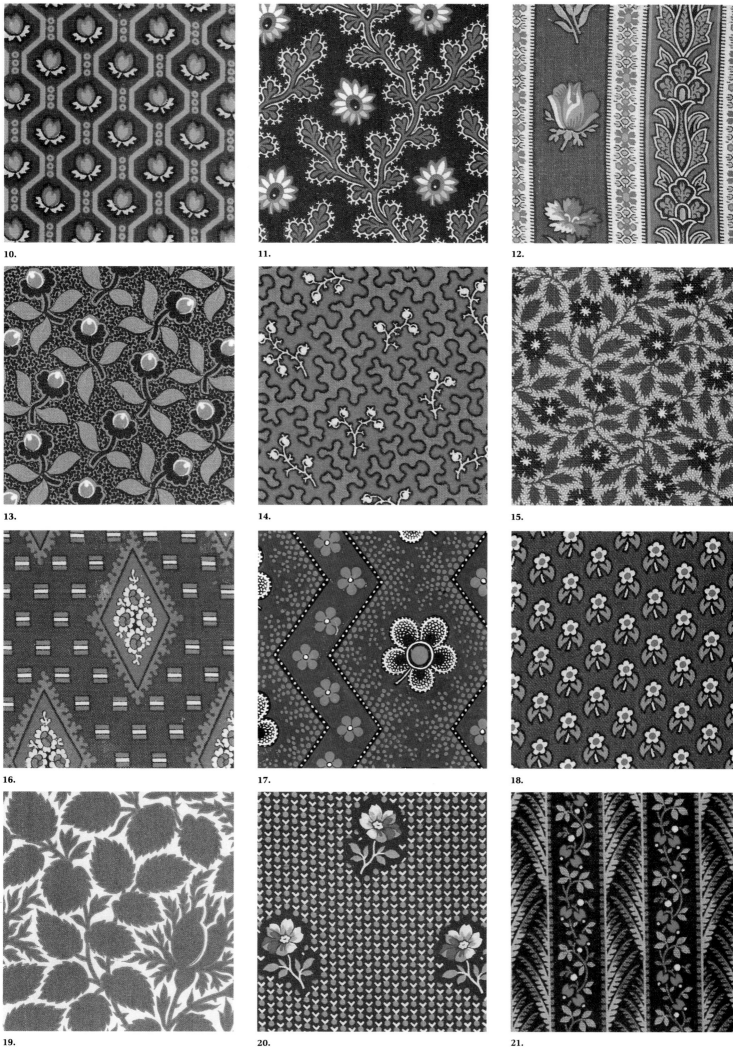

10.

11.

12.

13.

14.

15.

16.

17.

18.

19.

20.

21.

MILL ENGRAVINGS

1, 3–5, 7, 9, 12, 13, 15, 17–20, 24, 28, 29, 31, 34, 40, 42, 45. France, c. 1810–20, RP cotton, AYG, 100%
2, 10, 11, 14, 16, 21–23, 25, 30, 32, 35, 37, 39, 41, 43. France, c. 1810–20, gouache on paper, AYG, 100%
6, 27. France, c. 1810–20, RP cotton, AYG, 120%
8, 33, 38. France, c. 1820–25, RP cotton, AYG, 100%
26. France, c. 1820–30, gouache on paper, AYG, 100%
36. England, c. 1810–20, RP cotton, AYG, 100%
44. France, 1829, RP cotton, AYG, 100%

THIS PRINTING METHOD based on steel engravings was employed when a small-scale design needed very finely defined detail. Mill engraving is a demonstration of the nineteenth-century printer's practical application of the properties of metals. Steel is very hard and difficult to engrave, but it is durable and accepts fine line work. Copper is softer and more easily engraved, but a finely etched pattern soon wears away with use. The engraver's solution was to engrave the pattern by hand on a small soft-steel roller, which was then hardened. This roller, called the die, was then set in a machine where it revolved against the mill, a second soft-steel roller of equal size, to which it transferred the pattern in relief. After being hardened, the mill was then rotated against a larger copper printing roller to impress the pattern, and the process was repeated again and again to cover the entire copper surface. The actual printing of cloth could then begin. If the engraving began to wear thin, the copper roller could be "turned off" (ground smooth) and reengraved from the original mill, or the mill could be reused with a new design altogether.

1.

2.

3.

4.

5.

6.

7.

8.

9.

10.

11.

12.

13.

14.

15.

16.

17.

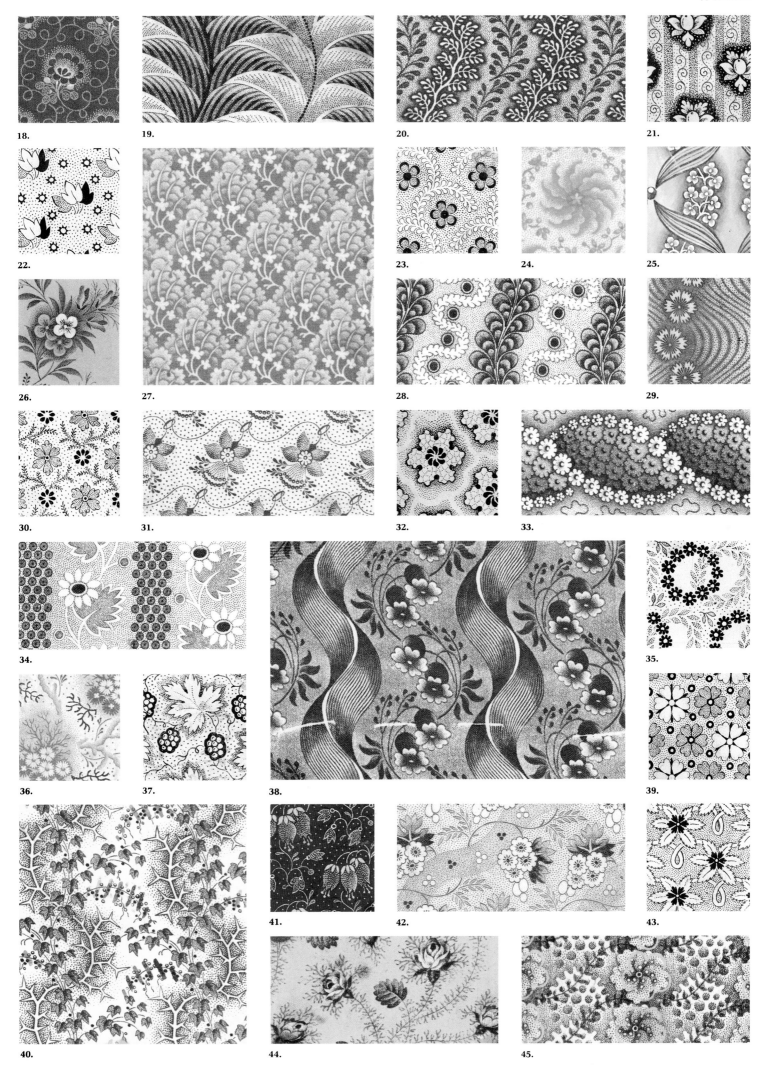

18.

19.

20.

21.

22.

23.

24.

25.

26.

27.

28.

29.

30.

31.

32.

33.

34.

35.

36.

37.

38.

39.

40.

41.

42.

43.

44.

45.

MOIRÉ

1. France, c. 1920, gouache on paper, HFYG, 50%
2. France, 1909, RP cotton sateen, HFYG, 29%
3. France, 1900–1920, gouache on paper, AYG, 100%
4. France, c. 1920, gouache on paper, HFYG, 46%

GENUINE MOIRÉ IS a dyeless form of printing. The cloth, usually silk, is run through rollers that crush the pattern into it to make permanent waves in the way it reflects light. This cloth is also called watered silk. But the moiré look can be imitated by conventional printing on any textile, giving a modest cotton or rayon the look of a more expensive fabric. And as long as the rollers have already been engraved and the presses are running, why not make the moiré a background for a floral motif? The urge to embellish is difficult to resist, and often an "enriched" pattern does prove more commercially successful.

1.

2.

3.

4.

MONOTONES

1. France, 1930s–40s, gouache on paper, AYG, 50%
2. France, c. 1900, RP cotton, AYG, 80%
3. France, c. 1840, paper impression, AYG, 60%
4. France, c. 1890–1900, gouache on paper, AYG, 50%
5. France, 1930s, gouache on paper, AYG, 70%

PRINTING A FABRIC in a range of colors involves applying a succession of dyes—each in its own pattern and each on a screen or roller that must align perfectly with the one before. Monotone designs cut costs by requiring only one dye and thus only one screen or roller. The motifs in these designs are often dark against a light ground—again for reasons of economy. Light motifs against dark grounds are traditionally produced by more complicated and costly methods of resist and discharge printing.

1.

2.

3.

4.

5.

NEATS

1, 15. France, c. 1870, gouache on paper, AYG, 100%

2, 11, 17, 20. USA, c. 1880–90, RP cotton, AYG, 100%

3, 14. France, c. 1880–90, RP cotton, AYG, 100%

4. England, c. 1900, RP cotton, AYG, 100%

5, 9, 10. France, 1861, RP cotton, AYG, 100%

6, 19, 21. France, c. 1860, RP cotton, AYG, 100%

7, 18. France, 1899, RP cotton, AYG, 100%

8. France, 1887, RP cotton, AYG, 100%

12. France, 1896, RP cotton, AYG, 100%

13. France, 1892, RP cotton, AYG, 100%

16. France, c. 1870–80, RP cotton, AYG, 100%

SPACED LAYOUTS OF simple, small-scale floral or geometric motifs were a staple in the textile industry during the second half of the nineteenth century. Called neats, for obvious reasons, they were economical to print. Usually black, red, or blue figures were set on a white ground, or white figures appeared on a black, brown, red, purple, or blue ground. Inexpensive and basic, such fabrics were used to clothe the entire family, though floral ornaments were preferred for women, geometric motifs for men and boys.

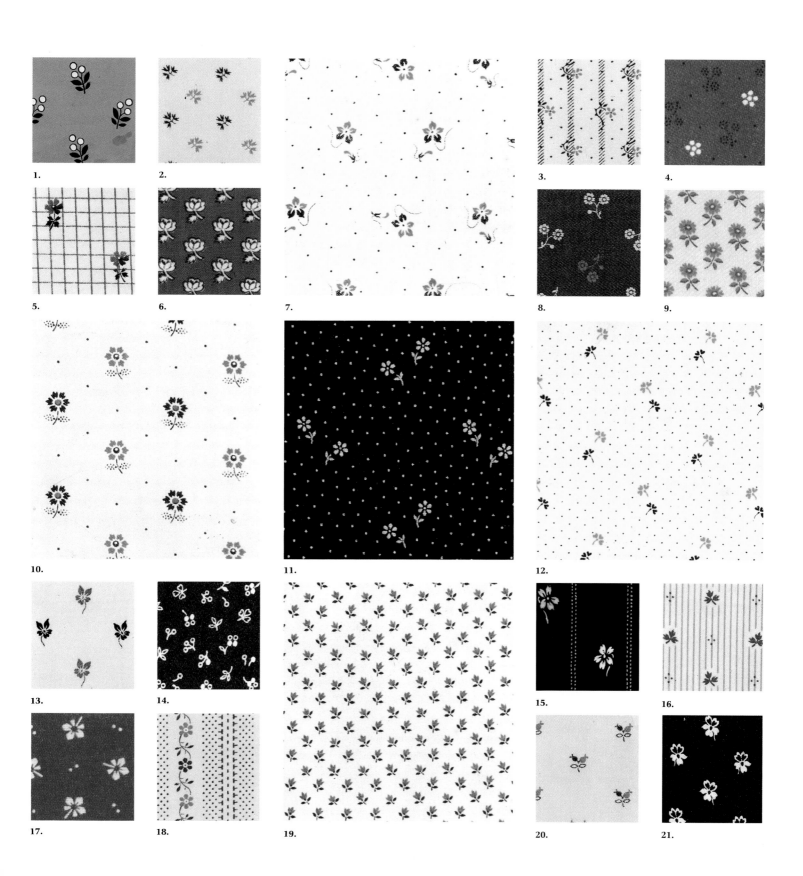

1. 2. 3. 4. 5. 6. 7. 8. 9. 10. 11. 12. 13. 14. 15. 16. 17. 18. 19. 20. 21.

OMBRÉ

1. **France, 1840–55, PP wool challis, AYG, 70%**
2. **France, 1840–55, PP wool challis, AYG, 110%**
3. **France, 1882, RP cotton, AYG, 80%**
4. **France, c. 1820, gouache on paper, AYG, 68%**
5. **France, c. 1820–30, gouache on paper, A (scarf pattern), 66%**
6. **France, c. 1820–30, gouache on paper, A (scarf pattern), 80%**
7. **France, 1840–55, PP wool challis, AYG, 100%**

ALSO KNOWN AS irisé, rainbow prints, and fondu, ombré patterns are distinguished by a gradual shading and blending of one color into another. The effect was achieved first in paper printing, and in the early 1800s the Alsatian wallpaper firm of Zuber became famous for its ombrés. The technique was soon applied to block-printed textiles, although it proved time-consuming and difficult. The look was particularly popular on cotton and wool-challis dress goods of the 1840s and 1850s. Because of its expense and complexity of manufacture, ombré is seldom seen in fabrics after the mid-nineteenth century.

1.

2.

3.

4.

5.

6.

7.

PATIO PRINTS

1. USA, c. 1940s, SP cotton, HFYG, 24%
2. USA, c. 1940s, SP cotton, HFYG, 30%

A GENRE OF large-scale floral patterns first produced in the 1940s and 1950s, patio prints often appear on a sturdy, heavyweight cotton called bark cloth because of its rough-textured surface. During World War II and for a while after, fine fabrics were scarce and weaves like bark cloth were a necessary substitute. Bright, bold prints helped to make them attractive. Tending to the tropical and the exotic, they also made the cloth a favorite for patio, sun-room, or porch furniture, even after wartime shortages were over. In fact, patio prints, once cherished for their cheapness, became popular again in the 1980s, at prices considerably higher than they originally commanded. What was once commonplace becomes precious when it is recycled as nostalgia.

1.

2.

PATTERNED GROUND: CHECKS AND PLAIDS

1. France, 1920s, paper impression, AYG, 50%
2. France, 1930s–60s, gouache on paper, AYG, 100%
3. France, 1920s, BP or SP wool challis, AYG, 100%
4. France, 1920s, BP or SP cotton, AYG, 70%

MOTIFS HAVE BEEN printed on patterned grounds since the first days of the textile-printing industry. Pattern upon pattern is a way to add interest, depth, and richness to a fabric. Contemporary designers like to play with this device in coordinated patterns, using the ground alone, say, in a sheet or a skirt and then both designs together in the matching pillowcase or blouse. And two-patterns-for-the-price-of-one is good value. Checks and plaids are often used in combination with flowers, since the mock-woven ground provides a striking contrast to the obviously printed floral motifs.

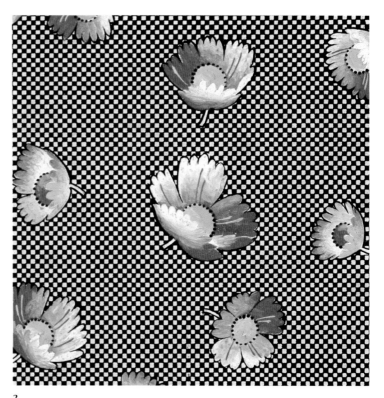

1.

2.

3.

4.

PATTERNED GROUND: DOTS

DOTTED GROUNDS ARE perhaps the most widely used—they fill up a background in a playful but unobtrusive way.

1. USA, 1920s–40s, RP cotton, AYG, 100%
2. USA, 1930s–40s, RP rayon, AYG, 100%
3. France, 1930s, gouache on paper, AYG, 80%
4. Probably England, c. 1900, RP cotton chintz, AYG, 76%

1.

2.

3.

4.

PATTERNED GROUND: FLORAL

FLOWERS ON FLOWERS can create a luscious layering of blossoms, or the background flowers can subtly enhance the mood of the main motif.

1. **France, c. 1920s, RP cotton, AYG, 80%**
2. **France, c. 1910, RP cotton, AYG, 90%**
3. **England or France, c. 1860–70, RP cotton, AYG, 100%**
4. **France, c. 1820–30, RP cotton, AYG, 100%**

1.

2.

3.

4.

PATTERNED GROUND: GEOMETRIC

FLORAL MOTIFS SUPERIMPOSED on a background of geometric shapes provide a study in contrasts. The two worlds can coexist in harmony, as they do in numbers 1, 3, and 4, or they can clash in a competition for dominance, as in number 2.

1. France, c. 1940s, gouache on paper, AYG, 100%
2. France, c. 1830–40, BP silk, AYG, 75%
3. France, c. 1900–1910, gouache on paper, AYG, 100%
4. France, c. 1870–80, RP cotton, AYG, 100%

1.

2.

3.

4.

PATTERNED GROUND: STRIPES

FLORAL MOTIFS ON striped grounds give the designer an opportunity to play with contrasting layouts: the carefree arrangement of tossed flowers, for example, against the rigid formality of stripes.

1. France, c. 1910–20, gouache on paper, AYG, 64%
2. France, 1888, RP cotton flannel, AYG, 90%
3. France, c. 1900, gouache on paper, AYG, 86%
4. France, c. 1850, gouache on paper, AYG, 70%

1.

2.

3.

4.

PATTERNED GROUND: TEXTURES

TEXTURED GROUNDS CAN complement a floral pattern without competing with it and at the same time add density to the appearance of the cloth.

1. France, 1930s, gouache on paper, AYG, 70%
2. France, 1930s, gouache on paper, AYG, 100%
3. France, late 19th C, gouache on paper, AYG, 100%
4. France, 1930s–40s, RP silk, AYG, 110%

1.

2.

3.

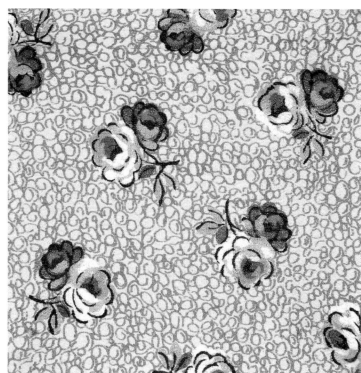

4.

PICOTAGE

1. France, 1840–45, BP cotton, AYG, 95%
2. France, c. 1900–1920, gouache on paper, AYG, 64%
3. France, c. 1840, RP cotton, AYG, 80%
4. France, 1830–40, gouache on paper, AYG, 50%

PICOTAGE, KNOWN AS "pinning" in England, dates back to the eighteenth-century block print. The carver, unable to cut very fine dots in relief, would stud the wooden block strategically with different-sized brass pins to create effects of shadow and highlight on the printed cloth. Though the original technique is no longer used, the look has remained a part of the design vocabulary. Picotage effects are seen most frequently today in traditional floral chintzes that aim to capture the old-fashioned block-printed look.

1.

2.

3.

4.

PILLEMENT LOOK

1. France, 1st half 19th C, gouache on paper, HFYG, 70%
2. France, c. 1830–40, watercolor and pencil on paper, AYG, 80%
3. France, c. 1910, gouache on paper, HFYG, 50%

JEAN BAPTISTE PILLEMENT, a court painter to Marie Antoinette, specialized in scenes of fanciful chinoiserie, which he painted on the walls of her various palaces to please her. Made to look Chinese by pagodas and Oriental figures, his landscapes were otherwise part French and part fantasy, with their little people sheltering under giant parasol plants and their flowers of butterfly wings and feathers. Pillement's murals were so popular that weavers in the late-eighteenth-century Lyonnais silk industry began to imitate them, and they were soon followed by the cloth printers. Pillement's elegantly playful style is still in demand today, mainly for furnishings textiles.

1.

2.

3.

PROVINCIAL

1. France, c. 1820–30, gouache on paper, AYG, 50%
2. France, c. 1820–30, gouache on paper, AYG, 58%
3. France, c. 1820–30, gouache on paper, AYG, 90%
4. France, c. 1820–30, gouache on paper, AYG, 100%
5–16. France, c. 1815–20, gouache on paper, AYG, 100%
17, 18. France, c. 1815–20, gouache on paper, AYG, 70%

THE NAME "PROVINCIAL" comes from the association of these designs with Provence, where it is hot and sunny and people wore these gay cotton prints as part of their traditional costume. Provincial patterns in fact mark the beginning of large-scale commercial textile printing. The type known as *mignonettes* (numbers 5–16) were produced by the thousands in the early 1800s (at first by laborious hand block-printing), and they were the bread and butter of the new industry. Christophe-Philippe Oberkampf's mill at Jouy, though better known for its sophisticated copperplate-printed scenic toiles, subsisted on these designs and exported them with great success. Napoleon is said to have visited the factory and to have told Oberkampf, "You and I wage good war on the English, you by your industry and I by my armies. But your way is the more effective."

1.

2.

3.

4.

5.

6.

7.

8.

9.

10.

11

12

13.

14.

15.

16.

17.

18.

PROVINCIAL BORDERS

1. France, c. 1810–20, gouache on paper, A (scarf pattern), 45%

2. France, c. 1810–20, gouache on paper, A (scarf pattern), 50%

3. France, c. 1810–20, gouache on paper, A (scarf pattern), 50%

4. France, c. 1810–20, gouache on paper, A (scarf pattern), 50%

5. France, c. 1810–20, gouache on paper, A (scarf pattern), 50%

A SQUARE COTTON scarf, or *mouchoir,* with a floral border was part of the traditional women's costume in Provence. The field was usually a small-scale motif that took second place to the more decorative border. The designs were generally block-printed. Scarf borders like these are now mass-produced and are a staple of the French country look, interpreted not only as scarves but as sheets, quilts, curtains, and tablecloths.

1.

2.

3.

4.

6012.

5.

RIBBON PATTERNS

1. France, c. 1850, gouache on paper, A, 100%
2. France, c. 1850, gouache on paper, A, 100%
3. France, c. 1850, gouache on paper, A, 100%
4. France, c. 1850, gouache on paper, A, 80%
5. France, c. 1850, gouache on paper, A, 100%
6. France, c. 1850, gouache on paper, A, 100%
7. France, c. 1850, gouache on paper, A, 80%
8. France, c. 1850, gouache on paper, A, 115%
9. France, c. 1850, gouache on paper, A, 80%
10. France, c. 1850, gouache on paper, A, 100%

SILK RIBBONS WERE necessary fashion items throughout the nineteenth century. They were usually made on a jacquard loom, with the pattern woven in, but less-expensive printed ribbons also had a market. These fancy trimmings could be as wide as twelve inches, for use as sashes, but most of them allowed the designer only a narrow strip of cloth with which to catch the customer's attention. They were an important accent on blouses, dresses, and hats, and a lot of attention was lavished on them. These particular examples are from Saint-Etienne, which was a major French ribbon-manufacturing center. Today this kind of design is more or less a vanished art, as are decorative ribbons.

1.

2.

3.

4.

5.

6.

7.

8.

9.

10.

ROSES

1. **England, 1902, RP cotton, HFYG, 74%**
2. **France, c. 1910–20, gouache on paper, A (ribbon pattern), 50%**
3. **France, c. 1920s, gouache on paper, HFYG, 35%**
4. **France, c. 1920, gouache on paper, AYG, 60%**
5. **France, 1920s, gouache on paper, AYG, 60%**
6. **France, c. 1920, gouache on paper, A (ribbon pattern), 74%**
7. **France, 1881, RP cotton, HFYG, 38%**
8. **France, c. 1900, gouache on paper, AYG, 80%**

FLORALS ARE THE most popular type of printed textiles, and of all floral subjects the favorite is the rose. Perhaps this reflects an unconscious collective desire for love and beauty, which roses symbolize in the ancient language of flowers. Of the countless rose motifs, a few are particularly notable. The first well-known fabric rose was the Tudor, emblem of the sixteenth-century rulers of England (number 1). Variations of this flat, stylized flower are often seen in designs by William Morris and other artists of the Arts and Crafts movement. More realistic are the roses painted by the French artist Pierre-Joseph Redouté (number 7), who was commissioned by the Empress Josephine to create a watercolor folio of all the species in her rose garden. The result, published between 1817 and 1824, earned Redouté the title "Raphael of the rose" and has influenced textile designers from the nineteenth century up to the present day. The best-known twentieth-century example is that of Paul Poiret, the French fashion designer of the pre–World War I years through the 1920s, who made a highly stylized rose his personal emblem (numbers 2 and 4). To design his fabrics, Poiret hired well-known artists such as Raoul Dufy and created a studio of untrained country girls, the Atelier Martine—thus combining refinement and spontaneity for a bright, flat, vibrant look.

1.

2.

3.

4.

5.

6.

7.

8.

SACKCLOTH

1. USA, c. 1930s, RP cotton, 100%
2. USA, c. 1930s, RP cotton, 70%
3. USA, c. 1930s, RP cotton, 80%
4. USA, c. 1930s, RP cotton, 70%
5. USA, c. 1930s, RP cotton, 80%
6. USA, c. 1930s, RP cotton, 100%

PRINTED SACKING IS a uniquely American product. During the Depression someone came up with the clever merchandising idea of printing gay allover patterns on sacks of chicken feed. Flour and grain sacks had long been bleached and converted into clothing by poor rural women, but this offered a much more appealing alternative. By buying X brand of chicken feed, one also got a "free" yard or so of cheerful fabric all ready to sew up. Since these patterns looked like store-bought cloth, many a child may have been spared the stigma of having to go to school in what the other kids recognized as sackcloth.

1.

2.

3.

4.

5.

6.

SCARVES

1. France, 1938, paper impression, A (scarf corner), 38%
2. Probably France, mid-19th C, paper impression, A (scarf corner), 25%
3. France, c. 1810–20, BP cotton, A (scarf corner), 50%

THE SQUARE OR rectangular format of the scarf frees designers from their usual obligation to create an infinitely repeating pattern: the border can frame a single image, like a painting. And since a silk scarf is a decorative luxury, bought more for its appearance than for any practical use, it gives the designer free rein to exploit its artistic potential. As an accessory, scarves offer women the chance to spice up their wardrobe without the expense of a whole new outfit, and they also make economic sense for the manufacturer, since a scarf can be priced high in relation to the small amount of fabric and construction it requires.

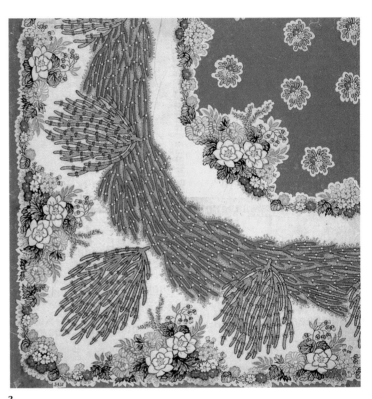

1.

2.

3.

SPACED DARK GROUND

1. France or USA, c. 1900–1930, gouache on paper, AYG, 50%
2. France, 1880–90, gouache on paper, AYG, 50%
3. France, 1880–90, gouache on paper, AYG, 56%

A SPACED LAYOUT reveals more ground than figure—the motifs have room around them. Relatively isolated against the field, they are more noticeable than in an allover or packed pattern and must be carefully conceived and drawn. Traditionally, dark grounds were used for fall and winter fashions and light grounds for spring and summer wear.

1.

2.

3.

SPACED LIGHT GROUND

1. France, 1930s–40s, RP silk crepe, AYG, 50%
2. France, 1888, RP wool challis, AYG, 80%
3. France, 1920s–30s, gouache on paper, AYG, 80%
4. France, c. 1890, RP silk, AYG, 86%

THE CHOICE BETWEEN light and dark grounds is not only made for seasonal reasons. There are also technical and cost considerations. It is usually simpler to print motifs on a background that is paler than they are. In order to print lighter motifs effectively on a darker ground, a chemical discharge process is often employed, and that involves additional cost.

1.

2.

3.

4.

SPRAYS

1. France, late 19th C, gouache on paper, HFYG, 25%
2. France, c. 1860–80, gouache on paper, AYG, 70%
3. France, 1888, RP wool mousseline, AYG, 88%
4. France, c. 1880, RP cotton, AYG, 86%

A BOUQUET IS a compact cluster of flowers; a spray is a freer, more casual arrangement. It may include long stems and grasses for an informal country look. A spray seems to have fallen into shape almost by accident. Or it can be a single branch with blossoms scattered along its length, as if no designer had had a hand in deciding where they went.

1.

2.

3.

4.

SPRIGS

1. France, c. 1880–90, RP cotton, AYG, 100%
2. France, c. 1880–90, RP cotton, AYG, 90%
3. France, c. 1880–90, gouache on paper, AYG, 70%
4. France, c. 1850, paper impression, AYG, 100%
5. France, 1899, RP cotton, AYG, 100%
6. France, 1895, RP cotton, AYG, 100%
7. France, 1895, RP cotton, AYG, 100%
8. France, c. 1860–70, RP cotton, AYG, 100%
9. France, 1888, RP wool mousseline, AYG, 100%

SPRIGS ARE SMALL single flowers, each on its own short stem, and they usually appear in a tossed layout. Informal yet demure, and always feminine, they were so popular in the eighteenth and nineteenth centuries for summer dresses that the cloth on which they were printed became known as sprigged cotton.

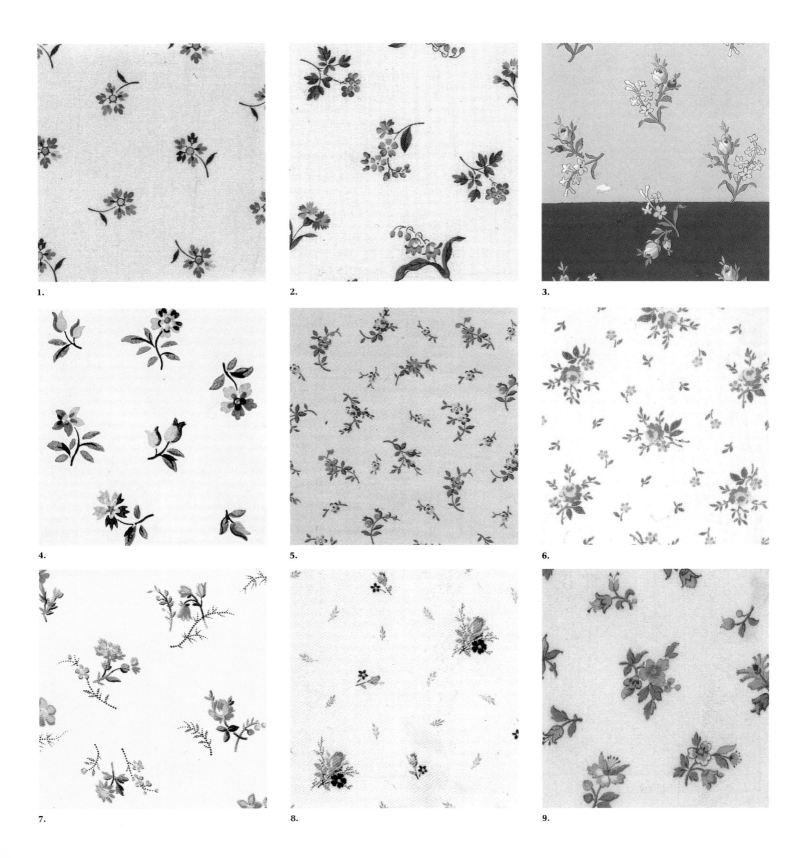

1.

2.

3.

4.

5.

6.

7.

8.

9.

STRIPES

1. **France, c. 1870–80, RP cotton, AYG, 86%**
2. **France, 1845, RP wool challis, AYG, 86%**
3. **France, c. 1830–40, gouache on paper, AYG, 100%**
4. **France, 1st half 20th C, RP silk moiré, AYG, 66%**
5. **France, 1930s, gouache on paper, AYG, 70%**
6. **France, 1930s, RP or SP silk crepe, 100%**

THE STRIPE, A basic geometric layout, can be decorated with flowers or actually made up of them. Stripes are a constant in both apparel and home-furnishing fabrics, but they were more common in the nineteenth century than they are today. Although they can run horizontally, vertically, or diagonally across a length of fabric, they can at most be only two-directional once one of these orientations has been chosen; twentieth-century manufacturers avoid directional patterns because they limit the options of the fabric cutter. Also, striped garments have to be carefully sewn so that the stripes meet. A busy allover pattern may hide a misalignment at the seam; a stripe makes it obvious.

1.

2.

3.

4.

5.

6.

STRIPES, SERPENTINE

1. France, c. 1820, gouache on paper, AYG, 66%
2. France, c. 1830, RP cotton, AYG, 100%
3. France, c. 1830, RP cotton, AYG, 100%

WAVY OR UNDULATING stripes were an eighteenth- and nineteenth-century device; they are seldom done today because of a twentieth-century prejudice against snakelike shapes. The strong sense of movement in stripes made sinuous may also be disconcerting. The complicated pattern of the first example on this page is actually a selection of different designs—a designer's sketch showing variations on a theme.

1.

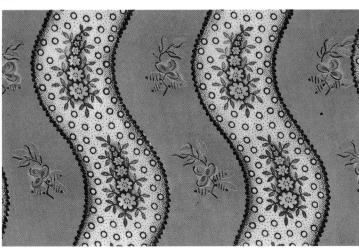

2.

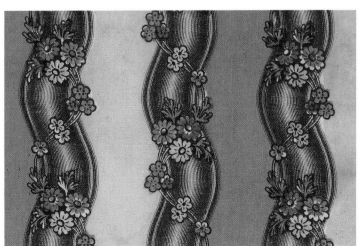

3.

TAPESTRY LOOK

1. France, 1884, RP cotton, HFYG, 50%
2. France, c. 1900, RP cotton, HFYG, 80%
3. France, c. 1880, RP cotton, HFYG, 50%
4. France, 1901, RP cotton, HFYG, 50%

MANY PRINTS ARE designed to imitate a more expensive fabric. These four examples emulate handwoven tapestry. A refined, labor-intensive art form, genuine tapestry has always belonged to the wealthy, and its aristocratic associations make it attractive to the designer wishing to create luxurious-looking prints. When printed on a machine-made cloth woven to resemble the tapestry weave, these patterns can be extremely realistic. In the eighteenth and nineteenth centuries, when the role of tapestry as a wall hanging was familiar to all, the tapestry look was mainly limited to furnishing fabrics. More recently, it has appeared in garments as well.

1.

2.

TH

5.

3.

4.

1.

7.   4.

TURKEY REDS

1. France, 1810–15, gouache on paper, A (scarf pattern), 88%

2. France, 1810–15, gouache on paper, A (scarf motif), 70%

3. France, 1810–15, gouache on paper, A (scarf motif), 70%

4. France, c. 1810–15, gouache on paper, AYG, 80%

5. France, 1810–15, gouache on paper, AYG, 80%

6. France, 1815, gouache on paper, A (scarf border), 40%

7. France, 1810–15, BP cotton, A (scarf border), 36%

8. France, 1810–15, BP cotton, A (scarf border), 90%

9. France, 1815, gouache on paper, A (scarf pattern), 54%

ALSO KNOWN AS Adrianople reds, these may be the most fanciful designs in all of textile printing. Though based on madder, Turkey-red dye was more complicated and time-consuming to produce. The 1801 edition of *Encyclopaedia Britannica* refers to "that beautiful red dye which distinguishes the cotton manufactured in the Ottoman empire," but the technique of processing it had probably arrived in Europe by the mid-eighteenth century. At first Turkey red was used only to dye fabrics a solid scarlet—the color was too strong to accept an overprinted pattern. In 1810, however, the Alsatian dyer Daniel Koechlin discovered a way to discharge a pattern chemically on Turkey-red cloth and at the same time to convert the pattern to blue or black. Later, yellow was added to the palette. The result was these exuberant starburst-like fantasies, with their sense of wheeling movement and their brilliant colors. Perhaps it was the new-found color freedom that called forth the wild patterns, or perhaps—to begin with, at any rate—it was the self-confident extravagance of France's first Empire period. Today Turkey reds are seldom seen except in toned-down cotton bandannas. The pulsating red may be sending out a subliminal message of intense emotion—passion or rage—that causes many people to remark, "It's too red!"

1.

2.

3.

4.

5.

6.

7.

8.

9.

WARP PRINTS

1. France, c. 1900, warp-printed silk, A (ribbon), 100%
2. France, late 19th C, warp-printed silk, A (ribbon), 70%
3. France, c. 1900–1910, warp-printed silk, AYG, 50%
4. France, c. 1860, warp-printed silk, AYG, 80%

THE WARP IS the yarn that is strung lengthwise on the weaver's loom; the weft, or woof, is the yarn threaded over and under the warp to fill it in crosswise. If the warp is printed with a pattern before the weft is woven into it, the finished design will have a blurry, out-of-focus look, softening the edges of the motif. The method is most often used with silk, and warp prints are also known as "shadow silks." The French call them *chinés*, from their word for variegated. A specialty of Lyons, particularly in silk taffeta, they were popular for women's apparel in the second half of the nineteenth century, but they are little seen in twentieth-century cloth. The technique is cumbersome and expensive: the warp threads are wound on a frame, printed with the pattern, then transferred to the loom, where the weft threads are woven in. The method is related to the traditional ikat technique, in which the warp threads are bound and dyed in a predetermined pattern before being strung on the loom.

1.

2.

3.

4.

WARP PRINTS, SIMULATED

THESE CONVENTIONALLY PRODUCED prints inexpensively mimic the warp-print effect. Most common at the end of the nineteenth century and in the first two decades of the twentieth, they are unusual today. What may seem pleasantly indistinct in a real warp print may look like an out-of-register printing job in the imitation if it is not meticulously executed.

1. France, c. 1900, gouache on paper, HFYG, 50%
2. France, 1895, gouache on paper, AYG, 100%
3. France, c. 1900–1910, gouache on paper, AYG, 100%
4. France, c. 1900, gouache on paper, AYG, 70%

1.

2.

3.

4.

WATERCOLOR LOOK

1. France, 1930s–60s, gouache and watercolor on paper, AYG, 100%
2. France, 1950s, gouache and watercolor on paper, AYG, 100%
3. France, 1930–40s, gouache and watercolor on paper, AYG, 100%

LIKE THE BRUSHSTROKE LOOK, these prints are a machine-age bow to painting, to the work of the hand, and to the aura of a traditional fine art. The light, fresh qualities of watercolor are particularly suited to flowing, delicate fabrics such as silk. The look became fashionable with the introduction of silk-screen printing in the late 1920s and early 1930s, for the fluid style of watercolor could be achieved much more effectively in silk screening than in roller printing.

1.

2.

3.

WILD FLOWERS

1. France, 1886, RP wool mousseline, AYG, 80%
2. France, c. 1920, gouache on paper, HFYG, 38%
3. France, 1878, RP cotton sateen, AYG, 100%

HUNDREDS IF NOT thousands of wild-flower patterns were produced each year during the nineteenth century. There was then such a passion for naturalism and a thirst for something new that in the first example even the lowly dandelion puff becomes worthy of reproduction. Numbers 2 and 3 show a threesome particularly dear to the French—the cornflower (*bluet*), daisy (*marguerite*), and field poppy (*coquelicot*). The blue, white, and red of the flowers are emblematic of the tricolor French flag.

1.

2.

3.

WREATHS

1. **France, c. 1880, gouache on paper, HFYG, 40%**
2. **France, c. 1810, gouache on paper, AYG, 50%**
3. **France, c. 1910–20, gouache on paper, AYG, 25%**
4. **France, 1810, gouache on paper, AYG, 52%**
5. **France, c. 1880, gouache on paper, HFYG, 54%**

THE WREATH COMBINES the dual symbolism of the flower and the circle. As a funerary emblem, it goes back at least to ancient Egypt; to set a ring of flowers on a grave is to involve the dead in the living cycle of nature. At their banquets, Romans wore wreaths of flowers on their heads to remind themselves of the ephemeral nature of life and the need to "eat, drink, and be merry." But wreaths also stand for victory (the Greek and Roman laurel wreath, revived by Napoleon), honor and peace (the symbol of the United Nations), and the rites of spring. Young girls and nymphs are often depicted dancing hand in hand in a circle with wreaths of flowers on their heads. Textile designers emphasize these positive meanings rather than the wreath's more melancholic associations.

1.

2.

3.

4.

5.

2. Geometric

TO CALL THE patterns in this chapter "geometric" is to use the vocabulary of the textile industry, but it also makes them sound rather like the subject of a mathematics class. And, in fact, the circles, squares, and triangles of euclidean geometry are all here—but so are crescents and cartouches, spirals and stars, pinwheels, polka dots, and many, many plaids. A geometric is an abstract or nonrepresentational motif, a shape that is not a picture of something out in the real world. A fleur-de-lis is a geometric: it is actually a stylized iris, but it is too removed from the flower form to be called a floral. Cube patterns are geometrics until an artist makes them into conversational images of a child's building blocks; a basket weave is a geometric until the artist makes it into a basket.

Whether as orderly as a hexagon or as visually electric as an optical or a serpentine stripe, geometric motifs have always been with us. The centuries have filled them with associations. It is hard to look at a triangle design, for example, without some echo of the Egyptian pyramid coming to mind, however subliminally. And its connection with the pyramid links the shape with immortality and eternity. The class of patterns called vermicular got its name in classical times from a Latin word that pointed out their resemblance to worm tracks in the earth, and though they have accrued a long and honorable history of nonrepresentational use since then, a contemporary designer may still dismiss a vermicular as "too wormy."

In modernist art, abstraction, at first controversial to the point of scandal, still retains an aura of difficulty, or, at the least, of intellectual weightiness—unless it reaches the point where people write it off as "merely decorative." In fabric patterns, abstraction has been around forever and is an entirely comfortable presence. The textile designer knows that abstraction is inherently, shamelessly decorative. The various symbolic meanings of geometric motifs are often antiquated matters of scholarship, and most people are probably oblivious to these meanings as they look at the cloth. (Some of these old symbolisms are outlined in the chapters that follow, but longer discussions than ours make no claim to have exhausted the subject.) Yet these motifs continue to attract their public. Perhaps they spark some sense of familiarity, some cultural memory that may not have to be articulated in order to be effective. Or perhaps they work as a blank slate for an interpretation of the viewer's own. In either case, they work well. The circle, in fact, is the most popular nonfloral motif.

And it is popularity that is really the issue here: the cloth must sell. It's doubtful that many in the chain of decision making are thinking about whether or not the triangle is a symbol of immortality. The extent to which geometrics are meaningful to us is suggested by the degree to which they earn their keep.

ABSTRACT

1. USA, 1940s–50s, gouache on paper, AYG, 70%
2. France, c. 1930s, RP silk crepe, AYG, 100%
3. USA, 1940s–50s, gouache on paper, AYG, 100%
4. USA, 1940s–50s, dye and gouache on paper, AYG, 100%
5. France, 1940s, paper impression, AYG, 100%

BECAUSE WESTERN PAINTING and sculpture had been representational for so much of their history, artists who began to make abstract art in the early twentieth century thought they had discovered something radically new. But abstract images had always been around—in the artifacts and objects of many different cultures and traditions, including fabric designs. A dot or stripe pattern, for example, is abstract, though designers don't use that term—they call it a dot or a stripe. The word "abstract" is used in the textile business to describe a nonobjective motif that can't be given any other name. If artists followed designers in working with abstraction, designers followed artists in developing particular styles and patterns. Art and design often cooperate to produce a period's "look." Fabrics inspired by abstract art appeared hand in hand with it between 1915 and 1920 and grew in popularity after World War II, which had swept away so much of the old Western order. During the 1940s and 1950s, a desire to be modern produced not only free-form coffee tables but also fabrics like those illustrated here, worn as bright, informal clothing by people who may never have gone to see abstract art in a museum.

1.

2.

3.

4.

5.

AIRBRUSH

1. France, c. 1920, gouache on paper, AYG, 100%
2. Germany, 1930s, gouache on paper, AYG (tie pattern), 70%
3. France, c. 1930s, gouache on paper, AYG, 50%
4. Germany, 1930s, gouache on paper, AYG (tie pattern), 50%

BESIDES MODERNITY, THE airbrush look also has a softness of outline that a designer can use to enhance the soft hand of the cloth. Long before a textile pattern reaches the ultimate buyer in the retail market, its creator must sell it within the textile industry, and since a design airbrushed on paper already has some of the blurring and indistinctness that a thick-napped fabric will give it when it is printed, the painting helps a potential buyer to imagine how it will look on cloth. The designs illustrated here were all intended to be printed on brushed cotton flannel. (See also *Floral: Airbrush,* page 28.)

1.

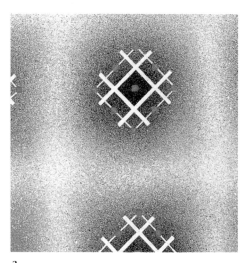

2.

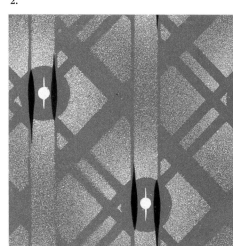

3.

4.

ALLOVER

1. France, late 19th C, RP cotton, AYG, 100%
2. France or USA, c. 1930s, gouache on paper, AYG, 100%
3. France, 1943, RP rayon, AYG, 100%
4. France, 1920s–30s, RP silk, AYG, 100%
5. France, c. 1840, gouache on paper, AYG, 100%
6. USA, 1920s–30s, RP cotton, AYG, 100%
7. France, 1920s–30s, RP silk, AYG, 100%
8. France, 1924, gouache on paper, AYG, 130%
9. France, 1920s–30s, RP cotton, AYG, 100%

As with allover floral layouts, these are designs in which the motif takes up more space than the ground behind it. The examples shown here are all nondirectional patterns based on a set (diagonal or grid) layout, but allover geometric designs, like allover florals, can be tossed or packed, one-directional or two-directional. (Abstract geometrical shapes, however, are often easier to work into nondirectional patterns than recognizable objects are.) What allovers of every type share is their full coverage of the cloth and the relative obscurity of the ground.

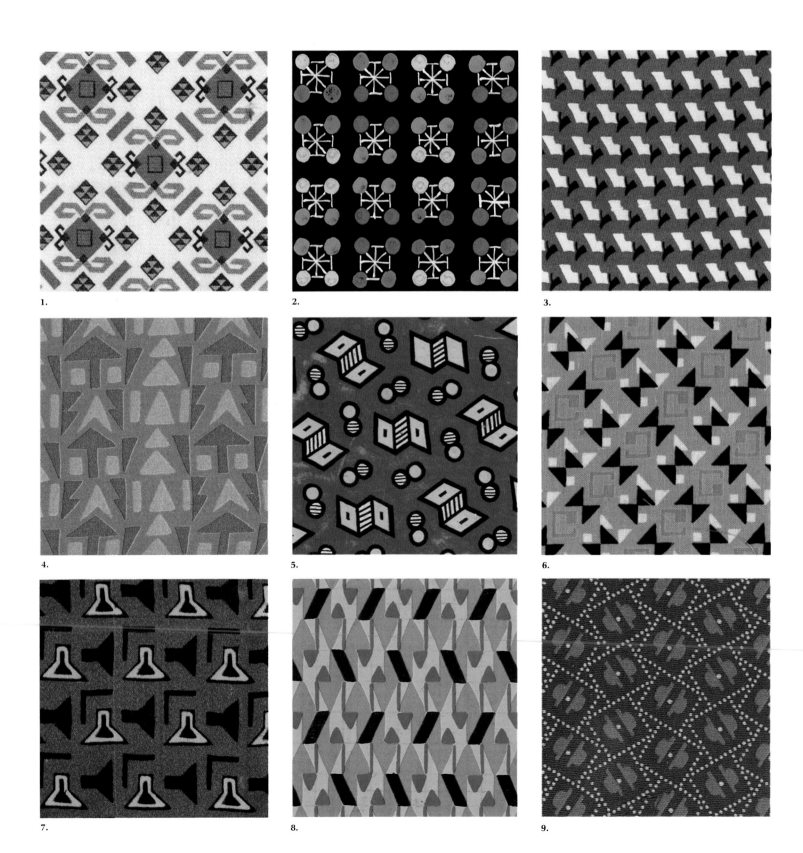

1.

2.

3.

4.

5.

6.

7.

8.

9.

ARABESQUE

1. France, c. 1850, RP cotton chintz, HFYG, 80%
2. France, c. 1880, gouache on paper, HFYG, 25%

THE INTRICATELY ENTWINED, curvilinear designs of the arabesque are derived mainly from Islamic art. Because Muslim law forbids the depiction of living creatures, Islamic artists have created highly stylized, complex geometric patterns, and it is from this kind of arabesque that number 2 is derived. But similar devices also appear in Greco-Roman decoration, from which they made their way to Renaissance art. Number 1 is an arabesque pattern with European roots.

1.

2.

BASKETWEAVE AND LATTICEWORK

1. USA, 1940s, RP cotton, AYG, 50%
2. France, 1886, RP cotton, AYG, 100%
3. France, 1886, RP cotton, AYG, 100%
4. France, 1895, RP cotton, AYG, 100%
5. USA, 1880s–90s, RP cotton, AYG, 120%
6. USA, 1880s–90s, RP cotton, AYG, 120%
7. USA, 1860s–80s, RP cotton, AYG, 120%
8. France, 1883, RP cotton, AYG, 100%
9. France, c. 1900, gouache on paper, AYG, 90%
10. France, 1881, RP cotton, HFYG, 100%

THERE IS SOMETHING psychically reassuring and pleasing about weaves and lattices. Nineteenth-century architects had patterns like these carved into the stone they built with, giving it the illusion of softness and a link with an older tradition of shelter. And on some level of the mind, perhaps, we see such designs as enlargements of the weave of cloth, with all cloth's ancient associations of protection and warmth. Maybe what is appealing is the sense of order in a form at the same time man-made and organic. In addition, these designs have the appeal of trompe l'oeil in the comfortable form of a familiar pattern.

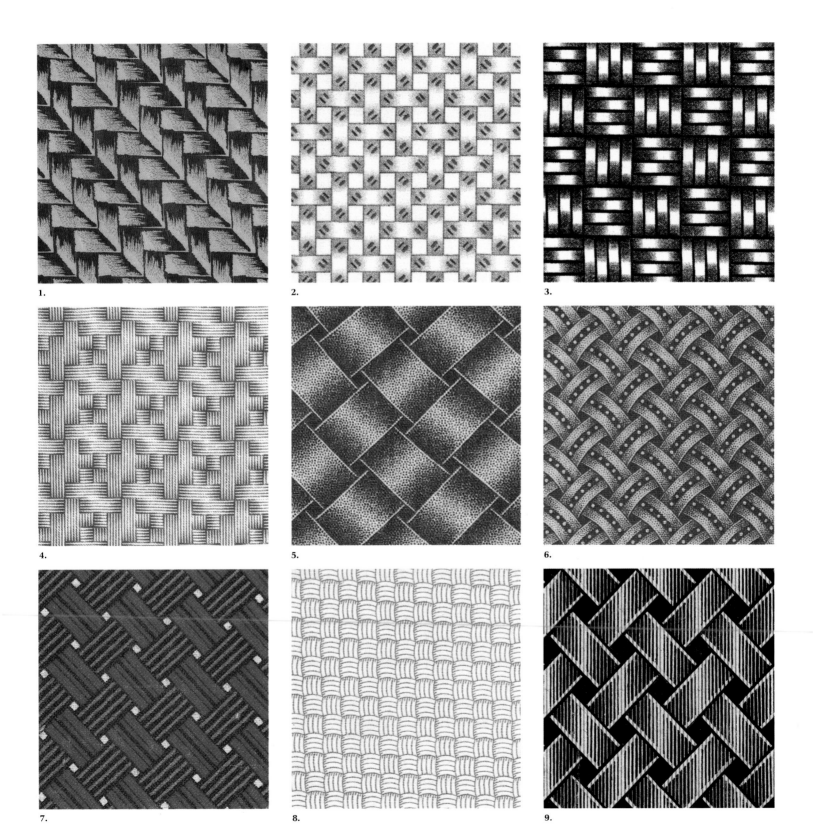

1.

2.

3.

4.

5.

6.

7.

8.

9.

10.

BLOCKS AND CUBES

1. **England or France, c. 1860, RP cotton, AYG, 100%**
2. **Probably USA, 1920s–40s, RP silk jacquard, AYG, 100%**
3. **France, 1886, RP cotton, AYG, 100%**
4. **France, 1889, RP cotton, AYG, 80%**
5. **France, 1887, RP cotton, AYG, 130%**
6. **France, c. 1910, gouache on paper, AYG, 60%**

FLAT SQUARE AND diamond shapes are easy to combine into the appearance of a three-dimensional object—the cube. This is one of the geometric forms, the solid extension of the square, that used to be called the Platonic Bodies, with various philosophical notions attached relating to the ideal world of the mind; today, more prosaically, geometry uses the term "regular solids." Except as the building blocks of childhood, cubes don't play a very visible role in everyday life. Household furnishings, such as books, tables, and beds, are almost always either longer than they are high or higher than they are long, as are the rooms that contain them, as are the buildings that contain the rooms. The isometric projection of the cube—in which the planes not flush with the picture surface do not narrow toward a vanishing point, as they do in perspectival renderings, but retain parallel edges—is a basic decorative device, used, for example, in the Baby Blocks quilt pattern. (See also *Geometric: Squares,* page 224.)

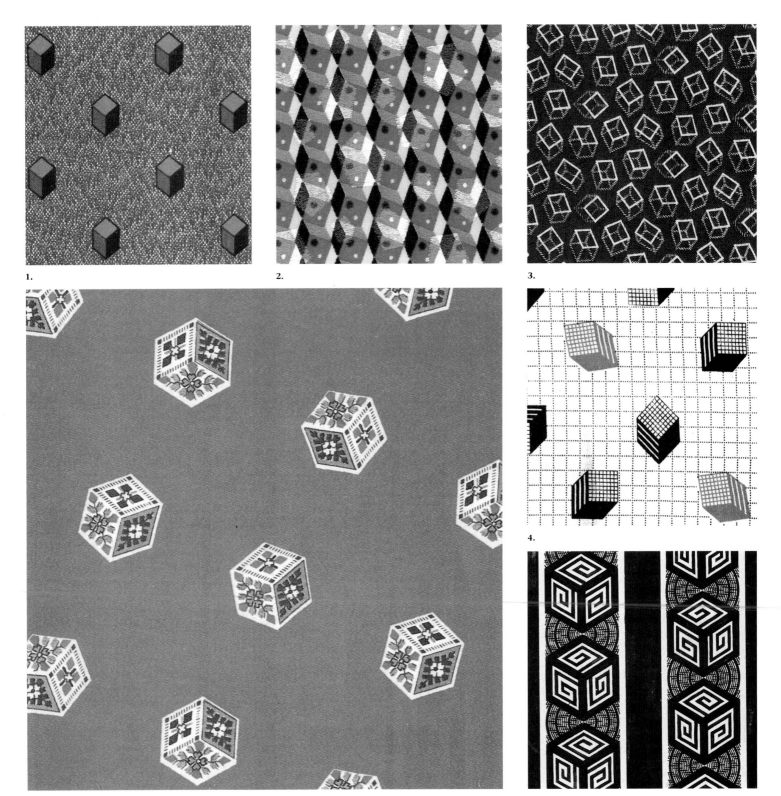

1.

2.

3.

4.

5.

6.

BORDERS

THE LESS SPACE a design takes up in a print, the harder it has to work to stand out. Border patterns are usually much more striking than the filler in the rest of the cloth.

1. **France, 2d half 19th C, RP cotton, A (scarf), 75%**
2. **France, c. 1910, gouache on paper, AYG, 70%**
3. **France, c. 1910, RP cotton, AYG, 115%**
4. **France, c. 1910, gouache on paper, AYG, 55%**
5. **France, c. 1920, RP cotton, AYG, 84%**
6. **France, c. 1910, gouache on paper, AYG, 70%**

1.

2.

3.

4.

5.

6.

BOX LAYOUT

1. France, c. 1920, gouache on paper, AYG, 100%
2. France, 1820–40, gouache on paper, AYG, 60%
3. France, c. 1920s, gouache on paper, AYG, 140%
4. Probably USA, 1920s–40s, gouache on paper, AYG, 110%
5. Germany, 1930s, gouache on paper, AYG (tie pattern), 50%
6. France, c. 1920, gouache on paper, AYG, 50%

SINCE BOX LAYOUTS are the easiest designs to weave into cloth—a natural consequence of the setup of the loom—they were classic in textiles long before mechanized printing. The plaid is a form of box layout. But woven-in patterns always add to the cost of production; printing makes such patterns more accessible to the public, and in doing so it speeds up the process by which the design is explored, developed, and transformed. Also, the print designer can elaborate a pattern to and beyond the point where it would become forbiddingly complicated to create on a loom. Thus a genre inspired by a weave and, at first, trying to imitate one, eventually looks only like a print. The box layout is capable of endless variations; in apparel, though, it is most successful when the boxes are relatively small in scale, so as not to "square off" the body.

1.

2.

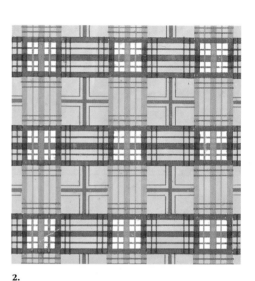

3.

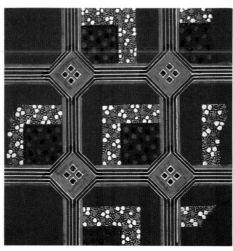

4.

5.

6.

BRUSHSTROKE LOOK

1. France, 1970s, gouache on paper, AYG, 100%

BRUSHSTROKE-LOOK FLORAL patterns make a print look like a painting of a flower. But if the aim is to suggest painted canvas, is the flower necessary? The brushstroke alone will do. (See also *Floral: Brushstroke Look,* page 53.)

1.

BULL'S-EYE

1. France, 1912, RP cotton, AYG, 100%
2. USA, 1930s, gouache on paper, AYG, 100%
3. USA, 1930s–40s, RP rayon, AYG, 50%
4. USA, c. 1930, gouache on paper, AYG, 80%

IN THE HINDU mandala, concentric circles are an instrument of contemplative meditation for purposes of the spirit. In the West their immediate association is with weaponry and the target—particularly when, as in number 2, they are combined with what look like the cross hairs of a gun sight. The motif has a strong feeling of movement, with the circles seeming to spin before one's eyes.

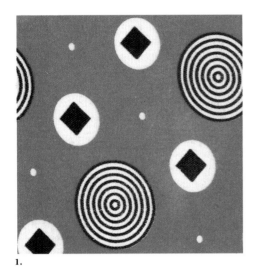

1.

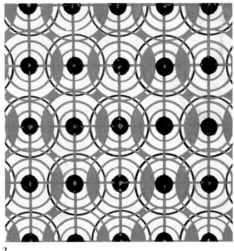

2.

3.

4.

CARTOUCHES AND LOZENGES

1. France, 1830s, gouache on paper, AYG, 100%
2. France, 1830s, gouache on paper, AYG, 50%
3. France, 1840s, RP and BP cotton, AYG, 50%
4. France, 1830s–40s, gouache on paper, AYG, 70%

THE CARTOUCHE (numbers 1 and 4), with its framework of Rococo curves, has a plainer cousin in the lozenge. The latter (numbers 2 and 3) is much less flamboyant and more regular in shape, with parallel sides of symmetrical dimensions. Both serve as a primary motif, often containing secondary motifs within them. The cartouche is associated more with Renaissance, Baroque, and Rococo designs than the lozenge, which reached its peak of popularity in a genre of rather somber, drab patterns of the 1830s and 1840s. (See also *Floral: Cartouches*, page 57.)

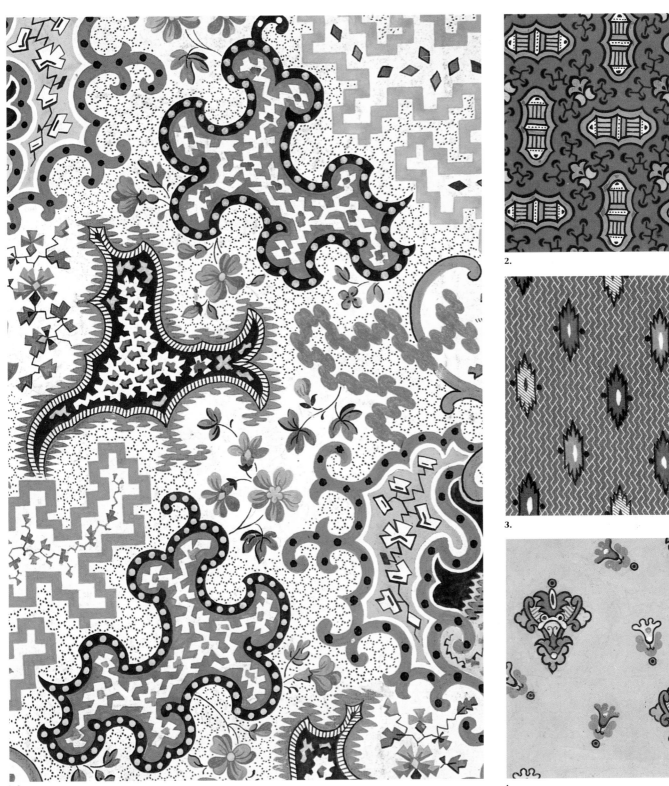

1.

2.

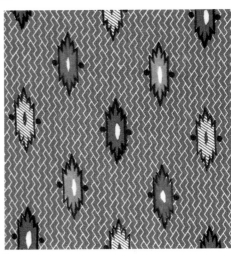

3.

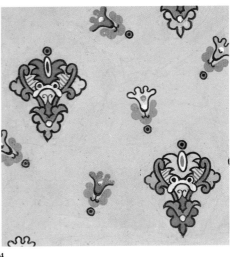

4.

CELLULAR

1. France, c. 1910, RP cotton, AYG, 100%
2. France, c. 1910, gouache on paper, AYG, 115%
3. France, c. 1920, gouache on paper, AYG, 80%
4. France, c. 1920, gouache on paper, AYG, 90%

VEINED AND LOBULAR designs like these appeared throughout the nineteenth century but had largely vanished by the early twentieth century. Their appeal to the Victorians may have been sparked by the development in the 1840s of compound microscopes that could be marketed to the general public—for a while, these instruments were magnetic shop-window attractions, making the microcosmic world available to any passerby. But by the twentieth century they were no longer a novelty, and the fleshiness of cellular patterns seems to have proved too morbid for the modern age, which considers it strange to use the inside of the body to decorate the outside.

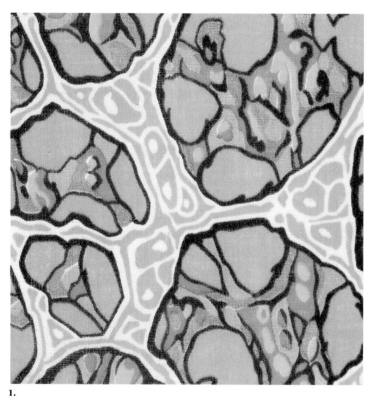

1.

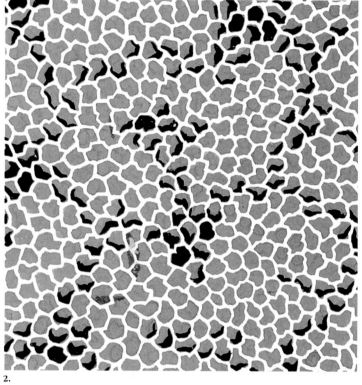

2.

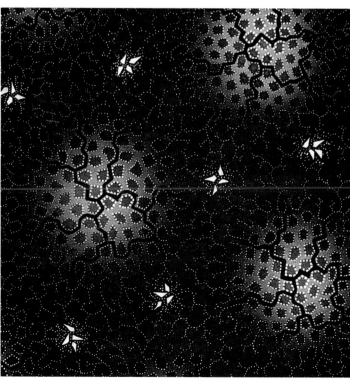

3.

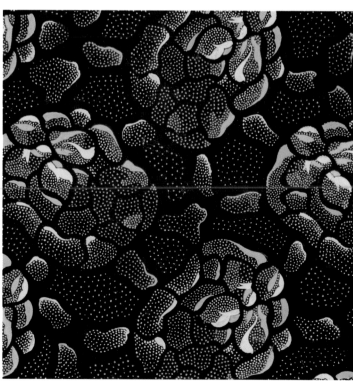

4.

CHALLIS

1. France, 1855, RP wool challis, AYG, 50%
2. France, 1850, RP wool challis, AYG, 70%
3. France, c. 1885, RP wool challis, A (scarf), 70%

A PATTERN USUALLY becomes a tradition by being marketed successfully over a long period of time. Usually something belongs to a tradition by resembling the tradition's other members. These mid-nineteenth-century challis designs, however, belong to the same tradition not by resembling each other but by resembling nothing else. Many are wildly inventive and various. What they have in common are the cloth itself and the rich hues of the aniline dyes customarily used on challis. Yet even before these dyes were introduced, in 1856, the shapes of challis patterns seemed to compete with their colors as to which was the more attention-grabbing. Perhaps because these fabrics were often used for morning dresses, apparel not worn outside the privacy of one's home, designers could afford to be especially daring with them.

1.

2.

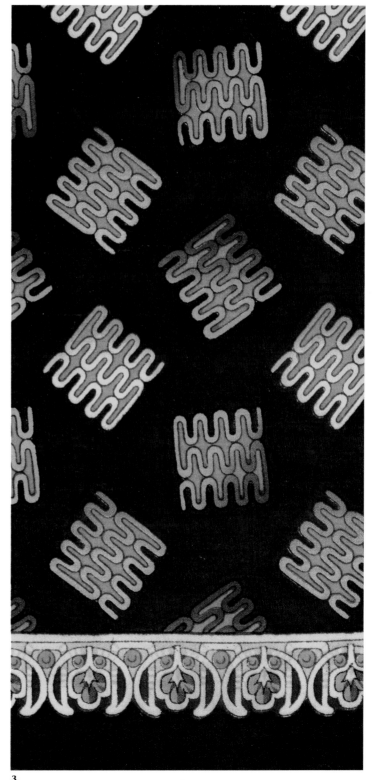

3.

CHECKERBOARD

1. France, c. 1920s, RP rayon crepe, AYG, 120%
2. France, c. 1920, gouache on paper, AYG, 70%
3. USA, 1920s–40s, RP silk, A (scarf), 64%
4. France, 1910–20, gouache on paper, AYG, 115%
5. France, 1880–84, gouache on paper, AYG, 109%
6. France, 1861, RP cotton, AYG, 125%

SOME OF THE ancient houses in Pompeii bear checkerboard signs on the outside, inviting Romans to drop in for some form of the game we still play today. But the pattern is universal, perhaps because the alternation of dark and light suggests a balance of opposites like yin and yang or, as in heraldic devices, the duality of the intellect and the spirit; or because their precise arrangement is a supreme symbol of order. (It could also be that this arrangement is simply one of the most basic variations possible in the decorative arts, whether of tile or loom.) Today the pattern is most likely to be associated with the checkered victory flag in grand-prix racing, with its implications of daring, winning, and youth. The grid in number 2 has been softened with an ombré effect; usually, though, the checkerboard's sharply defined boundaries suggest an unnuanced cast of mind—the world seen literally in black and white, with no in-between grays—that may reinforce the association with the young.

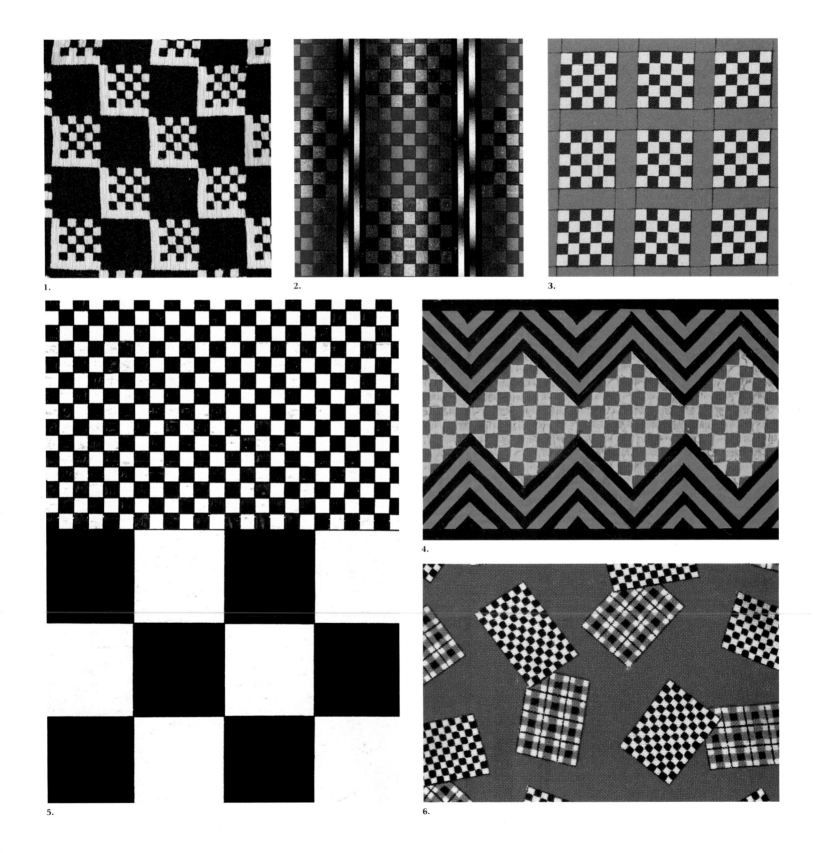

1.

2.

3.

4.

5.

6.

CHEVRON AND HERRINGBONE

1. France or USA, 20th C, gouache on paper, AYG, 100%
2. France, 1840, RP wool challis, AYG, 100%
3. USA, 1930s–40s, RP silk, AYG, 100%
4. Probably France, 1930s, RP silk, AYG, 70%
5. USA, c. 1950s, RP cotton, AYG, 135%
6. France, 1920s, gouache on paper, 125%
7. France, c. 1920, gouache on paper, 120%

ALL OF THESE designs are offspring of the herringbone weave, in which columns of short diagonal stripes meet in a line of Vs not unlike the skeleton of a fish. Some herringbone prints imitate a woven herringbone, complete with uneven lines that imply the roughness of woolly threads; others loudly declare their independence of their ancestor—for example, by setting the diagonals out of kilter, breaking up the V. Numbers 1–3 have fattened V's—bars like a sergeant's stripes—thereby becoming a pattern of their own, the chevron.

1.

2.

3.

4.

5.

6.

7.

CIRCLES AND DOTS

1. USA, c. 1930s, gouache on paper, AYG, 25%
2. France, c. 1890, RP cotton flannel, A (scarf pattern), 100%
3. France, c. 1910, gouache on paper, AYG, 100%
4. USA, c. 1930s, gouache on paper, AYG, 100%
5. France, c. 1910, gouache on paper, AYG, 130%
6. France, 1895, gouache on paper, AYG, 170%
7. Probably France, c. 1900, RP cotton, AYG, 110%
8. USA or France, c. 1880–90, RP cotton, AYG, 100%
9. USA or France, c. 1890–1900, RP cotton sateen, AYG, 155%

THE CIRCLE IS the most common geometric motif on printed cloth—far more popular than its closest competitor, the square. Its symbolism, of course, is ancient and universal, a sign of eternity, of oneness, of the cycles of human life and the natural world. Air, one of the four elements recognized by the classical Greek philosophers, is represented by a circle, as is heaven; in some cultures, the shape is also considered a masculine symbol of movement and activity. In Ptolemaic astronomy, the universe was held to consist of a series of revolving spheres; today, though the spheres are gone, the circle still dominates our idea of the universe, for it is the shape in which we imagine the planets, the sun, and the moon. The textile industry makes a distinction between circles and dots. Numbers 1–5 are all circles: the motifs are large enough to take interior patterns or variations of color, and the circular shape is the basic element of the pattern. In the dot patterns (numbers 6–9), the overall shapes need not be circular, though they are formed of circular dots. And the dots are too small to contain an interior pattern; they are solid color and suggest changes in shade by picotage effects of size and spacing. (See also *Floral: Picotage,* page 106; *Geometric: Polka Dots,* pages 212–13.)

1.

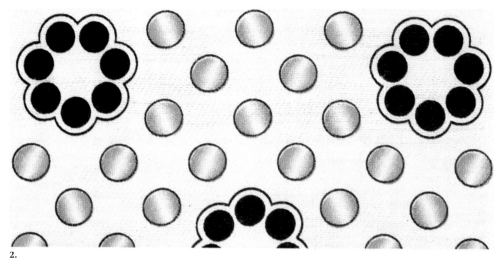

2.

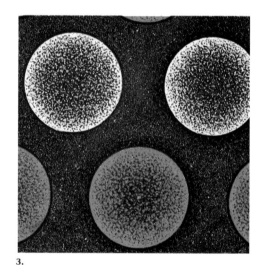

3.

4.

5.

6.

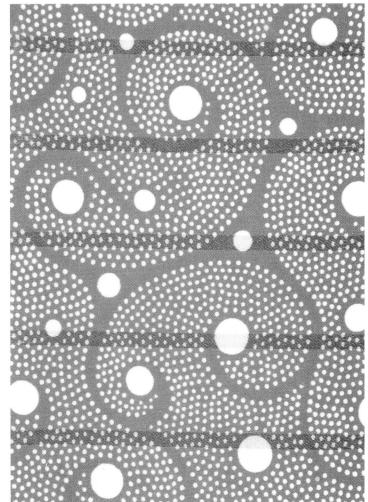

7.

8.

9.

COFFEE BEANS, SCREW TOPS, AND SPLIT PEAS

A BISECTED CIRCLE or dot is called a split-pea or screw-top motif. The dividing lines may align with or counter each other to create different vectors of movement. If you make the bisected circle an oval, the motif becomes a coffee bean.

1, 9. France or England, c. 1800–1810, BP cotton, AYG, 100%

2. England, 2d half 19th C, RP cotton, AYG, 100%

3. France, 1928, RP silk, AYG, 105%

4. France, 1820–40, gouache on paper, AYG, 100%

5. France or USA, c. 1930s, gouache on paper, AYG, 100%

6. France, 1930s, gouache on paper, AYG, 100%

7. France or USA, c. 1930s, RP or SP silk, AYG, 100%

8. France, c. 1860, gouache on paper, AYG, 100%

10. USA, c. 1920s–30s, gouache on paper, AYG, 100%

11. USA, 1930s–40s, gouache on paper, AYG, 90%

1.

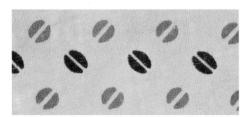

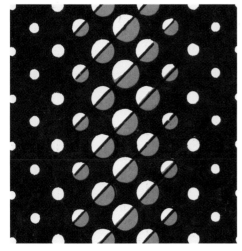

2.

3.

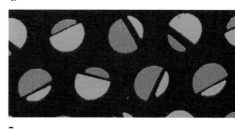

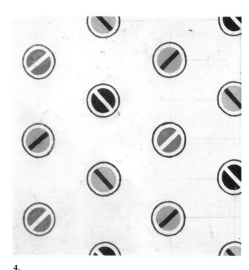

4.

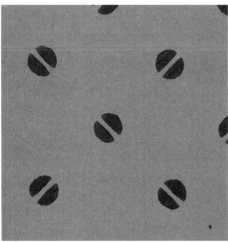

5.

6.

7.

8.

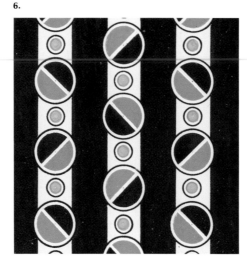

9.

10.

11.

COMMAS

1. France, c. 1880–90, RP cotton, AYG, 100%
2. England, 1872, RP cotton, AYG, 140%
3. France, c. 1880–90, RP cotton, AYG, 110%
4. France, c. 1910–20, gouache on paper, AYG, 62%

TO THE CHINESE, nature is dualistic. Traditionally, their concept of two interdependent principles—dark, cold yin and bright, hot yang—is represented by an interlocking-comma motif. One comma alone may be thought of as yin without yang or, if the comma is light instead of dark, yang without yin. In number 4, the yin-yang symbol is replaced by a wavelike curl, giving the motif a sense of surging spin. The combination of three commas in number 1 is a Japanese Buddhist symbol. All of these patterns have an Eastern aura, with numbers 1 and 3 in particular echoing Japan's *mon* tradition of the family or business heraldic crest. But *mon* designs are isolated on their grounds; they do not repeat, as Western prints do. The designer of number 2 has hedged his bets: the motif may be Japanese, but the regularly spaced layout almost turns it into a circle pattern, for customers not desiring an ethnic look.

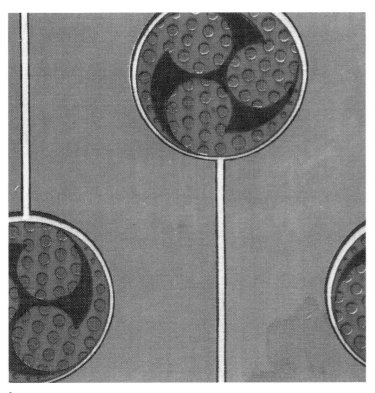

1.

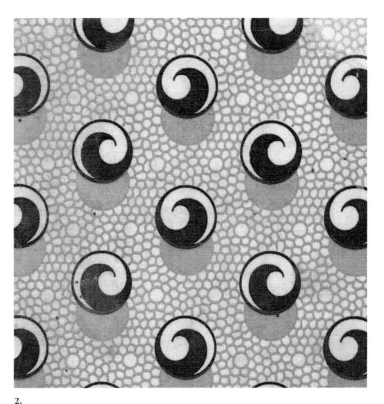

2.

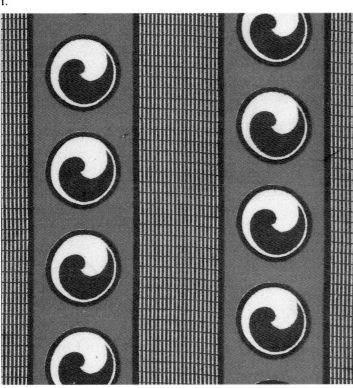

3.

4.

CONFETTI

1. **France, c. 1910, paper impression, AYG, 50%**
2. **France, 1928, RP silk, AYG, 110%**
3. **France, c. 1860, RP cotton, AYG, 130%**
4. **USA, 1980s, felt-tip pen on paper, AYG, 100%**
5. **USA, c. 1920s, RP cotton, AYG, 110%**
6. **USA, 1920s–30s, gouache on paper, AYG, 100%**

WHEN POLKA DOTS go berserk they become confetti. In the nineteenth century, these brightly colored patterns of randomly tossed dots and other speckles would have been called spotted cotton; twentieth-century buyers find "confetti" a catchier term (and perhaps less suggestive of measles).

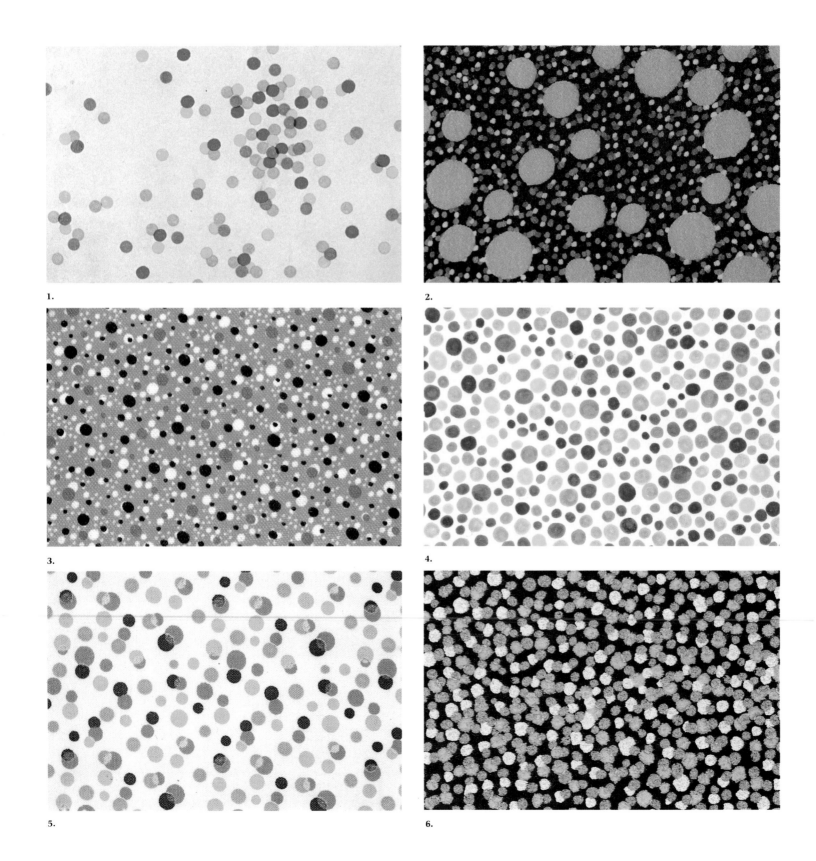

1.

2.

3.

4.

5.

6.

CRESCENTS

1. France, 1889, RP cotton, AYG, 80%
2. France, 1890, gouache on paper, AYG, 100%
3. France, c. 1880–90, RP cotton, AYG, 80%
4. France, 1886, RP cotton, AYG, 90%
5. France, 1880–84, gouache on paper, AYG, 74%

FROM ITS CLASSICAL association with the moon goddesses Selene and Diana and, even earlier, with the Middle Eastern Ashtaroth, the crescent moon became a symbol of the Virgin for medieval Christians. And it was also part of the crest of Constantinople, supposedly because, when the Macedonian king Philip, father of Alexander the Great, was laying siege to the city (then called Byzantium) in the fourth century B.C., a crescent moon revealed to the defenders his plot to undermine the walls. But when in 1453 Constantinople fell to the Turks, the crescent became the standard of the Ottoman Empire. It was consequently feared and reviled in Europe, and was rarely used in printed textiles until the late nineteenth century, when the Turkish empire was in decay and the Near East had developed into an exotic tourist destination for affluent Victorians. Perhaps because of its old links with the goddesses of myth, the crescent moon has often been connected to the mysterious powers of magic. Given these political and mystical associations, the crescent motif is seldom used today unless a deliberate celestial theme is desired.

1.

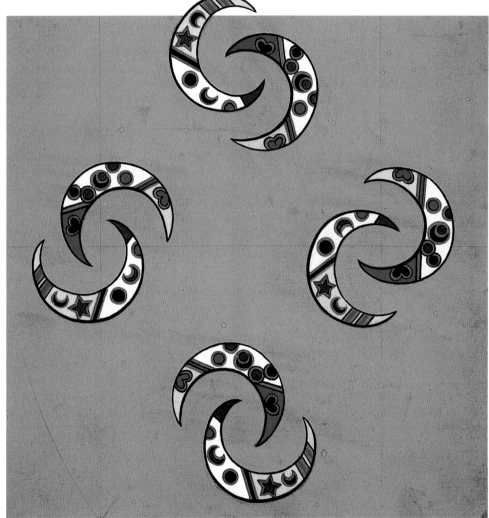

2.

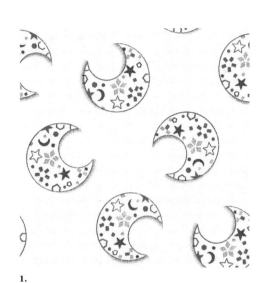

3.

4.

5.

DIAMONDS AND HARLEQUINS

1. France, 1845, RP cotton, AYG, 105%
2. France, c. 1930s, SP silk, AYG, 40%
3. France, 1890, gouache on paper, AYG, 56%
4. France, 1880–84, gouache on paper, AYG, 100%
5. France, c. 1910, gouache on paper, AYG, 80%
6. France, c. 1920s, paper impression, AYG, 70%

SQUARES SKEWED INTO parallelograms are a basic building block for the designer and a constant in textile prints. Spaced out against a field, as in numbers 3–5, they are called diamonds or lozenges (not to be confused with the framelike lozenge that is a cousin to the cartouche). Arranged to butt, in a lattice-like, diagonal version of the checkerboard, they become harlequin prints (numbers 1, 2, and 6). Number 6 actually suggests a commedia dell'arte harlequin by color shifts that reveal a human figure. But few designers of harlequin prints are out to make the wearer look like a clown . . . or are they?

1.

2.

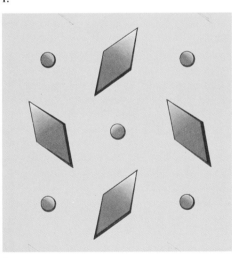

3.

4.

5.

6.

DIAPER

1. France, 1860, RP cotton, AYG, 100%
2, 11, 14, 17, 21, 24, 26, 28. France, c. 1910–20, RP silk, AYG, 100%
3, 13, 31, 35. USA, c. 1920s, RP cotton, AYG, 100%
4, 9. England, c. 1920s, RP cotton, AYG, 100%
5, 12, 20. USA, c. 1880, RP cotton, AYG, 100%
6, 8. USA, c. 1920s, RP silk, AYG, 100%
7, 33. France, c. 1920, gouache on paper, AYG, 100%
10, 23. USA, c. 1920s–30s, gouache on paper, AYG, 100%
15. USA, c. 1910–20, gouache on paper, AYG, 100%
16. France, mid-19th C, RP cotton, AYG, 100%
18, 22. France, c. 1910–20, RP cotton, AYG, 100%
19. France, 1835, RP cotton, AYG, 100%
25, 36. England, c. 1860, RP cotton, AYG, 100%
27. France, mid-19th C, RP wool challis, AYG, 100%
29, 32. USA, mid-19th C, RP cotton, AYG, 100%
30, 34. USA, c. 1910–20, RP cotton, AYG, 100%

IN TEXTILE LANGUAGE, the word "diaper" refers not, or not only, to the modern baby napkin but to a design genre of small-scale geometric figures in a set-layout of interlocking or closely aligned forms. In the fifteenth century, a diaper was an expensive linen, woven so that the lie of the thread created a lattice pattern. As the illustrations below show, the diaper print sometimes retains the original diamond shape, both explicitly and implicitly, but the term has broadened to describe a wide variety of small, tightly meshed geometric designs.

1. 2. 3. 4. 5. 6.

7. 8. 9. 10. 11. 12.

13. 14. 15. 16. 17. 18.

19. 20. 21. 22. 23. 24.

25. 26. 27. 28. 29. 30.

31. 32. 33. 34. 35. 36.

ECCENTRICS

1, 6, 12, 13. France, 1820–25, RP cotton, AYG, 135%
2. France, 1820–25, RP cotton, AYG, 155%
3, 9. France, 1810–20, RP cotton, AYG, 130%
4, 8. France, 1820–25, RP cotton, AYG, 140%
5. France, 1810–20, RP cotton, AYG, 100%
7. France, 1820–25, gouache on paper, AYG, 140%
10. USA, c. 1870–80, RP cotton, AYG, 120%
11, 14. France, 1820–25, RP cotton, AYG, 100%

ECCENTRICS, OR "EXCENTRICS" as they were called in the nineteenth century, are fine-lined geometrics that bend and twist what is essentially a stripe pattern into Op-Art–like waves and distortions. They are said to have been created by accident: in 1820, at the English factory of Messrs. Simpson & Co. of Foxhillbank, a run of cloth going through the rollers was incorrectly loaded, and the resulting creases transformed what had been a regular design into an out-of-kilter one—which went on sale and became an immediate success. This pattern, known as "Lane's Net," appears in numbers 10 and 11; it is reported that enough was sold to sew one hundred thousand dresses. Numerous designs followed its example, one of the most popular being "Hoyle's Wave" (number 4). Subsequently, an invention utilizing various-sized gears known as Perkins' Eccentric Lathe was used to design these patterns by mechanical means. Eccentrics were successfully marketed through much of the nineteenth century, particularly from the 1820s through the 1840s. They are seldom seen in twentieth-century prints in their original form but have been successfully interpreted in the bolder and larger-scale patterns of Op Art.

1.

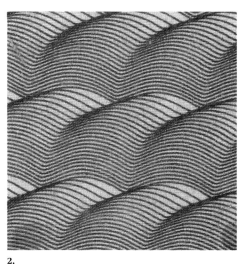

2.

3.

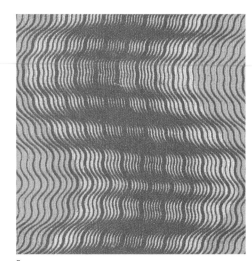

4.

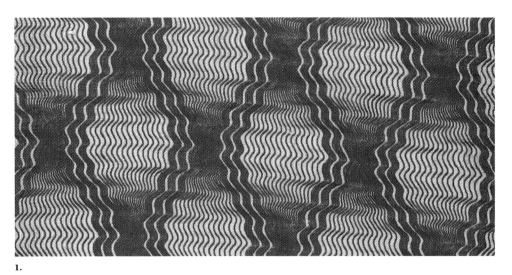

5.

6.

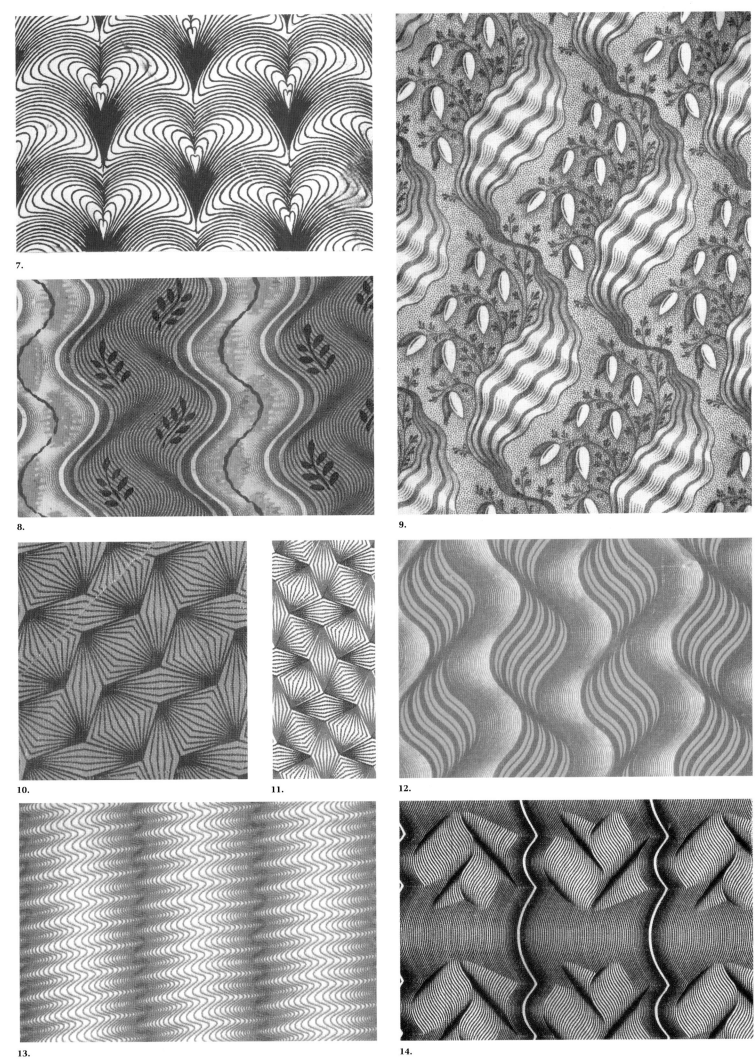

7.

8.

9.

10.

11.

12.

13.

14.

EMBROIDERED LOOK

LIKE THE FLORAL embroidered look, this is an imitation of hand-decorated cloth. Number 1 was a less expensive substitute for passementerie trimming. Number 2 mimics the cross-stitch of folk embroidery, and number 3 was probably a copy of an actual piece of elegant, hand-embroidered fabric.

1. France, c. 1910, gouache on paper, AYG, 94%
2. France, 1882, RP cotton, AYG, 75%
3. France, c. 1880–90, gouache on paper, AYG, 100%

1.

2.

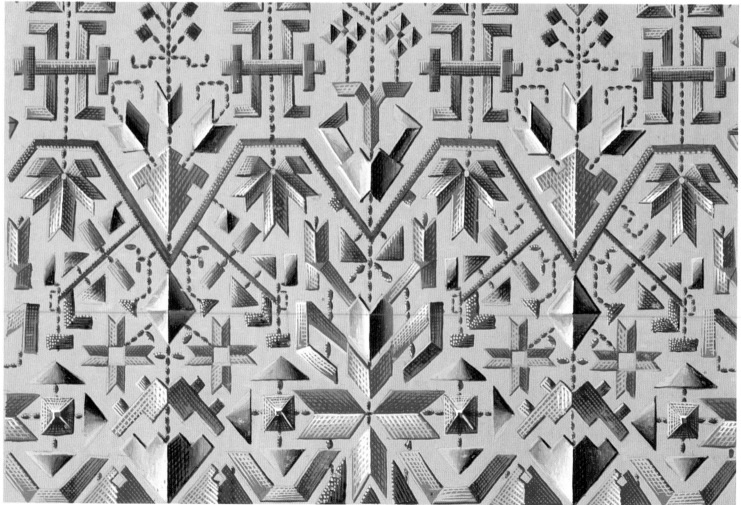

3.

FLEUR-DE-LIS

1. France, 1887, RP cotton, AYG, 125%
2. France, 1890, gouache on paper, AYG, 88%
3. Probably USA, late 19th C, RP cotton, 100%
4. Probably France, c. 1880–1900, RP cotton, AYG, 100%
5. USA, c. 1880–90, RP cotton, AYG, 100%
6. France, 1880–84, gouache on paper, AYG, 80%

THOUGH THE PRESENCE of the fleur-de-lis in France's royal coat of arms made this stylized iris a widespread symbol of that country's monarchy, the device itself is much older, going back at least to 1000 B.C. Austen Henry Layard's *Popular Account of the Discovery of Nineveh,* published in England in 1851, describes an image of a god in that ancient Assyrian city wearing "the square horned cap, surmounted by a point, or fleur-de-lys"; the shape is also found in the art of dynastic Egypt. In the Middle Ages it spread through Europe as a sign of the Virgin, for it is a form of cross (a central vertical shaft with a horizontal bar), and its leaflike outer elements suggest the lily or iris associated with Mary. The fleur-de-lis is now synonymous with French elegance, particularly outside France, which decapitated its royalty two centuries ago. Admirers of the fleur-de-lis may not know of its onetime association with the toad, or *crapaud,* deriving from a view of its topmost blade as the toad's head, the four curling leaves as the legs, and the downward-pointing spear as the rear. The sixteenth-century French astrologer Nostradamus, famous for his prophetic writings, referred to his countrymen as *crapauds;* the "toads" have since evolved into "frogs," though this English and American slang word for the French apparently comes from a well-known dish in their cuisine.

1.

2.

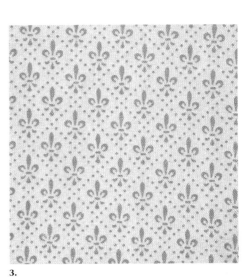

3.

4.

5.

6.

FOULARDS

1, 2, 5, 16, 17. USA, 1940s–50s, gouache on paper, AYG, 100%
3. France, c. 1950s, gouache on paper, AYG, 100%
4. USA, c. 1940s, RP cotton, AYG, 100%
6, 7, 9–11, 13, 15, 19, 20. England, c. 1950–70, RP silk, AYG, 100%
8. Germany, 1930s, gouache on paper, AYG, 80%
12. France, c. 1860, gouache on paper, AYG, 115%
14. France, 2d half 20th C, gouache on paper, AYG, 80%
18. USA, c. 1860, RP cotton, AYG, 100%
21. England, 2d half 20th C, RP wool, AYG, 100%

IN THE NINETEENTH century, the term "foulard" referred to a soft, lightweight silk cloth that was usually made into handkerchiefs and often block-printed in small-scale patterns. Today, the name refers more frequently to the patterns than to the fabric. Foulards are a steadfast motif in men's neckwear and dressing gowns, and most are printed by machine. Classic foulards are small regular-shaped geometrics, usually in set-layouts. Their traditional colors are deep-toned reds, blues, greens, and in some cases, genuine madder hues. Of course, foulards can be produced in any color or scale in keeping with fashion trends.

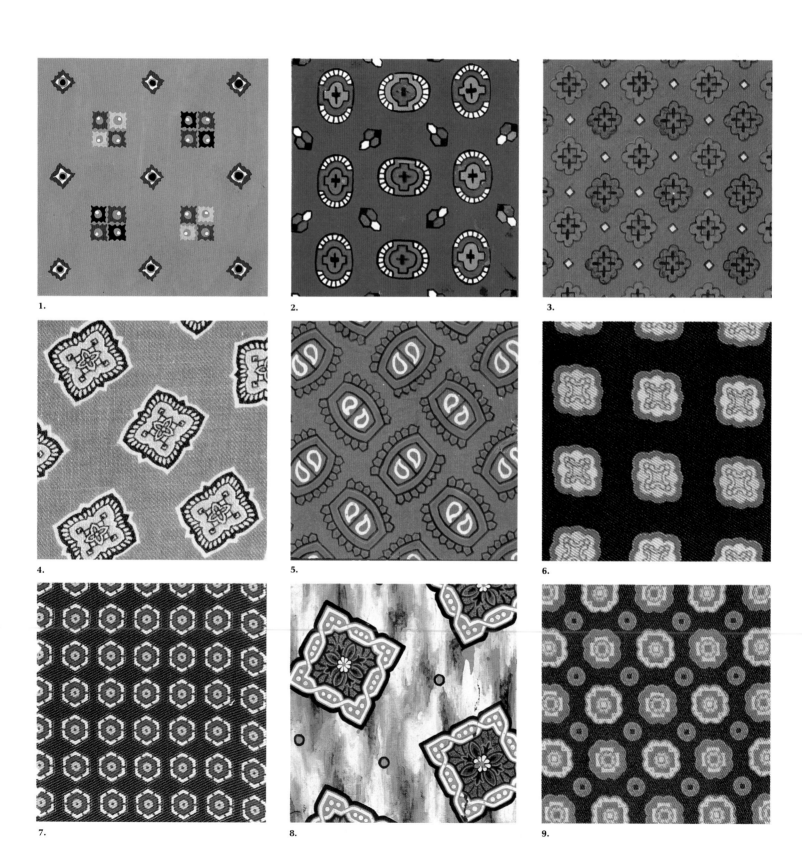

1.

2.

3.

4.

5.

6.

7.

8.

9.

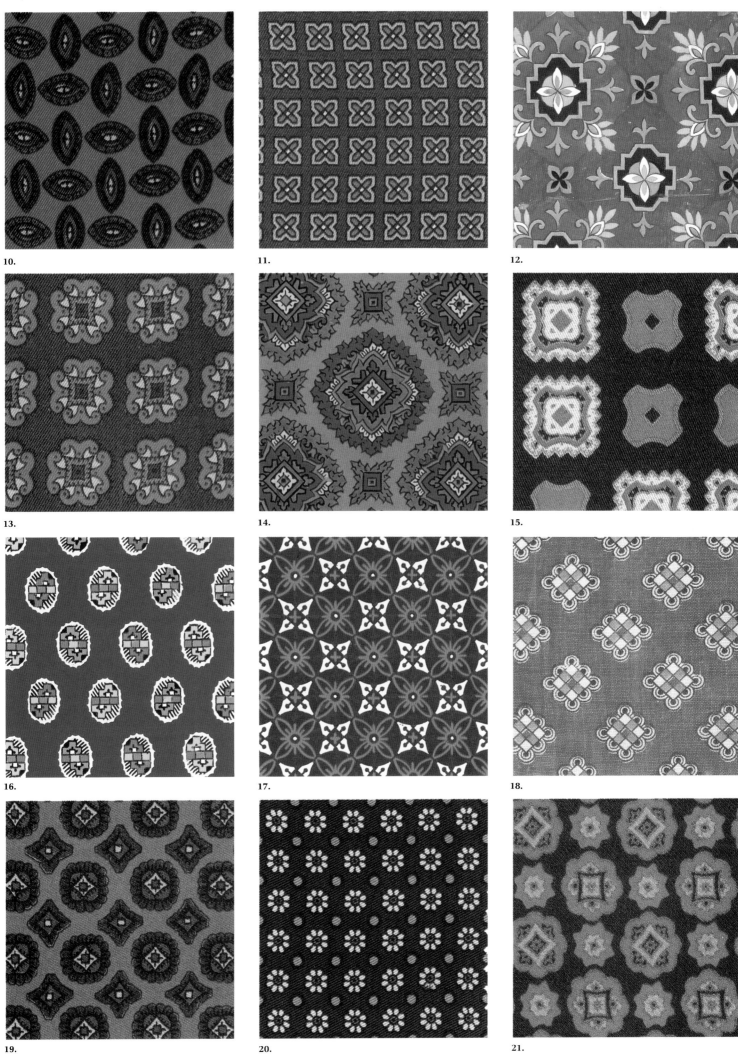

10.

11.

12.

13.

14.

15.

16.

17.

18.

19.

20.

21.

FRETWORK

1. France, c. 1910–20, gouache on paper, AYG, 135%
2. France, c. 1900–10, RP cotton, AYG, 80%
3. France, c. 1910–20, gouache on paper, AYG, 105%
4. France, c. 1850–60, gouache on paper, A (ribbon pattern), 100%

FRETWORK SYMBOLIZES ETERNITY, for it has no beginning and no end. The short, right-angled bars of fretwork usually interlock but don't quite meet, creating squares and grids but stopping short of sealing them off. In allover patterns, then, fretwork has an openness absent from checkerboard and box layouts, though it may also suggest a mazelike nest of cul-de-sacs. As an Oriental device, allover fretwork has the kind of ethnic undertone that designers like to avoid, except when that particular ethnicity is in vogue. The patterns are seen more often in linear border designs, and, in fact, the best-known fretwork motif is the Greek key, or Greek fret (see number 2, page 381), the row of dog-legged interlocking lines that runs along the entablatures of classical temples and still appears often in decorative art today.

1.

2.

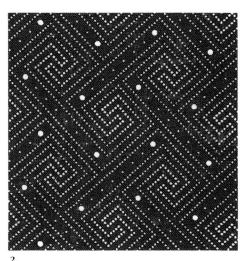

3.

4.

HEXAGONS AND OCTAGONS

1. France, c. 1840, gouache on paper, AYG, 105%
2. Probably France, c. 1880, RP cotton, AYG, 120%
3. France, c. 1880, RP cotton, AYG, 120%
4. France, c. 1820, gouache on paper, HF (carpet pattern), 80%
5. France, c. 1910, gouache on paper, AYG, 110%

LIKE TRIANGLES, SQUARES, and pentagons, hexagons can be arranged to fit together in an allover pattern that butts every individual form without leaving any space between them. Once the geometric forms have more than six sides, however, other shapes intervene: for example, the squares or diamonds among the octagons of numbers 4 and 5. The basic hexagon design is a harmonious complex of close-packed cells, as in numbers 1 and 3. Its organic feeling is borne out by its alternate names, the honeycomb and the tortoise-shell. But it can be infinitely elaborated: number 2, for example, has a hexagon ground covered with a grid of triangles, and it irresistibly tempts the eye to sort this overlay into larger hexagons, which themselves seem to accrue triangles on their outer facets to become the six-pointed stars known as the Solomon's seal or Star of David. Numbers 4 and 5 gain a certain formality from the juxtaposition of small squares with larger octagons; the designer of number 4 has taken advantage of this quality to turn the octagon into a decorative medallion.

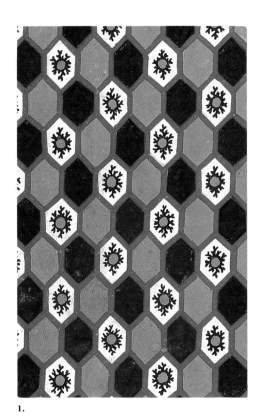

1.

2.

3.

4.

5.

HOUNDSTOOTH

1, 3, 5, 6, 8. France, c. 1910–20, gouache on paper, AYG, 100%

2, 4, 7, 9. France, c. 1910–20, gouache on paper, AYG, 115%

10. Probably France, c. 1940s, RP or SP silk, AYG, 100%

11. France, 1917, RP silk, AYG, 100%

12. USA, c. 1920s–40s, RP cotton, AYG, 125%

13, 20. USA, 1940s–50s, RP cotton, AYG, 100%

14. France, 1930s, gouache on paper, AYG, 80%

15, 16. France, 1920s–40s, RP or SP silk, AYG, 100%

17. France, c. 1920s, RP cotton, AYG, 125%

18. Probably France, 20th C, RP cotton, AYG, 100%

19, 21. France, c. 1910–20, gouache on paper, AYG, 68%

LIKE THE HERRINGBONE, the houndstooth pattern appeared as a weave long before textile printers developed it beyond the comfortable limits of weaving. A broken check of swastika-like squares with protruding arms, it has a classic, conservative look, though the designer can jazz it up by playing with its scale and coloring. A houndstooth motif is called by the French a *pied de poule* (chicken's foot); an extra-large houndstooth is a *pied de coq* (cock's foot). The English used to maintain the birdlike metaphor for houndstooth with the name "crow's foot," though this is now old-fashioned.

1.

2.

3.

4.

5.

6.

7.

8.

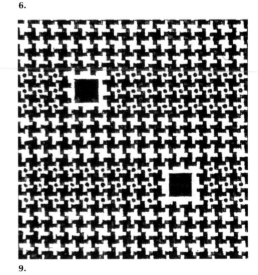

9.

10.

11.

12.

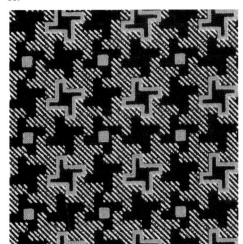

13.

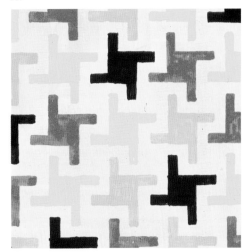

14.

15.

16.

17.

18.

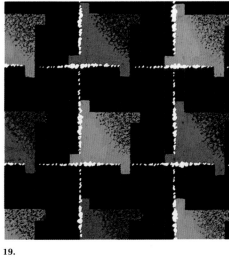

19.

20.

21.

INDIGOS

1. USA, c. 1880–1900, RP cotton, AYG, 140%
2. USA or France, c. 1880–1900, RP cotton, AYG, 100%
3. Probably France, late 19th C, RP cotton, AYG, 100%
4. USA, mid-19th C, RP cotton, AYG, 135%
5. France, c. 1830–40, RP and/or BP cotton, AYG, 100%
6. France, 1912, RP or BP cotton, AYG, 90%
7. USA, c. 1860–80, RP cotton, AYG, 105%

As with the floral indigos, the essential element of these designs is their color—indigo, with the motifs usually standing out in contrast against the dark blue ground of the cloth. For centuries the dye has been used on fabric made into practical everyday clothing for all ages and sexes, as typified by an offering in the 1925 Sears, Roebuck catalog: "Calico, dyed genuine indigo blue. Patterns suitable for men's work shirts and women's house dresses." Genuine indigo, made with the vegetable dye instead of its modern chemical substitute, usually releases a distinctive fruity aroma when the cloth is steam ironed, regardless of age. (See also *Floral: Indigos,* pages 80–81.)

1.

2.

3.

4.

5.

6.

7.

INTERLOCKING

1. France, 1930s, gouache on paper, AYG, 64%
2. France, c. 1910–20, RP cotton, 100%
3. USA, c. 1880, RP cotton, AYG, 120%
4. France, c. 1900–1910, RP wool, AYG, 120%
5. France, 1885, RP cotton, AYG, 140%

MOTIFS CAN INTERLOCK in two ways: through an illusion of depth, with lines that pretend to twist over and under each other, as in numbers 1, 4, and 5; or simply by contiguity, as in numbers 2 and 3. Interlocking circles are a symbol of friendship and union, notably in the five-circle symbol of the Olympic games and in the traditional Double Wedding Ring quilt pattern. But number 1 has the puzzling, conundrum quality of a magician's mysteriously linked steel rings.

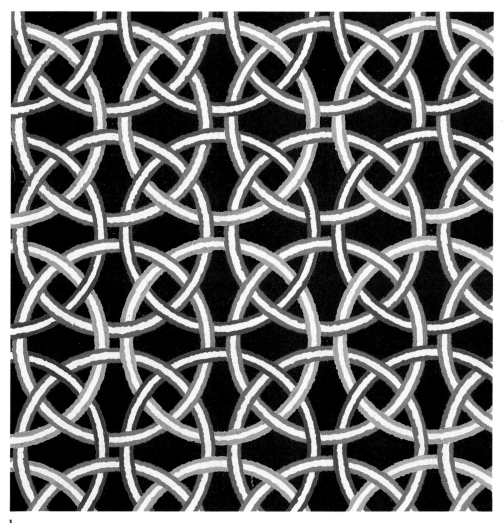

1.

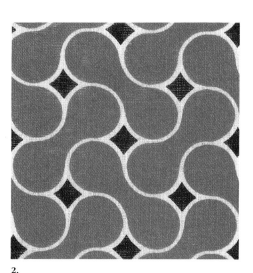

2.

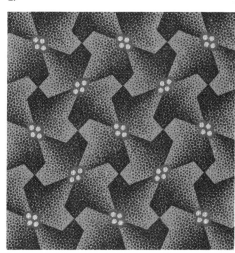

3.

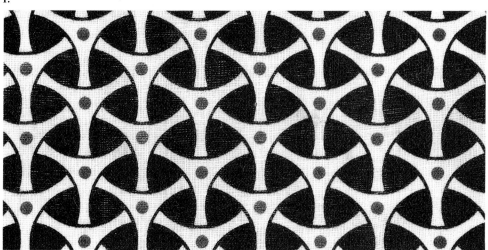

4.

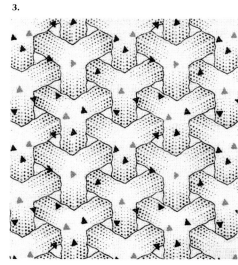

5.

LOOPS AND SCRIBBLES

1. France, 1890, gouache on paper, AYG, 100%
2. USA, 1940s, gouache on paper, AYG, 100%
3. USA, 1940s, RP rayon, AYG, 100%
4. France, 1929, RP silk, AYG, 70%
5. France, c. 1840, gouache on paper, AYG, 86%
6. USA, 1930s–40s, RP or SP rayon, AYG, 100%

SCRIBBLED WHORLS OF lines are the first designs a child can manage with crayon and paper, and few adults outgrow the habit of doodling. The doodle, in fact, dates to prehistory: it is preserved in the neolithic scribbles called macaronis, created by ancient folk running their fingers through patches of wet mud. Made orderly and neatly repeating, the scribble becomes a loop pattern in numbers 1 and 2. Though they are inspired by different degrees of ambition, numbers 3 and 4 both suggest calligraphy; number 6 is the scribble transferred from an ink to a fabric metaphor, seeming to show the loose coils of thread or yarn on their way to becoming knots. Number 5 is an odd combination of a randomly ranging line and a regular striped ground.

1.

2.

3.

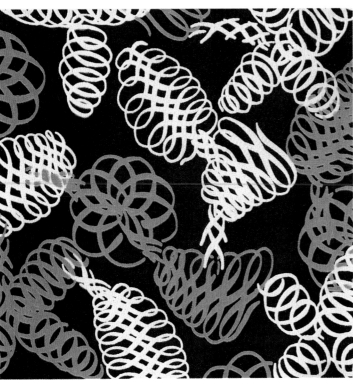

4.

5.

6.

MADDERS

1, 5. France, c. 1860, RP cotton, AYG, 135%
2. France, 1843, RP cotton, AYG, 100%
3, 7, 13–15. France, c. 1860, RP cotton, AYG, 100%
4. USA, c. 1860–80, RP cotton, AYG, 100%
6, 10. USA, 1873, RP cotton, AYG, 100%
8. USA, c. 1870–80, RP cotton, AYG, 100%
9. USA, c. 1840–50, RP cotton, AYG, 100%
11. USA, c. 1870–80, RP cotton, AYG, 125%
12. France, 1861, RP cotton, AYG, 135%

MADDER-DYED CLOTH combines richness of color with a dark palette that makes it practical—neither bright nor light, it doesn't show dirt. Throughout the eighteenth and nineteenth centuries madders were a staple of women's everyday wear. The patterns changed with the decades but the palette remained the same. From the mid-nineteenth century through the 1880s, madder-dyed geometrics were probably the most widely produced genre of prints in Europe and America. (See also *Floral: Madders,* pages 88–89.)

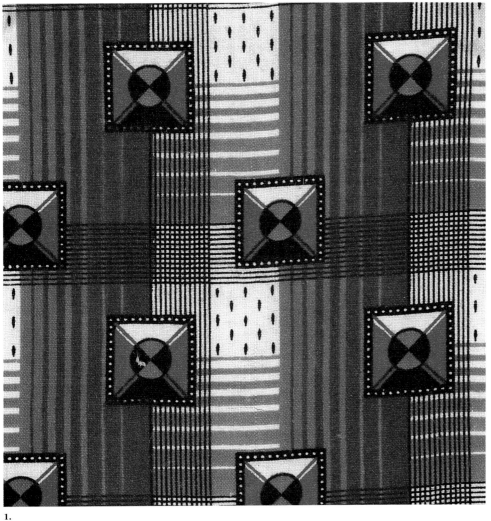

1.

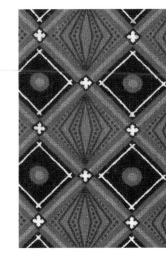

2.

3.

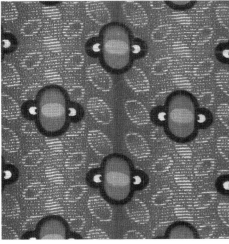

4.

5.

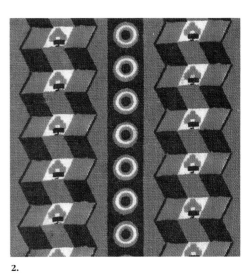

6.

7.

8.

9.

10.

11.

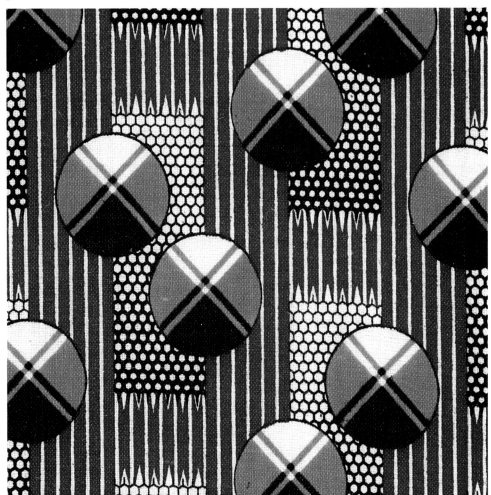

12.

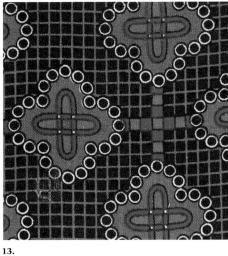

13.

14.

15.

MARBLEIZED LOOK

1. **France, c. 1840–50, RP wool challis, AYG, 130%**
2. **France, c. 1870–90, RP cotton, AYG, 110%**
3. **USA, c. 1930s, RP silk, AYG, 110%**
4. **Probably USA, c. 1940s, gouache on paper, AYG, 70%**
5. **Probably France, 2d half 19th C, RP cotton, AYG, 115%**
6. **A hand-marbleized silk made by the traditional technique**
7. **USA, c. 1930s, RP or SP silk satin, AYG, 100%**
8. **USA, c. 1930s, RP or SP silk satin, AYG, 100%**
9. **Probably France, c. 1950s–60s, RP or SP silk, AYG, 105%**

THE ENDPAPERS OF eighteenth- and nineteenth-century books were often decorated with swirling colors in imitation of marble. To create this effect, nonsoluble inks were floated across the surface of a tank of water, then transferred to paper by means of a quick dipping. Number 6 is an example of cloth marbleized by this traditional method. But it isn't feasible to apply this technique to large rolls of cloth, so in order to simulate the look, a fabric designer must create an image of veins and swirls, building into the pattern a way for it to repeat. On paper, this look may imitate marble. On cloth, it usually imitates not marble but marbleized paper.

1.

2.

3.

4.

5.

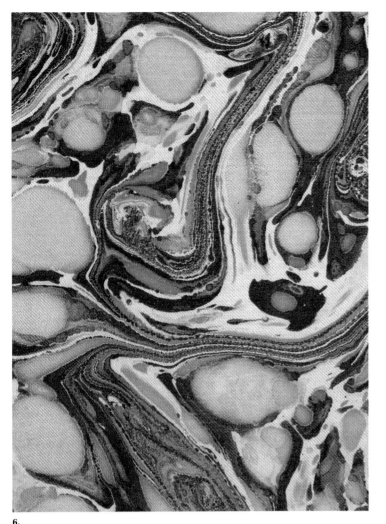

6.

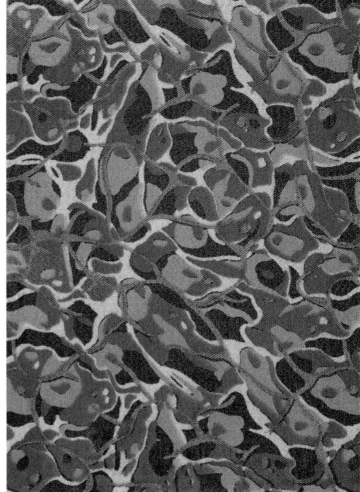

7.

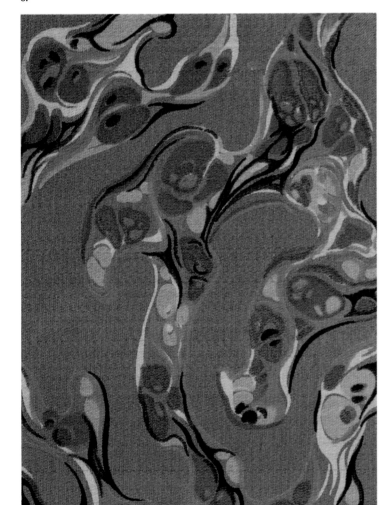

8.

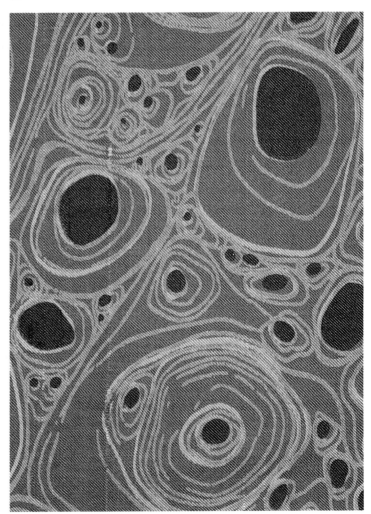

9.

MEDALLIONS

1. France, 1890, gouache on paper, AYG, 80%
2. France, c. 1815, gouache on paper, HF (carpet pattern), 85%
3. France, 1815, gouache on paper, AYG, 100%
4. France, c. 1920s, gouache on paper, AYG, 70%
5. France or England, 2d half 19th C, RP cotton, AYG, 86%
6. France, 1810–15, gouache on paper, A (scarf pattern), 70%

MEDALLIONS ARE CIRCULAR devices of a certain formality. They were popular in the late eighteenth century and early nineteenth century and often relate to the aristocratic neoclassical and Empire styles of decor (numbers 2 and 6). Star shapes and floral themes such as rosettes were favored, but coinlike and medal-like motifs also appeared. Number 4 is an unusual medallion design with Persian overtones, perhaps inspired by the colors and costumes of the Ballets Russes.

1.

2.

3.

4.

5.

6.

MOSAICS

1. France, c. 1900–1930, gouache on paper, AYG, 125%
2. France, c. 1920s, gouache on paper, AYG, 80%
3. France, c. 1920s, gouache on paper, AYG, 100%
4. USA or France, 1st half 20th C, RP cotton, AYG, 140%
5. Probably France, c. 1930s–40s, RP or SP silk, AYG, 100%
6. France, 1st half 20th C, gouache on paper, AYG, 100%

CURIOUSLY, MOSAIC PATTERNS are seen more often in apparel textiles than in home furnishings, though they are inspired by decorations for buildings rather than for the body. The jigsaw-like intricacy of the mosaic translates well into cloth; the countless tiny, brightly colored fragments, so painstakingly fitted together, produce movement and a tactile feeling quite absent from, say, bricks and mortar. And because the technique has flourished in many European cultures since the days of Alexander the Great, contemporary designers have a rich tradition to draw upon. Number 1, with its black tracery, may look toward stained glass as much as toward mosaic for its inspiration.

1.

2.

3.

4.

5.

6.

NEATS

1. **France, c. 1860, gouache on paper, AYG, 100%**
2. **France, mid-19th C, RP cotton, AYG, 100%**
3. **France, mid-19th C, paper impression, AYG, 100%**
4, 17, 23. **USA, c. 1880, RP cotton, AYG, 100%**
5–9, 12, 14, 18–20, 22, 24. **France, c. 1900, gouache on paper, AYG, 100%**
10, 11, 13, 16. **France, c. 1880, RP cotton, AYG, 100%**
15. **Probably France, c. 1900, RP silk satin, AYG, 100%**
21. **France, c. 1830, gouache on paper, AYG, 100%**

GEOMETRIC NEATS WERE as commonplace in the second half of the nineteenth century as floral ones. They were inexpensive to produce, usually having only one or two colors and simple motifs, all less than a quarter of an inch in size. Also, the regular layouts and small repeats required no ingenuity to design, cutting down on the artists' time and salary. In late-nineteenth-century America, an imported cotton neat cost eight cents a yard, a domestic one even less. These restrained, orderly designs were worn by men, women, and children.

1. 2. 3. 4. 5. 6.

7. 8.

9. 10. 11. 12.

13. 14.

15. 16. 17. 18.

19. 20. 21. 22. 23. 24.

OGEE

1. France, c. 1850, RP wool challis, AYG, 24%
2. France, c. 1920, RP cotton, AYG, 50%
3. USA, c. 1880, RP cotton, AYG, 100%
4. France, c. 1900, RP cotton, AYG, 130%

TRANSFERRED TO CLOTH, the architectural molding called the ogee, or ogive, forms a graceful, eye-shaped oval that narrows at each end to a point and then opens into the repeat pattern in a sinuous rhythm of S-shaped waves. The ogee design can be imagined, in fact, as an S shape constantly repeated and reversed by a series of mirror reflections. The space in the center of the curves is a natural enclosure for a decorative device such as a medallion. Ogival patterns often appeared in sixteenth-century Turkish, Persian, and Italian brocades. When designed for larger-scale, more elaborate home-furnishing fabrics, they tend to reflect either their Middle Eastern or their Renaissance roots.

1.

2.

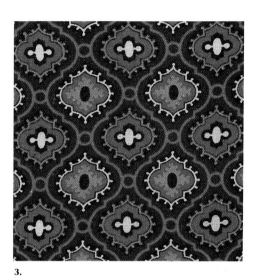

3.

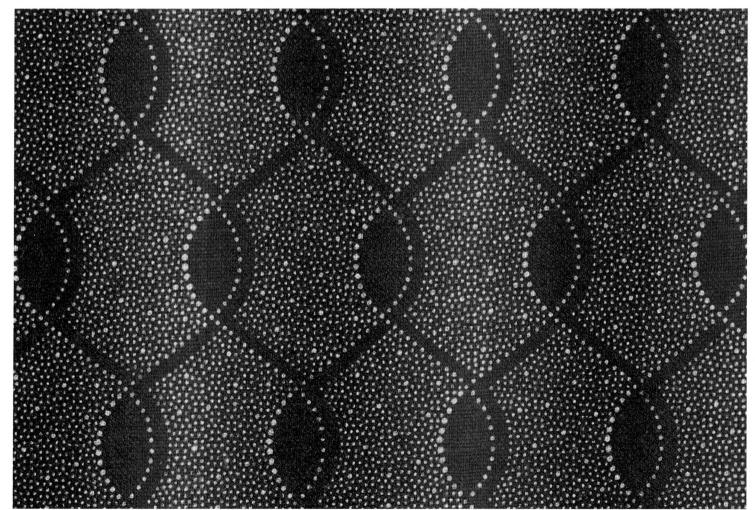

4.

OMBRÉ

1. France, 1927, silk, AYG, 90%
2. France, 1855, PP wool challis, AYG, 90%
3. France, 1855, PP wool challis, AYG, 90%
4. France, 1855, PP wool challis, AYG, 90%
5. France, 1855, PP wool challis, AYG, 76%
6. France, 1855, PP wool challis, AYG, 90%
7. France, 1880, gouache on paper, AYG, 130%
8. France, 1880, gouache on paper, AYG, 130%
9. France, 1880, gouache on paper, AYG, 130%
10. France, 1880, gouache on paper, AYG, 130%

THESE DESIGNS ILLUSTRATE the sophistication achieved with the ombré process in the nineteenth century. The ground of number 6, for example, is a basic stripe made elegant and subtle by the ombré method of blending one color into another. Superimposed over it is a conventionally printed serpentine stripe broken down into elongated loops, and this second stripe includes a third, another ombré, set so that its gradations of light into dark stand out in counterbalance to the similar transitions in the ground—in other words, a double ombré. Such a print must have been arduous and expensive to produce; it is easy to see why the ombré technique fell into disuse by the mid-nineteenth century. (See also *Floral: Ombré,* pages 96–97.)

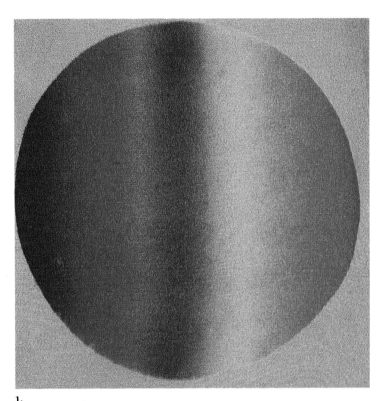

1.

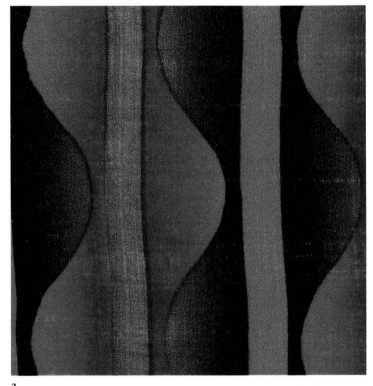

2.

3.

4.

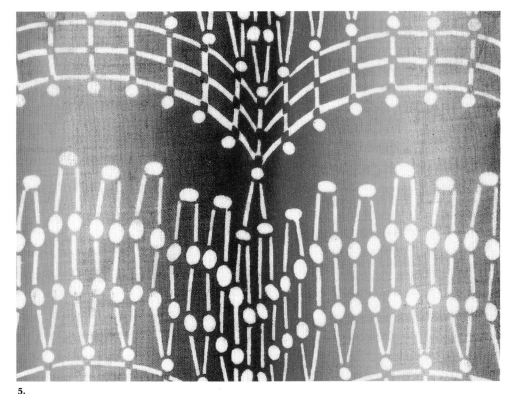

5.

6.

7.

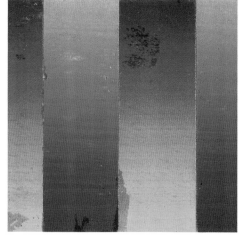

8.

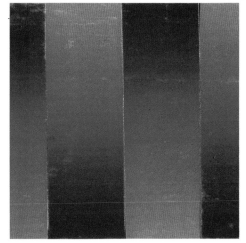

9.

10.

OPTICAL

1. **Probably France, c. 1900, RP cotton, AYG, 140%**
2. **Probably France, c. 1880–1900, RP cotton, AYG, 120%**
3. **USA, 1960s, ink on paper, AYG, 50%**
4. **Probably France, c. 1880–1900, RP cotton, AYG, 90%**
5. **Probably France, c. 1900, RP cotton, AYG, 100%**
6. **Probably France, c. 1900, RP cotton, AYG, 100%**
7. **USA, 20th C, gouache on paper, AYG, 96%**
8. **Probably France, c. 1900, RP cotton, AYG, 110%**
9. **Germany, 1930s, gouache on paper, AYG (tie pattern), 120%**
10. **France, 1912, RP cotton, AYG, 92%**
11. **France, 1930s–40s, gouache on paper, AYG, 100%**

THE DISTORTED-LOOKING images in these optical prints may seem to have been inspired by the paintings of twentieth-century artists such as Bridget Riley and Victor Vasarely, but all the examples here, except for number 3, were produced decades before. Designs resembling Op Art actually predate the modern printing industry altogether, for they arise easily out of the grid imposed by loom weaving. Numbers 2, 7, and 9 in particular resemble centuries-old woven patterns. Woven designs suggesting Op Art were being made in the early nineteenth century, at the same time as the earliest printed opticals, in the German and early American tradition of the overshot coverlet. Optical prints are novelties—they are too disquieting to the eye to have caught on as a mass taste. Though most of these patterns are variations on the square or the check, number 1 stretches and squeezes a houndstooth motif. (See also *Geometric: Eccentrics,* pages 164–65.)

1.

2.

3.

4.

5.

6.

7.

8.

9.

10.

11.

OVALS AND SEEDS

1. France, 1890, gouache on paper, AYG, 66%
2. France, 1886, RP cotton, AYG, 100%
3. France, 1845, RP cotton, AYG, 74%
4. France, c. 1930s, gouache on paper, AYG, 100%
5. France, c. 1830–40, gouache on paper, AYG, 74%
6. France or USA, c. 1880, RP cotton, AYG, 100%
7. France, 1949, paper impression, AYG, 50%
8. France or USA, c. 1930s, RP silk, AYG, 130%
9. France, c. 1830–40, gouache on paper, AYG, 100%

OVALS ARE CLEARLY related to circles, but they appear far less often in textile design. Given pointed ends to make them into almond or seedlike shapes (numbers 5 and 9), they become the mandorla, a mystical form signifying the union of heaven and earth. But this too has never been a popular motif. Perhaps, for modern customers at any rate, the oval can too easily recall pills; the designer of the pattern illustrated in number 8 seems to have tried to fight that association by wrapping the forms in dots and stripes that suggest the foil around chocolates. Number 3 can't really stand accused of being an oval pattern—clearly these are circles, receding into the distance.

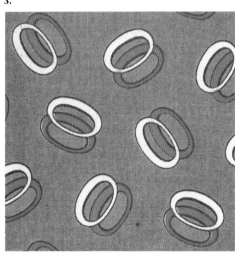

1.

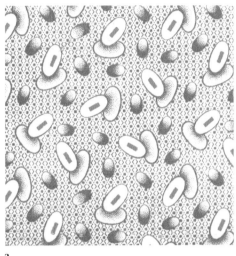

2.

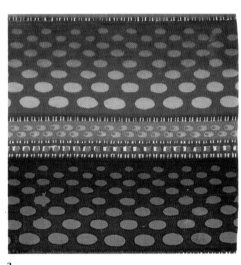

3.

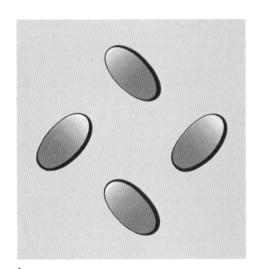

4.

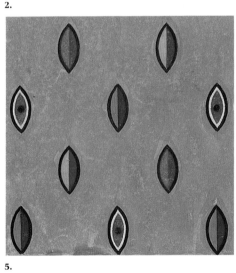

5.

6.

7.

8.

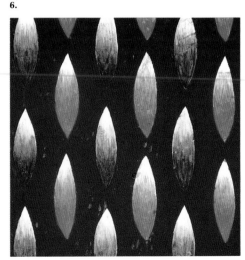

9.

PATTERNED GROUND

1. USA, c. 1930s, gouache on paper, AYG, 100%
2. France or USA, c. 1920, RP cotton, AYG, 100%
3. France, c. 1840, RP and BP cotton, AYG, 100%
4. France, c. 1860, gouache on paper, AYG, 100%
5. France, 1900–1920, gouache on paper, AYG, 110%
6. USA, 1920s–30s, gouache on paper, AYG, 80%

GRIDS, DOTS, AND textures—the same variety of grounds used as the backdrop for floral motifs—can also support geometrics. Or almost the same, for though a flower often floats against a geometric ground, a geometric device is rarely superimposed on a floral print. At least in cloth, the natural still seems to have some claim to precedence over the artificial.

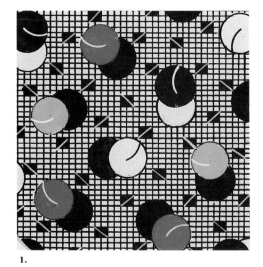

1.

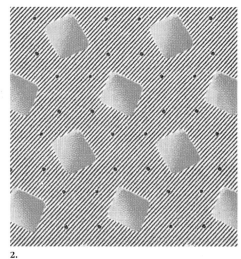

2.

3.

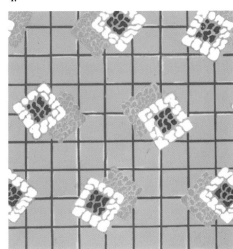

4.

5.

6.

PINWHEELS AND SPIRALS

1. France, c. 1890, gouache on paper, AYG, 90%
2. France, c. 1810–20, gouache on paper, AYG, 74%
3. France, c. 1890, gouache on paper, AYG, 90%
4. France, c. 1810–20, gouache on paper, AYG, 74%
5. France, c. 1810–20, gouache on paper, AYG, 110%
6. France, 1883, RP cotton, AYG, 100%
7. France, c. 1900–1920, gouache on paper, AYG, 96%
8. France, c. 1820, BP cotton, AYG, 115%
9. France, c. 1890, gouache on paper, AYG, 100%
10. France, c. 1900–1920, gouache on paper, AYG, 115%
11. France or USA, c. 1930s, gouache on paper, AYG, 170%

THE SPIRAL IS a continuous line circling an axis, a pinwheel is a set of spokes radiating from a hub. The spiral can seem to spread outward or to contract, expanding like a nebula in the galaxy or pulling vortically inward like a whirlpool. In number 2 it is static, like the shell of a snail. An age-old shape, found repeatedly in prehistoric art, the spiral is still capable of a larger meaning, symbolizing the evolution of the universe and growth. But it is also a natural, playful doodle. The pinwheel usually suggests whirling movement, its arms curved as if bent by the wind of their own spin. Starfish, flower, or electric fan—it is a protean motif.

1.

2.

3.

4.

5.

6.

7.

10.

8.

9.

11.

PLAIDS: BLACK AND WHITE

1. France, c. 1920s, gouache on paper, AYG, 400%
2. France, c. 1920s, gouache on paper, AYG, 130%
3. France, c. 1920s, gouache on paper, AYG, 130%
4. France, c. 1920s, gouache on paper, AYG, 130%
5. France, c. 1920s, gouache on paper, AYG, 110%
6. France, c. 1920s, gouache on paper, AYG, 94%
7. France, c. 1920s, gouache on paper, AYG, 130%
8. France, c. 1920s, gouache on paper, AYG, 130%

THE PLAID IS a box layout of stripes, usually horizontal and vertical, and almost always crossing at right angles. This simple definition is scarcely very descriptive, but plaids have been produced in such vast variety since the beginning of modern textile printing that a more searching definition might not cover them all. Their origin is in the threads of the loom, the warp set up lengthwise, the woof or weft filling it in horizontally. Print designers building on the tradition of woven plaids can make patterns into fantasies that the loom cannot manage. Black-and-white printed plaids get over the issue of color simply by ignoring it, revealing the complexities possible with nothing but lines and right angles. Essentially they are monotones, one-tone designs that could have been printed in any single color on white. But black is particularly effective for its stark high contrast.

1.

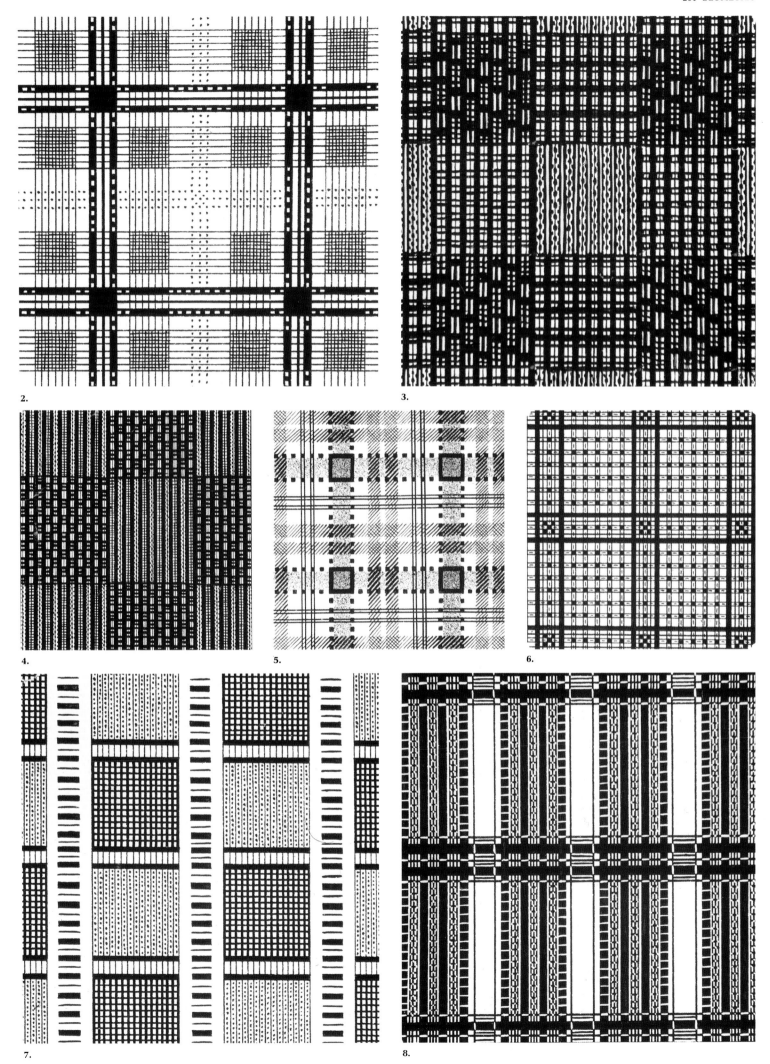

2.

3.

4.

5.

6.

7.

8.

PLAIDS: CHALLIS

1. **France, c. 1850, RP wool challis, AYG, 100%**
2. **France, 1850, RP wool challis, AYG, 50%**
3. **France, c. 1850, RP wool challis, AYG, 80%**
4. **France, c. 1850, RP wool challis, AYG, 100%**

BECAUSE IT HAS usually been cheaper to print a pattern than to weave it, many printed plaids try to look like wovens, using the technology of printing to make an expensive style affordable but not to explore the visual possibilities of the style. For these rich-colored challis, however, the plaid layout was only a starting point. They had their own tradition to draw upon, a tradition not of weaving but of printing—or rather a tradition within printing, for challis designs have a look all their own. (See also *Geometric: Challis,* page 153.)

1.

2.

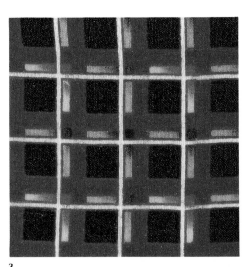

3.

4.

PLAIDS: CHECKS, GINGHAM CHECKS, AND WINDOWPANE CHECKS

1. France, c. 1920s, gouache on paper, AYG, 100%
2. "California," France, 1851, RP cotton, AYG, 86%
3. USA, 1960s, gouache on paper, AYG, 110%
4. Europe, 2d half 20th C, RP cotton velvet, AYG, 100%
5. France, 1883, RP cotton, AYG, 110%
6. USA, c. 1880, RP cotton, AYG, 100%
7. USA, 1960s, RP cotton, AYG, 100%
8. France, 1880–90, RP cotton, AYG, 100%
9. France, c. 1920, gouache on paper, AYG, 100%

THE STRIPES IN a plaid are often uneven in width; squared off, a plaid becomes a check (numbers 1–3). Number 2, printed in 1851, was given the name "California" (probably to cash in on the allure of the California gold rush) by its French maker, Koechlin of Alsace; alongside the swatch a sales agent of the company wrote, "It will not have success. It will not sell much in Paris, they are afraid of the color." A gingham check (numbers 4–6) is an allover pattern of solid-color squares made by overlapping stripes of the same width (the word "gingham" has its roots in the Malayan *ginggang,* meaning striped). When the checks are oversize, as in the cloth from which the traditional red-and-black lumberjack's jacket is cut, it is called a buffalo check. A gingham check is a classic, unpretentious design, simple to weave or to print. A windowpane check (numbers 7–9) is a plaid in which the squares are created by thin lines, suggesting the framework of a window.

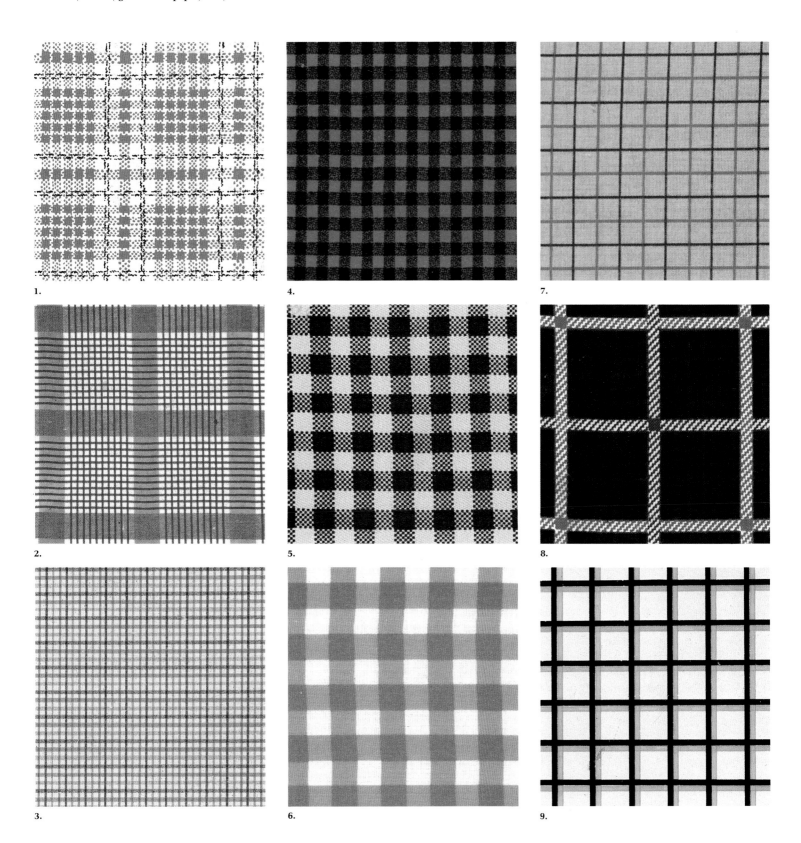

1.

2.

3.

4.

5.

6.

7.

8.

9.

PLAIDS: DRESS SHIRTING

1, 7. France, c. 1860, RP cotton, AYG, 100%
2–4, 8. USA, c. 1920s, RP cotton, AYG, 100%
5. France, 1931, gouache on paper, AYG, 100%
6. France or USA, c. 1920s, gouache on paper, AYG, 110%
9. France, 1929, gouache on paper, AYG, 100%

PLAIDS: DRESS-SHIRTING DOBBIES

10, 13. France, c. 1900–1920, gouache on paper, AYG, 110%
11, 12, 14. USA, c. 1900–1920, RP cotton, AYG, 100%

DRESS-SHIRTING PLAIDS of the late-nineteenth century and early-twentieth century, when printing technology allowed for finer detail than it does now, were sometimes indistinguishable from more costly woven plaids on all but the closest inspection, going so far as to reproduce the texture of the weave. Today a pattern this detailed would be more expensive to print than to weave. Around the turn of the century, however, it was a boon to the new legions of low-level office workers and country folk dressing up in their Sunday best.

A DOBBY IS a small geometric figure, originally created on a dobby loom, as a woven-in textile pattern. Dobbies added to the cost of the cloth, but print designers can scatter faux dobbies at no extra expense wherever they choose, usually on men's shirting patterns, creating illusion upon illusion.

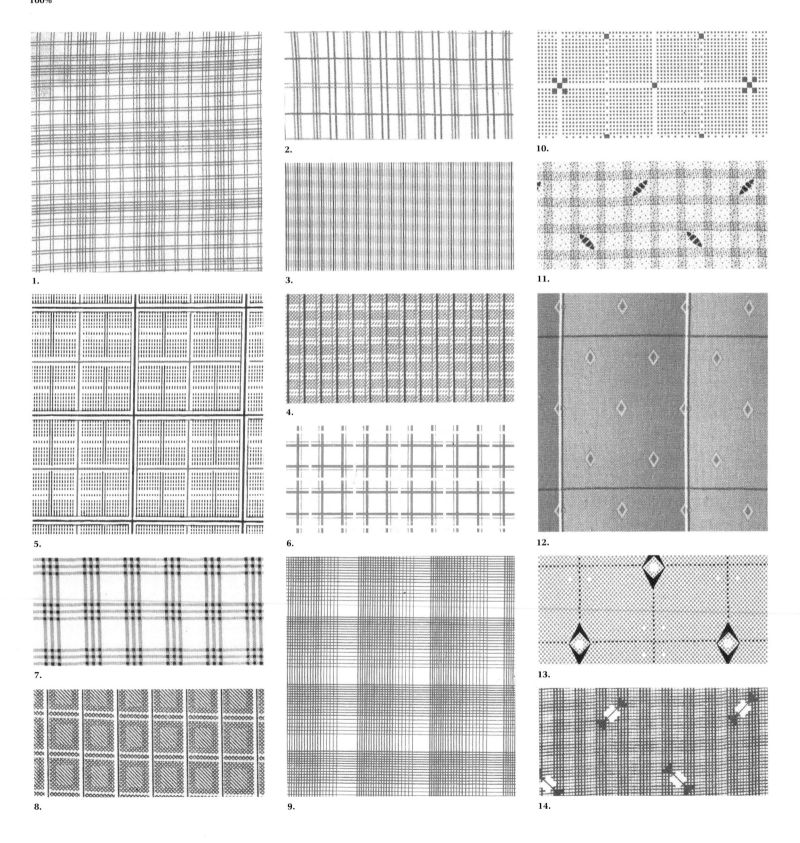

1.

2.

3.

4.

5.

6.

7.

8.

9.

10.

11.

12.

13.

14.

PLAIDS: FLANNEL

A TYPE OF bold, rather coarse plaid designed to be printed on flannel, these textiles were usually made into sturdy work or sport shirts for boys and men. Less expensive than the woven plaids they imitated, they have remained a staple at the low end of the market throughout the twentieth century.

1. Europe, 2d half 20th C, RP or SP cotton flannel, AYG, 70%
2. Europe, 2d half 20th C, RP or SP cotton flannel, AYG, 70%
3. Europe, 2d half 20th C, RP or SP cotton flannel, AYG, 70%
4. Europe, 2d half 20th C, RP or SP cotton flannel, AYG, 70%

1.

2.

3.

4.

PLAIDS: MADDER

1. France, 1843, RP cotton, AYG, 80%
2. France, 1843, RP cotton, AYG, 100%
3. France, 1843, RP cotton, AYG, 90%
4. France, 1851, RP cotton, AYG, 100%
5. France, 1843, RP cotton, AYG, 100%
6. France, c. 1840–50, RP cotton, AYG, 80%
7. France, 1843, RP cotton, AYG, 90%
8. USA, c. 1860–80, RP cotton, AYG, 115%
9. France, 1843, RP cotton, AYG, 80%

THE DISTINCTIVE COLOR range of madder dyes separates these fabrics from their woven models. Though the designs themselves could for the most part have been created on a loom, their overall appearance puts them firmly in the world of printed cloth.

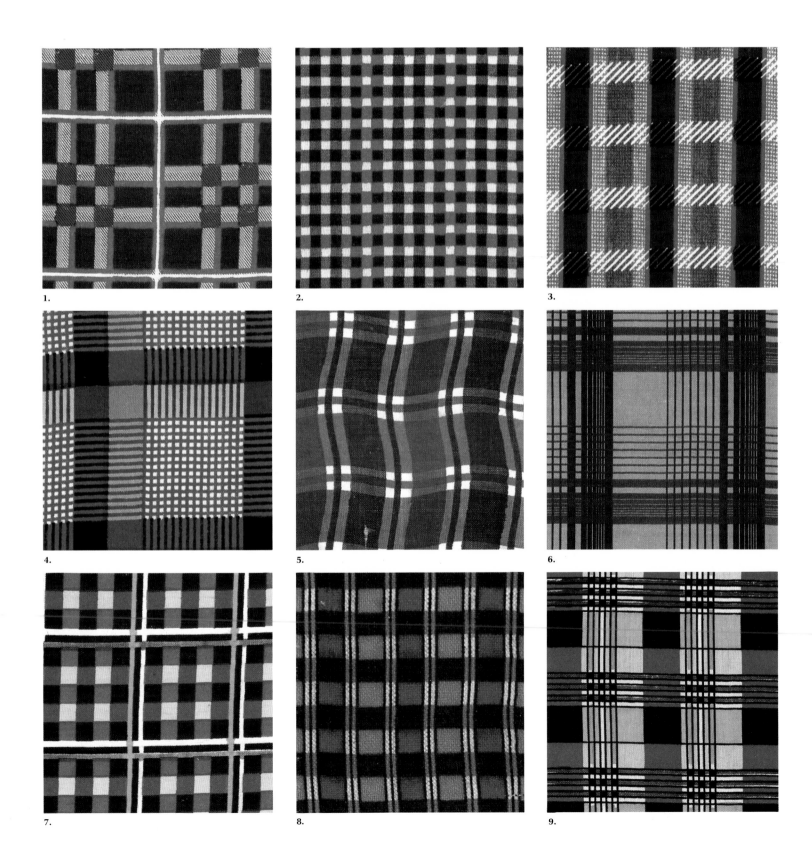

1.

2.

3.

4.

5.

6.

7.

8.

9.

PLAIDS: NOVELTY

1. France, c. 1910–20, gouache on paper, AYG, 110%
2. France, c. 1920s–30s, gouache on paper, AYG, 100%
3. France, 1930s, gouache on paper, AYG, 90%

PRINTED PLAIDS COME into their own in bright and witty novelty plaids like these, which a weaver would never attempt. They were particularly popular for inexpensive summer dresses in the 1930s, 1940s, and 1950s.

1.

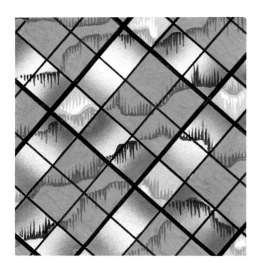

2.

3.

PLAIDS: PROVINCIAL

1. France, c. 1810–20, gouache on paper, AYG, 100%
2. France, c. 1810–20, BP cotton, AYG, 105%
3. France, c. 1810–20, gouache on paper, AYG, 100%
4. France, c. 1810–20, gouache on paper, AYG, 130%
5. France, c. 1810–20, BP cotton, AYG, 115%
6. France, c. 1810–20, BP cotton, AYG, 115%
7. France, c. 1810–20, gouache on paper, AYG, 110%
8. France, c. 1810–20, gouache on paper, AYG, 88%

THESE FRENCH DESIGNS from the early nineteenth century were created with the same bright palette as the floral provincial prints, and in fact the plaids and florals were often worn together in the traditional costume of Provence. Like the challis plaids, they are not so much imitations of wovens as a genre to themselves.

1.

2.

3.

4.

5.

6.

7.

8.

PLAIDS: SPORT SHIRTING

INEXPENSIVE PRINTED COTTONS for men's and women's casual and work clothes, plaid sport shirtings were introduced in the nineteenth century and are still made today, though on a much reduced scale. They were a hardy presence in the American market up until the 1960s, when it became as cheap to import woven plaids as to print them domestically. An item of economy rather than of fashion, printed plaid shirting lost its market when it could no longer compete pricewise with the real thing. A faux plaid on a haute-couture shirt in a Paris boutique can be appreciated precisely for its sham quality, but put the same plaid in a shopping-mall discount store and the chic disappears.

1. France, c. 1880–90, RP cotton, AYG, 80%
2. France, 1899, RP cotton, AYG, 80%
3. France, 1899, RP cotton, AYG, 90%
4. Probably France, c. 1900, RP cotton, AYG, 100%
5. USA, 1950s, RP cotton, AYG, 70%

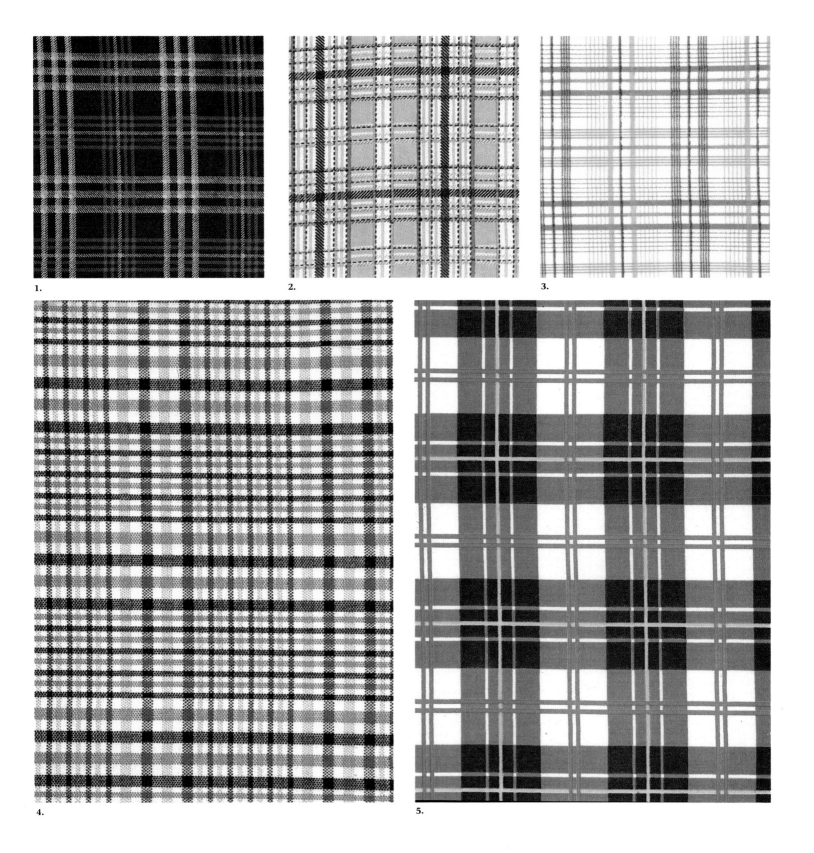

1.

2.

3.

4.

5.

PLAIDS: TARTAN

1. USA, 2d half 20th C, RP or SP cotton, AYG, 94%
2. USA, 2d half 20th C, RP or SP cotton, AYG, 105%
3. USA, 2d half 20th C, RP or SP cotton, AYG, 90%
4. USA, 2d half 20th C, RP or SP cotton, AYG, 84%

TARTANS ARE PLAIDS with a particularly strong association with Scotland (the word "plaid" comes from the Scottish Gaelic for blanket). Historically, each Scottish clan has been an extremely tight-knit group and fiercely proud of its particular woven wool tartan, including a dress tartan and a hunting tartan. This makes tartan plaids unique in the realm of geometric-patterned dress goods, for other geometrics gratify the eye but tend to leave the heart unmoved. Many tartans are new inventions, capitalizing on an authentic look but lacking Celtic ancestry. The printed cottons shown here are double impostors: not only do they try to claim the name of a traditional and honored clan tartan, they also pretend to be woven. Yet, like the skirl of electronic bagpipes, these parvenu plaids can also evoke strong associations and emotions.

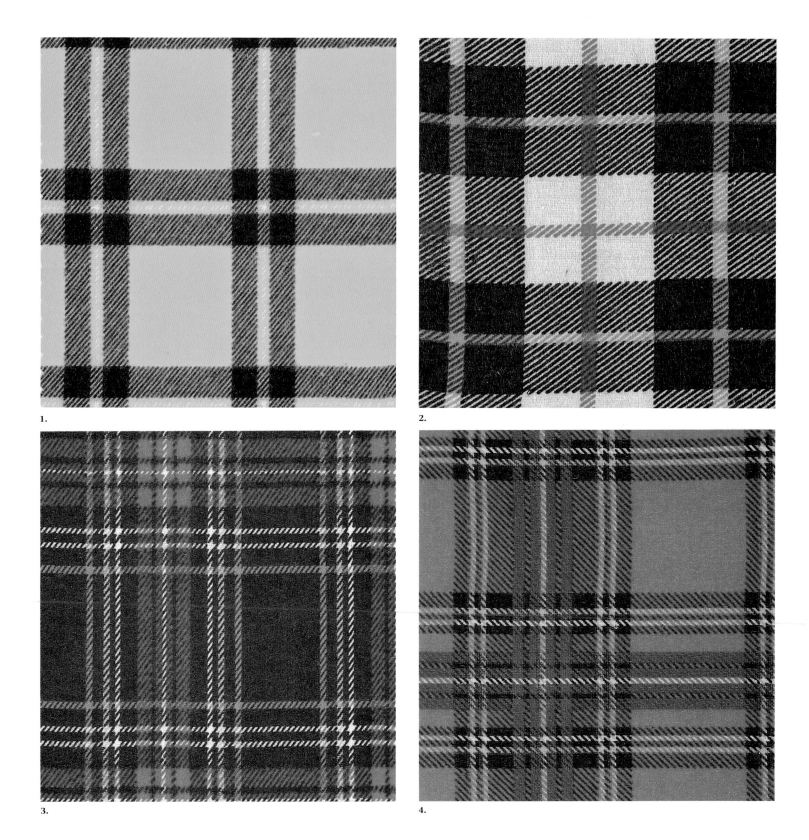

1.

2.

3.

4.

PLAIDS: TEXTURES AND TWEEDS

THESE PATTERNS REPRODUCE not only the layout of the plaid but the weave, texture, and pile of stout, nubby cloth. Even a rough tweed's stray curls of thread appear. Unlike the printed shirting patterns, these designs represent not so much an attempt to produce a more economical substitute for their woven competitors as a fashion trend for trompe-l'oeil effects.

1. France, c. 1900–1920, gouache on paper, AYG, 100%
2. France, c. 1900–1920, gouache on paper, AYG, 100%
3. France, c. 1900–1920, gouache on paper, AYG, 80%
4. France, c. 1900–1920, gouache on paper, AYG, 100%
5. France, c. 1900–1920, gouache on paper, AYG, 68%

1.

2.

3.

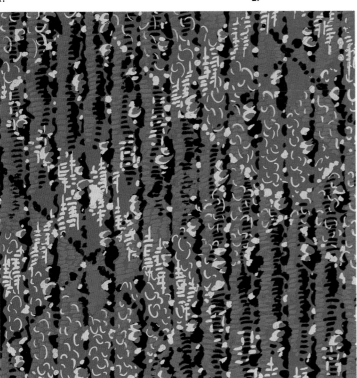

4.

5.

POLKA DOTS

1. **France, 1873, RP cotton, AYG, 80%**
2, 3, 6, 8, 11–15, 26, 29. **France, 1886, RP cotton, AYG, 100%**
4, 5. **France, c. 1900, RP silk, AYG, 100%**
7, 17, 19–21. **Europe, 20th C, RP or SP silk, AYG, 100%**
9, 24, 28. **USA, 20th C, RP cotton, AYG, 100%**
10. **France, 1932, gouache on paper, AYG, 110%**
16. **France, 1888, RP wool challis, AYG, 100%**
18. **USA, c. 1920s–30s, gouache on paper, AYG, 100%**
22. **France, c. 1930s, gouache on paper, A (scarf pattern), 100%**
23. **France, 1829, BP cotton, AYG, 100%**
25. **France, 1st quarter 19th C, BP cotton, AYG, 70%**
27. **France, 1890, gouache on paper, AYG, 100%**

THE POLKA DOT has always been and always will be. A basic favorite among textile patterns, it has never been out of style. To the print designer, the difference between the polka dot and the circle is that circles contain some internal motif, or are empty outlines; the polka dot is a round of solid color. And unlike the solid dots in the dot pattern, which are used as the elements of some other motif, the polka dot is arranged in random or set-layouts. The smallest polka dot is the pin dot (numbers 6, 11, and 13); the largest standard polka is the coin dot (number 22). But bigger ones also appear, in which case they are called outsized dots. The polka dot is a classic spring pattern, particularly in the colors of navy and white. It takes its name from a Bohemian folk dance, first performed in Prague in 1837 and brought to Paris in 1840; by 1845 the polka had spread to England, the United States, and even India. It became such a craze that numerous consumables were named after it—puddings, hats, fishing lures, drapery arrangements, dot patterns—in the hope that they would share its popularity.

1.

2.

3.

4.

5.

6.

7.

8.

9.

10.

11.

12.

13.

14.

15.

16.

17.

18.

19.

20.

21.

22.

23.

24.

25.

26.

27.

28.

29.

PROVINCIAL

1. France, c. 1810, gouache on paper, AYG, 100%
2. France, c. 1810, BP cotton, AYG, 90%
3. France, c. 1810, gouache on paper, AYG, 105%
4. France, c. 1810, gouache on paper, AYG, 100%
5. France, c. 1810, gouache on paper, AYG, 100%
6. France, c. 1810, gouache on paper, AYG, 160%
7. France, c. 1810, gouache on paper, AYG, 96%
8. France, c. 1810, gouache on paper, AYG, 70%

GAILY COLORED GEOMETRIC provincials were printed in quantity in early-nineteenth-century France as yard goods for ladies' wear. Another common use was as the filler for *mouchoirs,* or scarves, in combination with a border of another pattern. In Provence, geometrics and florals in this palette may be worn together, a rich layering of many different patterns sharing the same color scheme. Number 7, a stylized coral pattern, seems to anticipate a "postmodern" look of the 1980s; recurrences like this, both accidental and deliberate, are a constant in textile design. (See also *Floral: Provincial,* pages 108–9.)

1.

2.

3.

4.

5.

6.

7.

8.

QUATREFOILS AND TREFOILS

1. France, 1850, RP wool challis, AYG, 100%
2. France, 1850, RP wool challis, AYG, 78%
3. France, c. 1850, paper impression, AYG, 100%
4. France, 1892, RP cotton, AYG, 100%
5. France, 1840–45, RP silk and wool, AYG, 90%

IN TRADITIONAL SYMBOLISM, the quatrefoil (numbers 1 and 3–5) depicts the number four, with all that number's inherent significance—the four elements, the four cardinal points, the four seasons. As a rounded cross shape, it is also an architectural device (found, for example, in the tracery of Gothic cathedrals) and a heraldic charge. The trefoil (number 2) is a symbol of the number three and especially of the Trinity. The shapes may have had some of these antique and religious associations for Victorian designers (many Victorian churches in northern Europe, after all, are Gothic Revival), but they were also convenient medallion-like framing devices. They are seen less often now than in the nineteenth century, except in small-scale foulard prints.

1.

2.

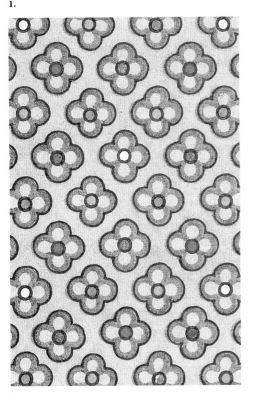

3.

4.

5.

RECTANGLES

1. **France, c. 1910–20, RP cotton, AYG, 100%**
2. **USA, c. 1930s, gouache on paper, AYG, 70%**
3. **Probably USA, c. 1940s–50s, RP or SP cotton, AYG, 100%**
4. **Probably France, c. 1920s–30s, RP silk, AYG, 100%**
5. **France, 1873, RP cotton, AYG, 100%**
6. **France, c. 1950–70, gouache on paper, AYG, 100%**

IN EVERYDAY LIFE, we are surrounded with more rectangular shapes than any other geometric form. Yet print designers are partial to squares; rectangles are relatively little seen in textiles. In part, at least, this is because designs based on them tend to be two-directional—the prints below could be turned upside down and no one would notice, but most would have quite a different aspect if they were laid sideways. Directional patterns are less economical in the cutting of garments than nondirectionals. Perhaps the equal proportions of the square offer some psychic satisfaction and sense of order that the rectangle distorts.

1.

2.

3.

4.

5.

6.

SCALE PATTERN

1. France, 1925, paper impression, AYG, 100%
2, 9. France, c. 1840, gouache on paper, AYG, 100%
3, 8. USA, c. 1880, RP cotton, AYG, 115%
4. Probably France, 1920s–30s, RP silk, AYG, 185%
5. France or USA, c. 1930s, gouache on paper, AYG, 150%
6. France, 1928, RP silk, AYG, 125%
7. France, c. 1800, paper impression, AYG, 100%
10, 13. France, c. 1860–80, RP cotton, AYG, 100%
11. France or USA, 2d half 19th C, RP wool, AYG, 155%
12. France, 1920s–30s, RP silk chiffon, AYG, 100%
14. France, c. 1880–90, gouache on paper, AYG, 195%
15. USA, 1873, RP cotton, AYG, 100%

THESE OVERLAPPING ARCS are also known as the clamshell pattern and the scallop pattern, though they can be made to look like architectural vaulting as easily as like the scales of a fish. The design is ancient and universal, found in Roman mosaics, Oriental brocades, the Indian hand-painted cottons called palampores, and American quilts. When based on fish and reptile scales, feathers of birds, or architectural trimming, the scales are usually arranged with the curved side down as if to form a protective covering. When based on shells or growing plant forms or simply nonobjective decorative shapes, the curved side most often points upward, as in all the examples on this and the following pages.

1.

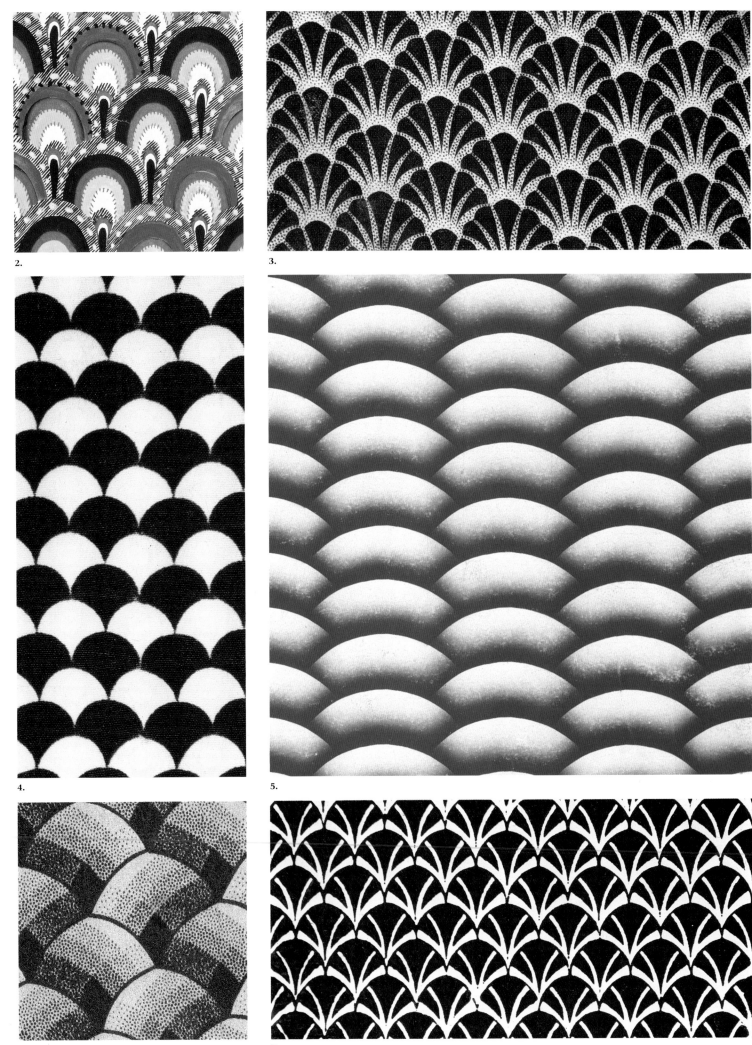

2.

3.

4.

5.

6.

7.

8.

9.

10.

11.

12.

13.

14.

15.

SCARVES

1. France, c. 1880, RP cotton, A (scarf corner), 64%
2. France, c. 1850, BP cotton, A (scarf corner), 50%
3. France, c. 1880, RP cotton, A (scarf corner), 50%

AN ORNAMENTAL BORDER is a natural presence on a printed scarf—a kind of frame, and a more satisfying way to finish the central pattern than simply to run it off the edge of the cloth. Often the border pattern is a stronger design than the field of the scarf, but the designer tries to prevent it from overpowering by integrating the two subtly with each other. The border design may pick up motifs from the filler and then do something more ambitious with them.

1.

2.

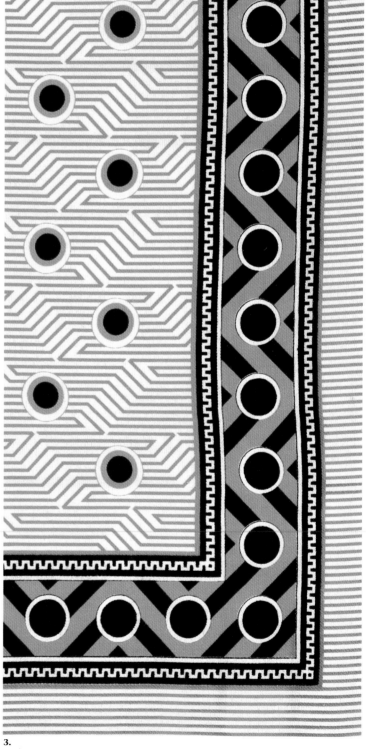

3.

SCROLLWORK

1. France, 1849, RP cotton, AYG, 60%
2. France, 1898, gouache on paper, AYG, 210%
3. France, c. 1855, gouache on paper, AYG, 50%
4. U.S.A., 20th C (after a 19th-C French pencil sketch), gouache on paper, AYG, 50%

IN THE WORDS of Auguste Racinet (*L'Ornement Polychrome*), the "irrepressible acanthus has passed through twenty-two centuries without losing one of its leaves and has covered with its branches the whole monumental world." Its scrolled leaf has been the basis of many a scrollwork pattern. Scrollwork has appeared constantly in printed textiles from the eighteenth century on, sometimes quite acanthus-like (number 4), and sometimes stylized into an almost abstract impression of looping vines and leaves. It combines allover coverage with graceful lightness and is usually nondirectional.

1.

2.

3.

4.

SPACED

1. France, c. 1840, PP cotton, AYG, 76%
2. USA, c. 1930s, RP or SP rayon, AYG, 100%
3. USA, c. 1930s–40s, gouache on paper, AYG, 100%
4. France, c. 1920–30s, paper impression, AYG, 100%
5. France, 2d half 19th C, gouache on paper, AYG, 100%
6. France, 1890, gouache on paper, AYG, 76%
7. France, 1890, gouache on paper, AYG, 100%
8. France, 1930s, gouache on paper, AYG, 100%
9. USA, c. 1930s, RP rayon, AYG, 74%
10. France, c. 1920s, paper impression, AYG, 64%

WHAT CHARACTERIZES A spaced layout is less motif than ground. Like flowers, geometric devices of any kind can be set in spaced layouts, floating apart from each other on a relatively empty field. The ground in this kind of design is usually a solid color, but the same motifs in the same arrangements could be set against some kind of pattern. The design would then be called a spaced geometric on a patterned ground. (See also *Geometric: Patterned Ground,* page 197.)

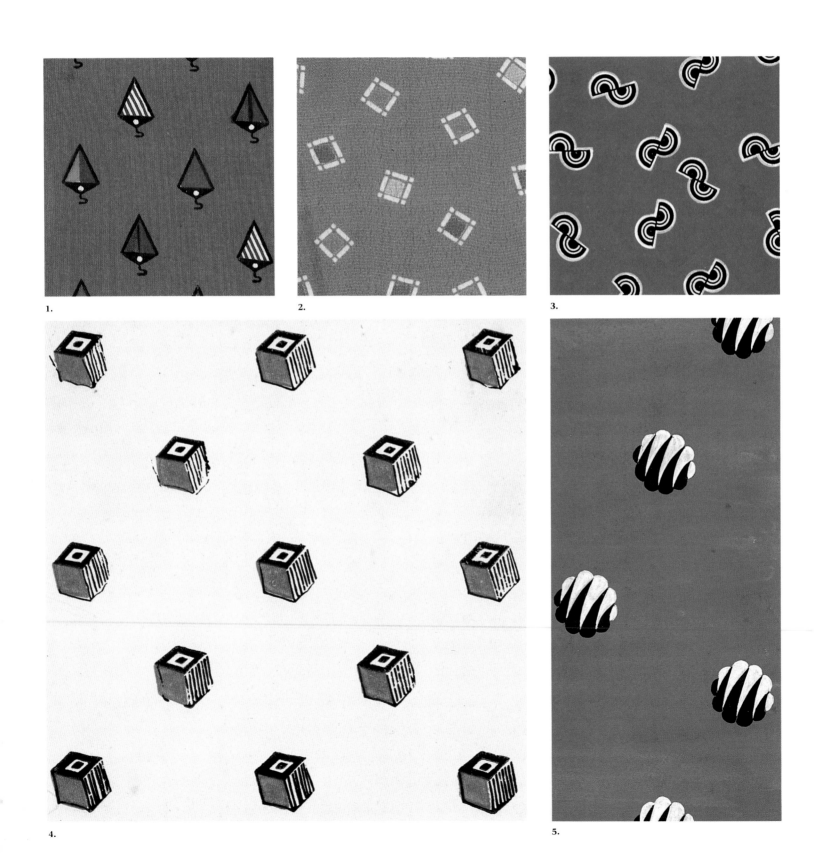

1.

2.

3.

4.

5.

6.

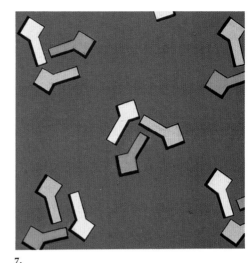

7.

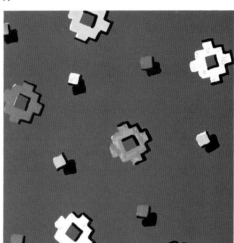

8.

9.

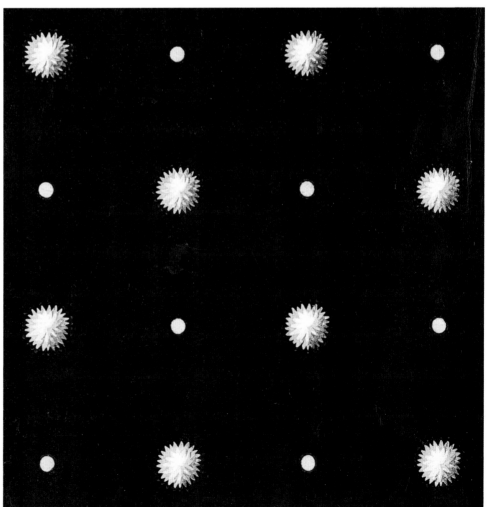

10.

SQUARES

1. **Germany, c. 1920–30s, gouache on paper, AYG (tie pattern), 100%**
2. **Germany, c. 1920s–30s, gouache on paper, AYG (tie pattern), 130%**
3. **France, c. 1920s–30s, gouache on paper, AYG, 150%**
4. **France, c. 1930s, gouache on paper, AYG, 50%**
5. **France, c. 1910–20, gouache on paper, AYG, 200%**
6–8. **France, 1886, RP cotton, AYG, 100%**
9. **France, 1830, BP cotton, AYG, 100%**
10, 13. **USA, c. 1930s, gouache on paper, AYG, 120%**
11. **France, c. 1910–20, gouache on paper, AYG, 100%**
12. **France, 1885, RP cotton, AYG, 100%**

AFTER THE CIRCLE, the square is the most common geometric form printed on textiles. The equal proportions of the square give it a strong feeling of stability, firmness, and rationality—a square must be carefully measured if it is not to become a rectangle. In Chinese, Hindu, and other traditions it is symbolic of one of the four elements, earth, and as such has feminine characteristics ascribed to it, while the circle is a masculine image emblematic of air or heaven. Squares within squares, squares butting into a grid, squares scattered, squares on top of squares, squares skewed into diagonals—designers have found infinite variety in this simplest of shapes. All of the patterns here play with the square as a motif in itself rather than as the basic constituent of a box layout, check, or plaid.

1.

2.

3.

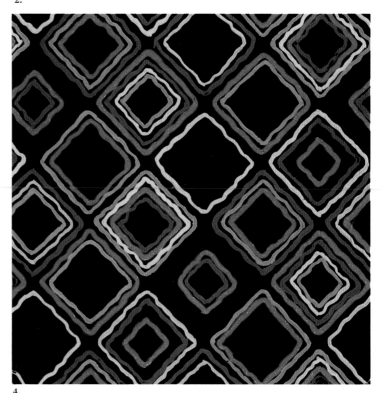

4.

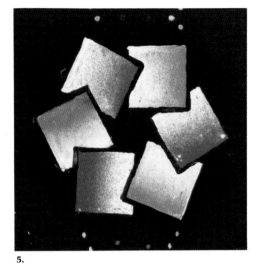

5.

6.

7.

8.

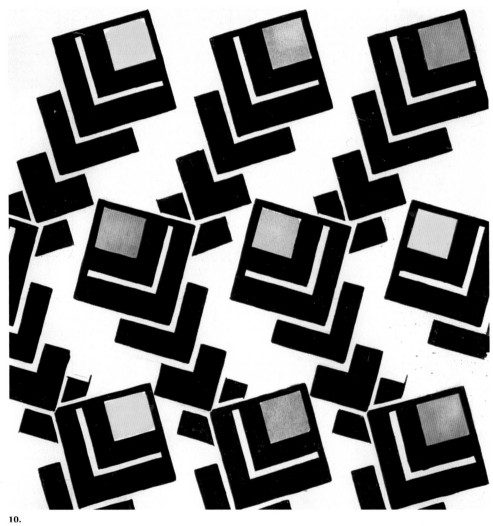

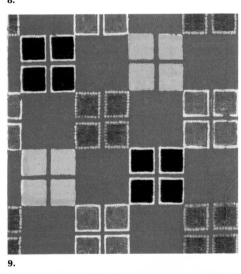

9.

10.

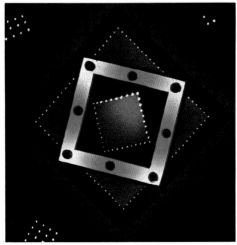

11.

12.

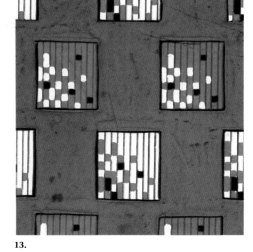

13.

STARS

1. **France, c. 1880, gouache on paper, AYG, 92%**
2. **France, 1887, RP cotton, AYG, 115%**
3. **Probably France, late 19th C, RP wool flannel, AYG, 36%**
4. **France, c. 1880, RP cotton, AYG, 100%**
5. **France, c. 1810–20, gouache on paper, AYG, 100%**
6. **France, c. 1810–20, paper impression, AYG, 90%**
7. **France, c. 1810–20, gouache on paper, AYG, 200%**
8. **France, mid-19th C, RP cotton, A (bandanna pattern), 100%**

THE CONVERSATIONAL PRINTS that designers call celestials often include stars, but the patterns on this page show them minus the night sky. Removed from their galactic surroundings, they become a geometric shape, as does the crescent. Stars generally have from five to eight points; those with more tend to be called starbursts. Once, of course, stars were thought to have a powerful influence on human affairs (hence such phrases as "thank your lucky stars"). They were also a sign of nobility—incorporated, for example, among the symbols of every order of British knighthood—and of the spiritual struggle of light against dark. Stars got a boost as decorations for cloth in 1777, during the American Revolution, becoming a symbol of freedom and the overthrow of tyranny when the American flag was designed with thirteen of them. Stars are also frequently combined with nautical motifs.

1.

2.

3.

4.

5.

6.

7.

8.

STRIPES

1. **France, c. 1930s–40s, gouache on paper, AYG, 100%**
2. **France, c. 1850–60, gouache on paper, AYG, 100%**
3. **France, c. 1840, gouache on paper, AYG, 120%**
4. **France, c. 1920, gouache on paper, AYG, 100%**
5. **USA, 20th C, gouache on paper, AYG, 105%**

IN THE TEXTILE industry, the term "striped" refers not to the straight bands of color called stripes but to a type of layout where the motifs line up to form stripes. Number 4, for example, would be a regular stripe but for its orderly arrangements of squares; number 5 makes its stripes out of stacks of triangles. Whatever form the stripe takes, it is almost always vertical, particularly in apparel designs. Vertical stripes accentuate the body's height, while horizontal stripes make it look wider.

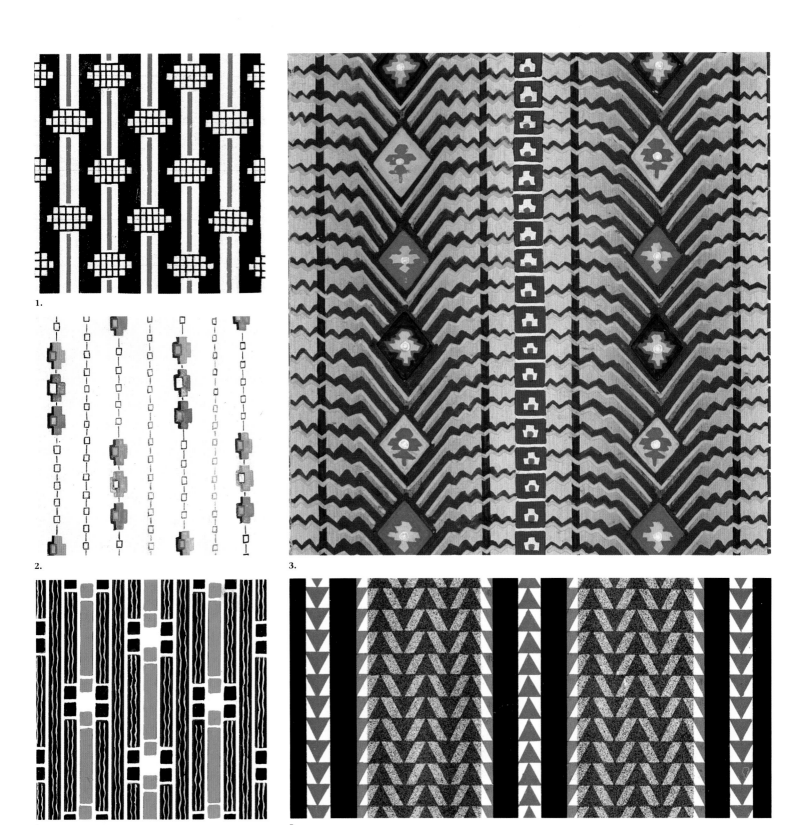

1.

2.

3.

4.

5.

STRIPES: DRESS SHIRTING

1, 9, 11. USA, c. 1880–1900, RP cotton, AYG, 100%
2, 8. USA, c. 1920s, gouache on paper, AYG, 100%
3, 7. France, 1885, RP cotton, AYG, 100%
4. Probably England, c. 1880–1920, RP cotton, AYG, 100%
5, 6, 12. England, c. 1920s, RP cotton, AYG, 100%
10. France, 1895, gouache on paper, AYG, 100%

STRIPES: DRESS-SHIRTING DOBBIES

13, 14, 17. France, 1899, RP cotton, AYG, 100%
15, 16, 18. USA or England, c. 1920, gouache on paper, AYG, 100%

STRIPES LIKE THESE have a timeless look, but they were most popular as a genre of prints during the two decades before and after the turn of the century, when many men in Europe and America were moving from the farm to manufacturing and office jobs that allowed them more leisure time. Now they had a need for neat, good-looking clothes to wear during work and off-work hours and a modest income to buy such clothes. The shirting prints of that time reproduce the texture of woven patterns so closely that only an attentive look will reveal the stripes as a dye. Despite the care the artists lavished on these designs, they were produced cheaply in great quantity. Their fine detail depended on the technique of the mill engraving. (See also *Floral: Mill Engravings*, pages 90–91.)

THE DOBBY IS considered to be almost any small-scale geometric motif added to enliven a basic stripe and to simulate a more expensive dobby-woven cloth. On dress shirtings, it usually remains subtle and understated, often in white or the same color as the stripe. Its purpose is to add interest and texture to the shirt without competing with the basic stripe pattern.

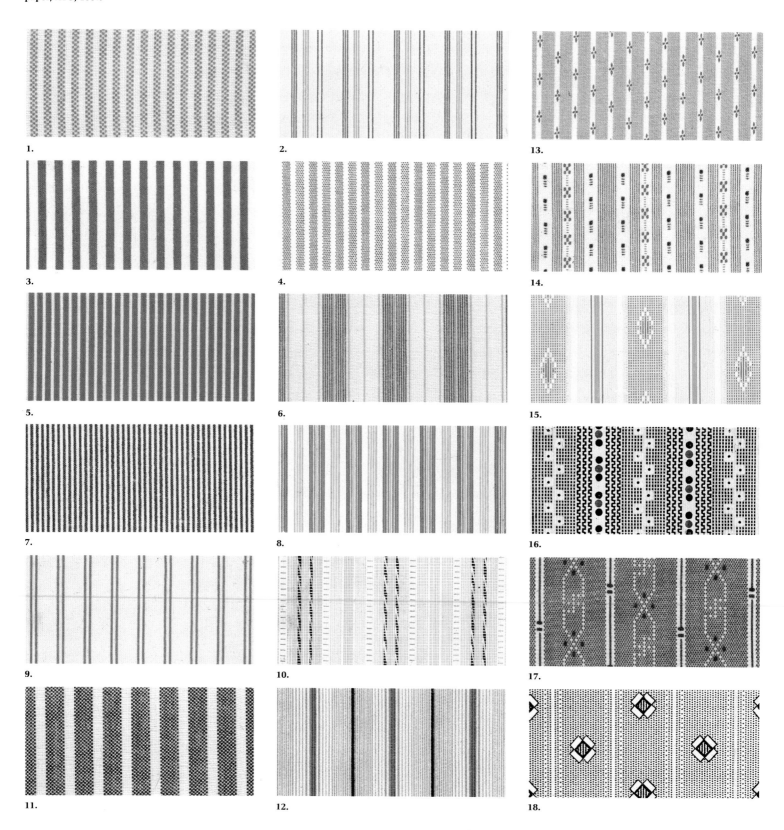

1.

2.

13.

3.

4.

14.

5.

6.

15.

7.

8.

16.

9.

10.

17.

11.

12.

18.

STRIPES: MADDER

1, 5, 8, 9. France, 1858, RP cotton, AYG, 100%
2. France, c. 1850–60, RP cotton, AYG, 115%
3. France, c. 1850, RP cotton, AYG, 100%
4. France, 1842, RP cotton, AYG, 100%
6. USA, 1873, RP cotton, AYG, 100%
7. USA, c. 1860–80, RP cotton, AYG, 100%
10. France, c. 1850, RP cotton, AYG, 100%
11. USA, c. 1880, RP cotton, AYG, 105%
12. USA, c. 1880, RP cotton, AYG, 110%

THESE PATTERNS ILLUSTRATE the rich but somber colors of natural madder dyes. Printed madder stripes and plaids usually do not simulate woven patterns but instead, like the challis plaids and challis stripes, are a look unto themselves.

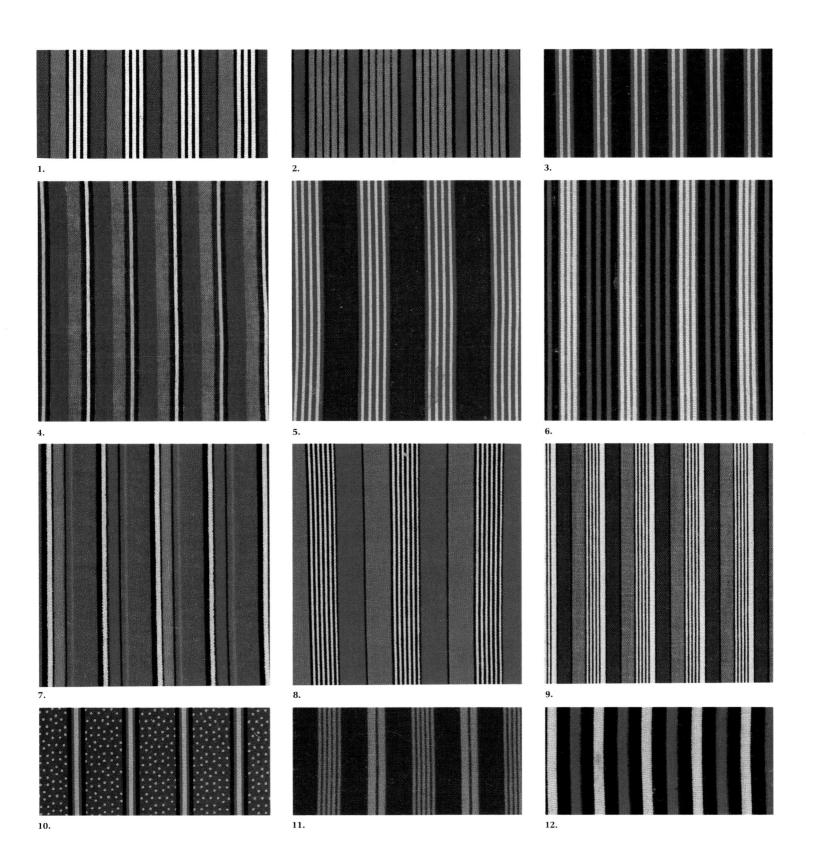

1.

2.

3.

4.

5.

6.

7.

8.

9.

10.

11.

12.

STRIPES: PROVINCIAL

1–5, 7, 9–11, 13, 15–18. France, c. 1820, gouache on paper, AYG, 100%
6, 8, 14. France, c. 1820, gouache on paper, AYG, 110%
12. France, c. 1820, RP cotton, AYG, 100%

FRENCH PROVINCIAL FLORALS, plaids, stripes, and other geometrics were immensely popular in the 1810s and 1820s as a cheerful alternative to the more formal look of Empire-style clothing. Originally inspired by the traditional folk costume of Provence, they kept their association with the countryside even when they were worn all over France. Their vogue eventually faded, but they survived as a regional print made specifically for Provence.

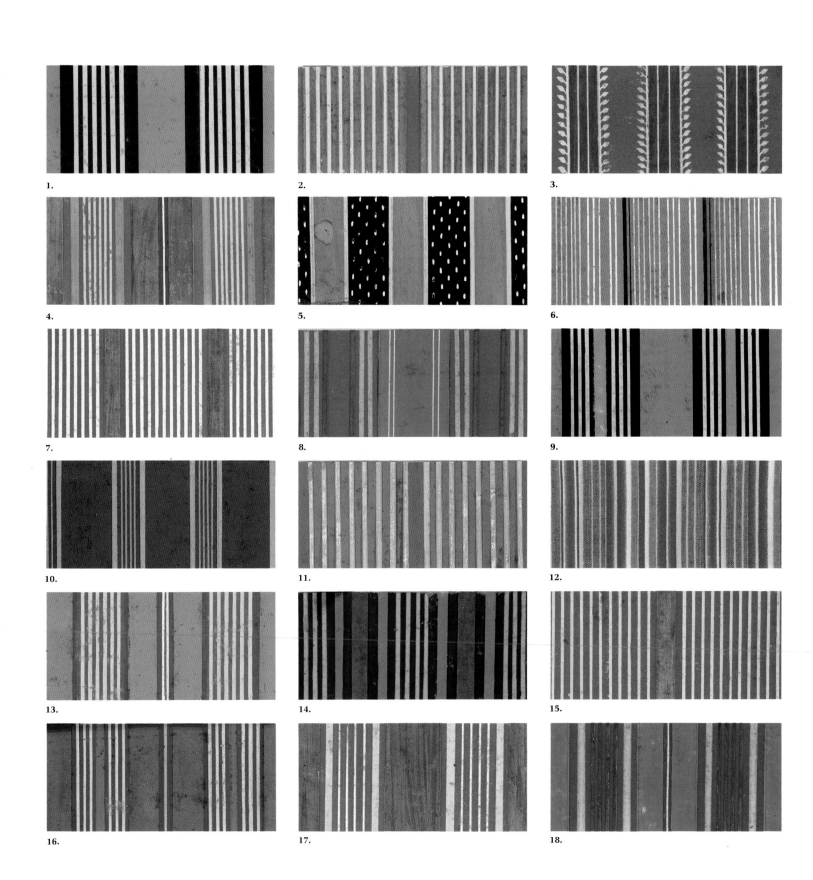

1.

2.

3.

4.

5.

6.

7.

8.

9.

10.

11.

12.

13.

14.

15.

16.

17.

18.

STRIPES: SERPENTINE AND WAVY

1. France, 1888, RP cotton, AYG, 100%
2. France, c. 1840, RP wool challis, AYG, 56%
3. France, 1820–25, BP cotton, AYG, 170%
4. France, 1895, RP cotton, AYG, 100%
5. France, c. 1840, RP wool challis, AYG, 100%

UNDULATING OR MEANDERING stripes like these were used often in the eighteenth century and the early nineteenth century, but most of them are considered too "snaky" for the market of today. Yet they can suggest rippling water as much as they do the serpents that give them their name, or a stylized version of the ruffle, or an abstract optical effect predating Op Art.

1.

2.

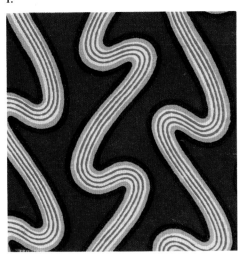

4.

3.

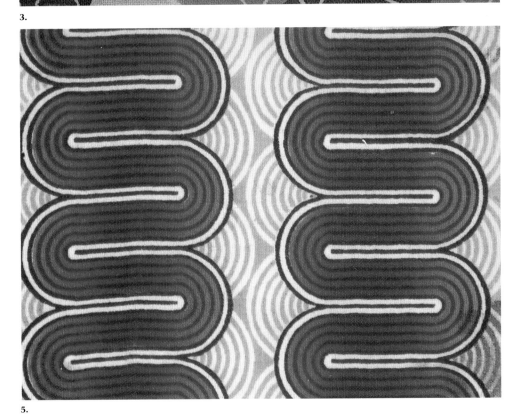

5.

STRIPES: SPORT SHIRTING

IN THE NINETEENTH century, stripes like these would mainly have been produced for women's wear; with the boom of the sport-shirt industry since World War II, they have become an option for men. They are bolder and more colorful than dress-shirting stripes and are designed for informal situations (most neckties would clash with them).

1. France, 1899, RP cotton, AYG, 100%

2, 4, 5, 10, 11. USA, 1960s–70s, gouache on paper, AYG, 100%

3. France, c. 1930s, gouache on paper, AYG, 100%

6. France, 1880–90, RP cotton, AYG, 100%

7. USA, 1899, RP cotton, AYG, 100%

8. USA, c. 1920s–30s, RP cotton, AYG, 100%

9. USA, c. 1920s–30s, RP cotton, AYG, 100%

12. USA or France, 1st half 20th C, RP cotton, AYG, 100%

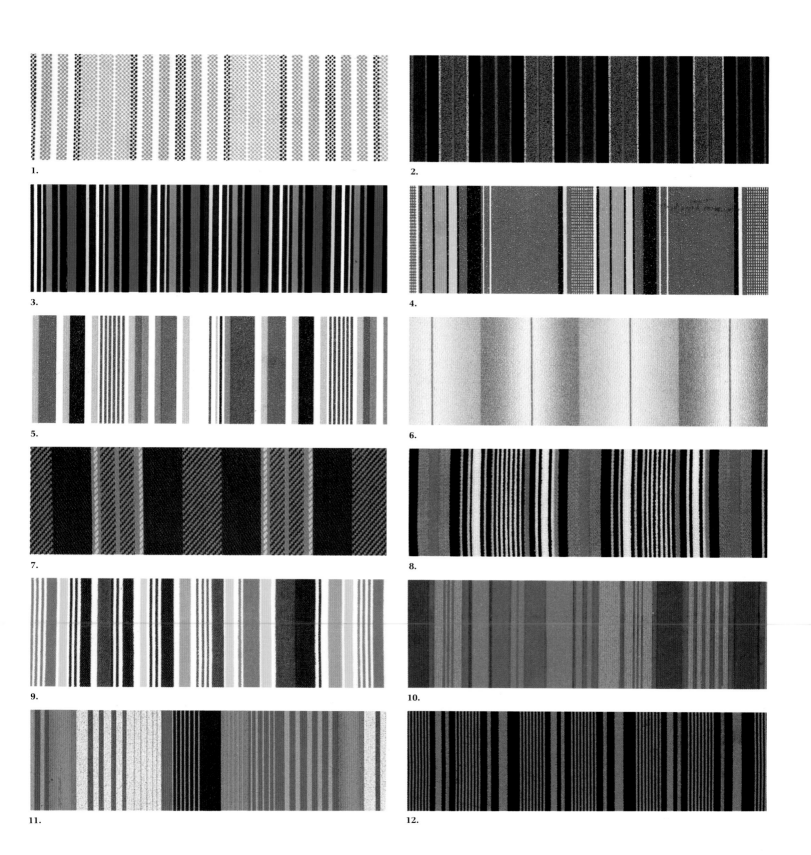

1.

2.

3.

4.

5.

6.

7.

8.

9.

10.

11.

12.

STRIPES: TEXTURED

1. France, 1895, gouache on paper, AYG, 120%
2. France, c. 1910, gouache on paper, AYG, 100%
3. France, 1899, gouache on paper, AYG, 120%
4. France, 1899, gouache on paper, AYG, 100%
5. France, 1899, RP cotton, AYG, 100%
6. France, c. 1900, gouache on paper, AYG, 80%
7. France, 1895, gouache on paper, AYG, 105%
8. France, c. 1900, gouache on paper, AYG, 100%
9. France, c. 1890, gouache on paper, AYG, 100%

AN ARTIST WHO tries to render the texture of cloth may end up working with a kind of stripe pattern; a weave, after all, is naturally a web of straight lines. Combine that trompe-l'oeil texture with an actual stripe and it can be hard to tell where the background pattern ends and the foreground begins. Many designers try to imitate woven-in patterns so that their cloth can substitute cheaply for the real thing. But these turn-of-the-century textured stripes were fashion items in themselves, playful exercises in the vocabulary of design.

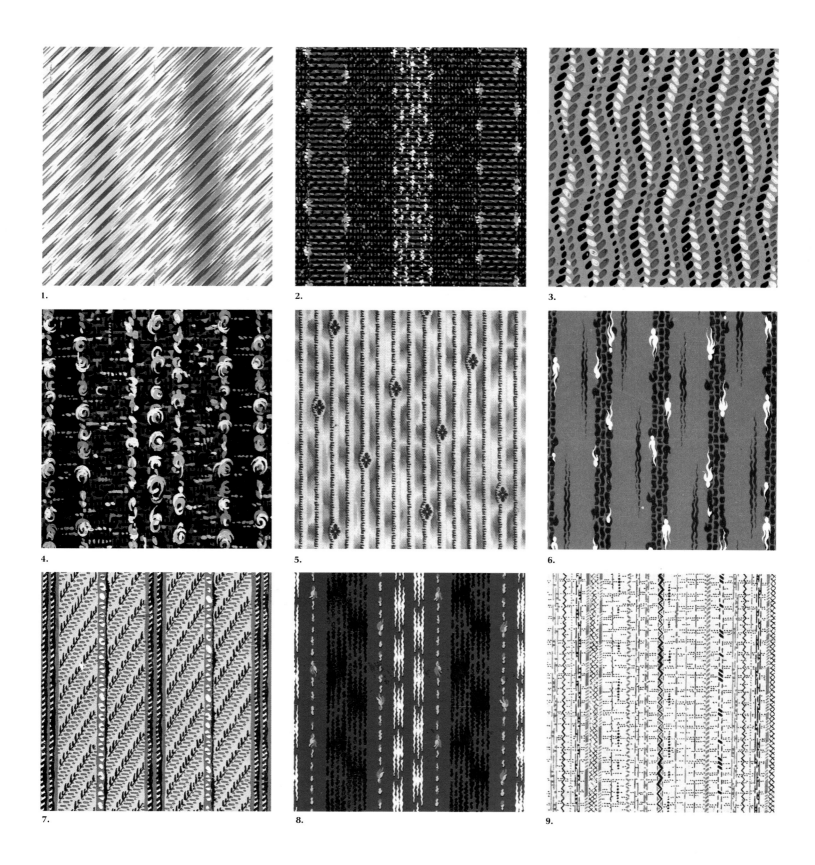

1.

2.

3.

4.

5.

6.

7.

8.

9.

TEXTURED

1. France, c. 1920s, gouache on paper, AYG, 80%
2. France, 1920s–30s, RP silk, AYG, 110%
3. France, 1928, RP silk, AYG, 110%
4. France, c. 1920, gouache on paper, AYG, 80%
5. Probably France, c. 1930s, RP or SP silk, AYG, 90%

THESE PATTERNS COMBINE a motif with the illusion of a woven texture, as though a nubby or thick-stranded cloth were showing through the pattern printed on it. They give an extra visual interest and density to what might otherwise be a simple design.

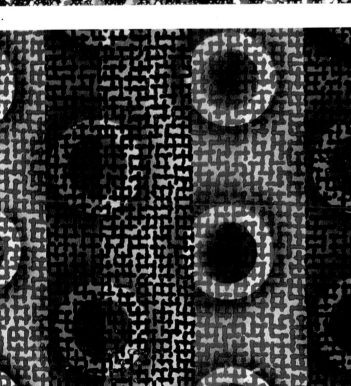

1.

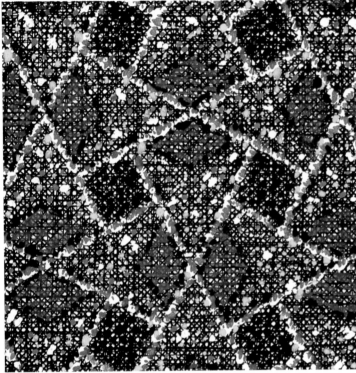

4.

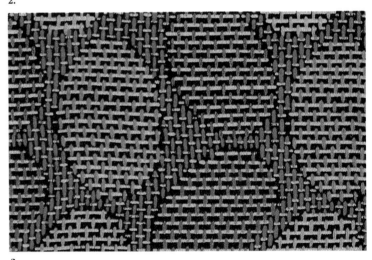

2.

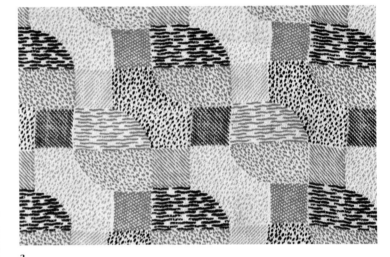

3.

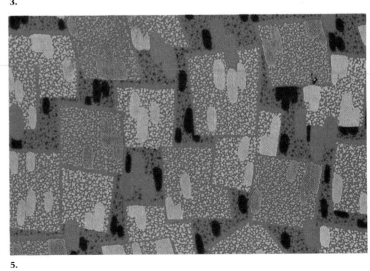

5.

TEXTURES

HAVING CREATED AN image of cloth to print on cloth, the designer has made his statement.

1. France, c. 1870–90, RP wool, AYG, 100%
2. USA, c. 1880, RP cotton, AYG, 100%
3. Probably France, c. 1920s–30s, RP silk, AYG, 100%
4. France, 1899, gouache on paper, AYG, 100%
5. France, 1896, RP cotton, AYG, 110%
6. France, 1888, RP cotton, AYG, 110%

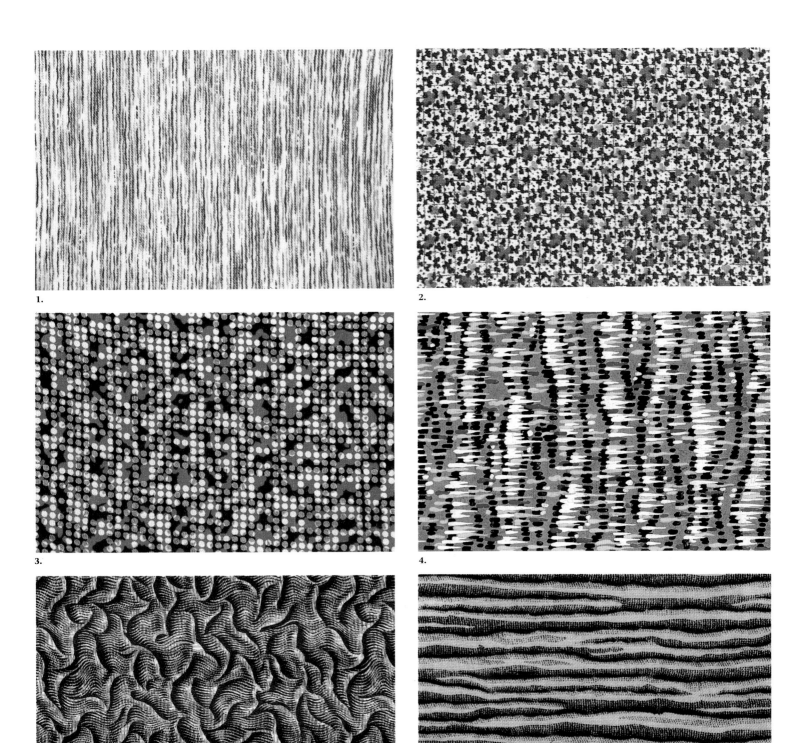

1.

2.

3.

4.

5.

6.

THREE-DIMENSIONAL

ANY GEOMETRIC MOTIF can appear in a three-dimensional design as long as it gives the impression of depth. Shading and highlighting suggest the shifts of light over a solid volume; a simple shadow added to a stripe makes it seem to spring up out of the flatness of the fabric. The same effects are used in conversational trompe-l'oeil prints, but there the objects pictured are of the real world. The abstract shapes of the geometric print exist only on cloth, but they come alive with the illusion of substance.

1, 15. France, c. 1860, RP cotton, AYG, 90%
2. France, 1926, RP or SP cotton, AYG, 100%
3. France, c. 1860–80, RP cotton, AYG, 120%
4. England, c. 1920s, RP cotton, AYG, 100%
5. France, 1892, RP cotton, AYG, 100%
6. Germany, c. 1880, RP cotton, AYG, 100%
7. Europe, 1957, RP cotton, AYG, 120%
8. Probably USA, c. 1930s, RP or SP silk, AYG, 100%
9, 14. France, c. 1880–90, RP cotton, AYG, 130%
10. France, 1866, RP silk, AYG, 72%
11. France, 1866, RP silk, AYG, 200%
12, 16. France, 1886, RP cotton, AYG, 100%
13. France, c. 1890, RP cotton, AYG, 500%

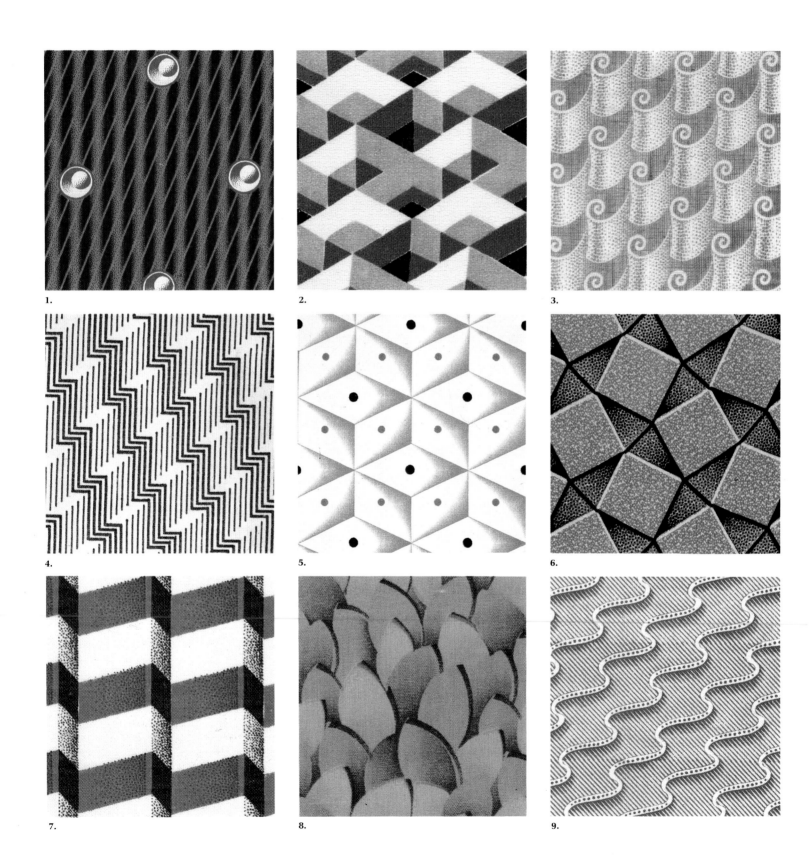

1.

2.

3.

4.

5.

6.

7.

8.

9.

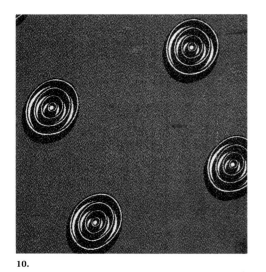

10.

11.

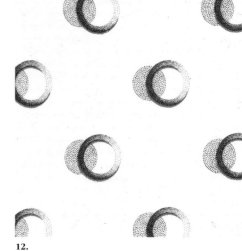

12.

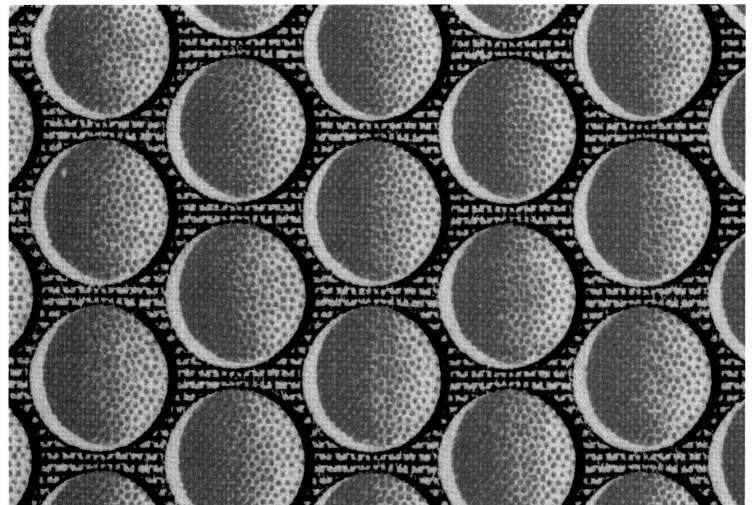

13.

14.

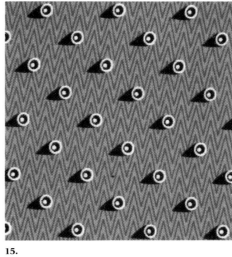

15.

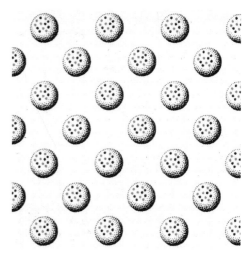

16.

TICKTACKTOE

1. France, c. 1920–30s, paper impression, AYG, 80%
2. France, c. 1940s–50s, RP or SP silk, AYG, 100%
3. France, c. 1850, RP wool challis, AYG, 130%
4. France, 1889, RP cotton, AYG, 100%
5. France, c. 1840–50, RP wool challis, AYG, 100%
6. France, c. 1840, gouache on paper, AYG, 100%
7. France, c. 1810–20, RP and BP cotton, AYG, 100%
8. USA, c. 1930s, RP rayon, AYG, 160%
9. USA, c. 1880–90, RP cotton, AYG, 110%

THE HATCHMARK USED for playing ticktacktoe, minus the *o*'s and *x*'s, appeared in prints as early as the first decade of the nineteenth century. It is still seen today, and it seems an appropriate motif to decorate cloth: as number 1 suggests, it is a stylized symbol of the basic unit of weaving. The word "tic-tac-toe" (its original spelling) did not appear until the 1860s, and then in connection with a different game, involving tapping blindfolded on a slate with a pencil, trying to hit a number to score. The English name "noughts and crosses" and the terser French "OXO" are more descriptive of the modern game.

1.

2.

3.

4.

5.

6.

7.

8.

9.

TIE PATTERNS

1. USA, 1940s, SP rayon jacquard, AYG, 60%
2. USA, 1940s, SP rayon jacquard, AYG, 74%
3. USA, 1940s, SP silk jacquard, AYG, 96%

A NECKTIE CAN carry virtually any motif; those shown here come from the late 1940s, when a generation of recently discharged servicemen shed their drab army uniforms. To compensate for the privations of the war years, men hurried into bright-patterned casual wear, which quickly became a new industry unto itself. Formal or office wear, however, was still relatively restrained. The only indulgence there was in the tie, lurid and wide enough to be called a belly-warmer. Large as these items were, the patterns were larger, so that the repeats were often invisible; the prints looked one-of-a-kind.

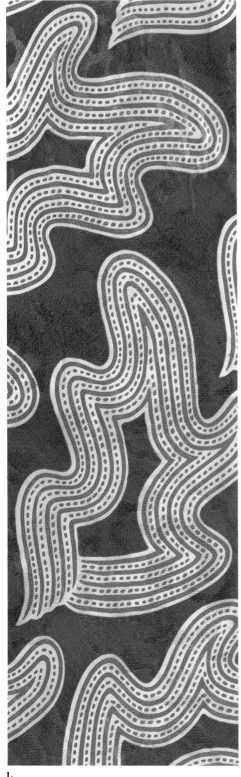

1.

2.

3.

TILE PATTERN

1. **France, c. 1950s, gouache on paper, AYG, 86%**
2. **England, c. 1920s, RP cotton, AYG, 150%**
3. **Probably USA, 1920s–40s, RP silk, AYG, 130%**
4. **France, c. 1920s, gouache on paper, AYG, 110%**

THOUGH THESE TEXTILES are based on tile patterns, they are cosmeticized somewhat: unlike mosaic designs, they don't show the interim spaces that in real tiling would be filled with grout or putty. But tiles are larger than the tiny tesserae of mosaics, and if the pattern were made too realistic, the cloth would begin to look hard and unyielding. Tile designs can be made simply by alternations of color, as in number 2, or each unit can become a surface for further ornament, as in numbers 1 and 4. Number 4 seems to be a Victorian interpretation of a Persian design; it is based on the square, but in the intricacies of the tile pattern the square blends into other shapes. Number 3 is taken from a Moresque tile pattern.

1.

2.

3.

4.

TRIANGLES

1. **France, 1886, RP cotton, AYG, 100%**
2. **Probably France, c. 1915, RP cotton, AYG, 100%**
3. **France, 1887, RP cotton, AYG, 160%**
4. **England or France, c. 1890, RP wool, AYG, 140%**
5. **Probably USA, c. 1930s, gouache on paper, AYG, 115%**

A BASIC GEOMETRIC form, the triangle is seen less often in textile patterns than the square or circle but more often than the rectangle. Symbolically, it represents one of the four elements, fire, and, on a spiritual plane, the Trinity. In the pyramid, whose sides are triangles, it is an emblem of immortality, and those mysterious tombs have left it a legacy of symbolic power, for example on the one-dollar bill. But for moderns it is just a decorative device, and perhaps too pointy to be worn with comfort.

1.

2.

3.

4.

5.

VERMICULAR

1. France, c. 1880–90, RP cotton, AYG, 100%
2. France, 1895, RP cotton, AYG, 92%
3. France, c. 1890, gouache on paper, AYG, 64%
4. France, 1899, RP cotton, AYG, 100%
5. England or France, c. 1850, gouache on paper, AYG, 80%
6. France, 1900, RP cotton voile, AYG, 60%

THE ANCIENT ROMANS used the word *vermiculatus* to describe a pattern "inlaid as if with the tracks of worms." This coral-like design has endured for centuries. Carved into stone as a surface ornament in architecture, it passed into a Western tradition of fabric design, reinforced by the popularity of Indian palampores, where similar motifs appear as background fillers. But it is little seen in twentieth-century cloth. The origin of the word—from the Latin *vermiculari,* to be full of worms—may suggest why squeamish modern designers avoid these patterns.

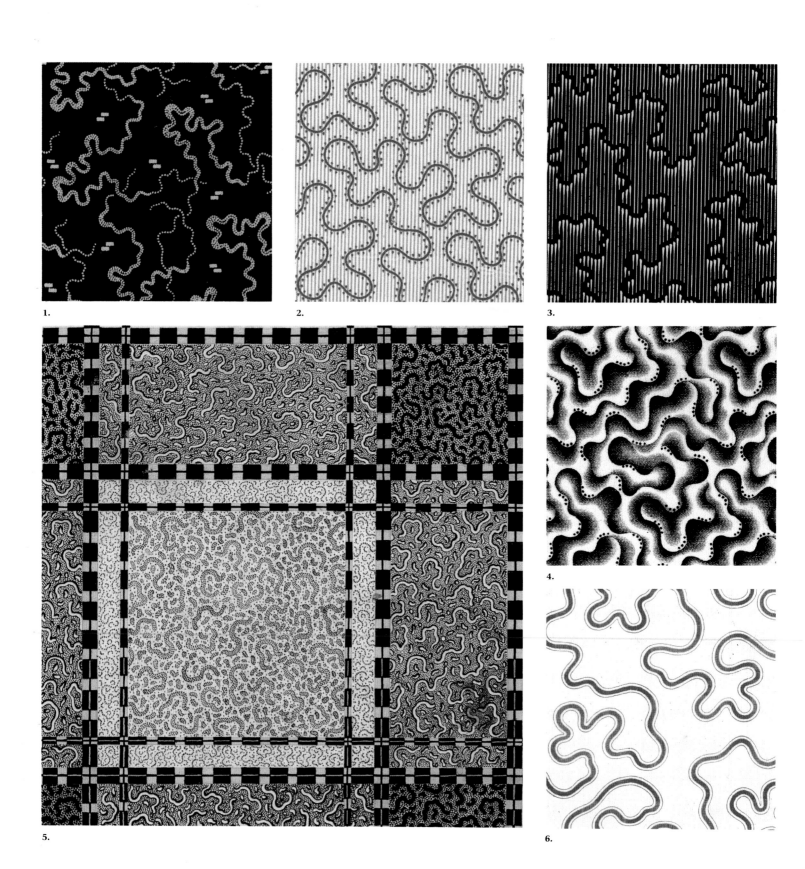

1.

2.

3.

4.

5.

6.

WARP PRINTS AND SIMULATED WARP PRINTS

THE WARP PRINT (numbers 1 and 2) is the product of Western printing technology, and its distinctive look is often used to give a Western design a hint of the exotic. In simulated warp prints (numbers 3–5), which aim to reproduce the warp-print effect, that touch of exoticism often becomes broader and bolder, so that the cloth has an ethnic feeling, often imitating Indonesian, Japanese, or Afghan ikats. (See also *Floral: Warp Prints,* page 132.)

1. France, c. 1900, RP silk, AYG, 110%
2. France, c. 1920, RP silk, A (ribbon pattern), 100%
3. USA, c. 1920, RP silk satin, AYG, 66%
4. France, 1851, RP cotton, AYG, 100%
5. France, c. 1840, RP wool challis, AYG, 100%

1.

2.

3.

4.

5.

WATERCOLOR LOOK

MOST WATERCOLOR-LOOK geometrics date from the 1950s or later. When they are successful, their beauty often comes from a translucent, jewel-toned palette of color.

1. **France, 1960s, dyes on paper, AYG, 75%**
2. **Probably France, c. 1940s, RP or SP silk, AYG, 100%**
3. **France, 1960s, dyes on paper, AYG, 100%**

1.

2.

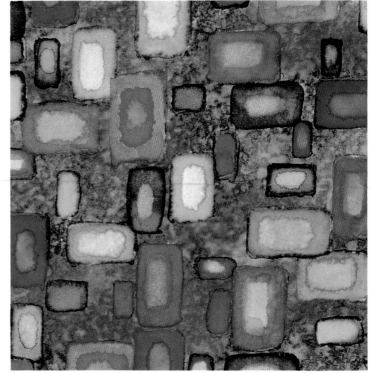

3.

ZIGZAG

1. France, c. 1840, RP wool challis, AYG, 130%
2. France, c. 1850, RP cotton, AYG, 110%
3. France, 1896, RP cotton, AYG, 140%
4. France, c. 1840, RP wool challis, AYG, 125%
5. France, c. 1850–60, gouache on paper, A (ribbon pattern), 100%

CHEVRON PATTERNS CAN look like zigzags, but the zigzag proper is freer and more irregular. Even made into a relatively tranquil stripe, it seems to want to be a diagonal (as in number 1), a desire that the conventional stripe usually manages to repress. The zigzag has a lightning-bolt zap, and Art Deco designers liked it for its electrical sense of energy. Otherwise, however, its frenetic quality makes it rather hard to live with. The stylized mountain range or graph in number 5 is a linear design for a ribbon.

1.

2.

3.

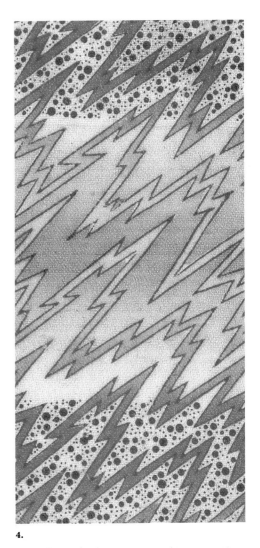

4.

5.

3. Conversational

A **CONVERSATIONAL PRINT** is one that depicts some real creature or object (excluding flowers, which are a family unto themselves). But a conversational doesn't have to be a picture of the world. It may show a whole scene—a landscape or cityscape—but just as often the designer removes a motif from its usual surroundings and arranges it in one of the formal layouts of fabric design—in a neat grid or stripe—or scatters it randomly. Conversationals are more, well, conversational, more attention-getting than most geometrics or florals. Fabric-printed versions of genre paintings, or of photographs, or even of architectural models may show up as conversationals. And more modest devices, such as clowns, may still have enough character and humor to become the talking point of a room, or of the street you're walking down when you wear them.

Conversationals are also called novelty prints, for their easily identifiable images tend to be more vulnerable than neutral motifs to the public's passing moods. An animal print of pandas, for example, may move in and out of fashion quite rapidly depending on how the zoo's amorous couple are doing in the news at the time. This family of subjects also includes the large class of designs known as commemoratives—prints made in honor of some special occasion. Virtually any sort of event that a large-enough audience feels enthusiastic about may earn itself a commemorative print, from elections to coronations to sporting competitions to historic anniversaries to advances in technology—each illustrated with some image relating to the great moment. Even more than conversationals in general, such designs are temporary novelties; they are usually dead in the market as soon as the event that launched them is over. Eventually, though, they may reacquire value as collectibles.

Some of the most lucrative of all contemporary patterns are conversationals of a relatively new kind: licensed motifs. Until this century, a designer could borrow at will from practically any source in the history of images. Motifs that a designer must pay to use are a modern innovation. Most of them are cartoons—like Mickey Mouse—and they are bound in with the marketing machinery of television and the movies.

Delightful as some of these characters can be, they are more like trademarks, logos, and copyright signs than artworks. Still, their life in the mass media—the vehicle of their existence, as flesh and blood is the stuff of ours—has made them immensely popular. Mickey is a charismatic chap, and we shouldn't be surprised that he's proven to be a sales animal. This mouse can move bed sheets and T-shirts like no man's business; it's no wonder that the textile industry has anted up to hire him and his graphics kin.

Conversationals are as old as any family in mechanical printing—they have been made since its beginnings. Among the earliest examples were the toiles, large-scale scenics that look like fine etchings in repeat. But what happens when a picture duplicates itself so many times on one piece of cloth that no one looking at it could have any illusion of looking out into a landscape? Or when, made into a shirt or a dress, the contours of fields and woods are shaped by the lines of the human body? Looking at textile patterns, we often see their actual motifs less clearly than we notice their colors and the symmetries and interplay of forms caused by the repeat. It's as if the uses to which these images are put hide them from attention at the same time that they lay them out for public view. Without their repeats, without their air of the everyday, would these pictures be reconsidered as the potential subject matter of art history? Or would they fall flat, like song lyrics without music?

AMERICAN WEST

1. USA, c. 1950s, SP rayon, AYG, 50%
2. USA, c. 1940s–50s, gouache on paper, AYG, 50%
3. USA, c. 1940s–50s, gouache on paper, AYG, 25%
4. USA, 1950s, SP rayon, HFYG, 38%

WESTERN PRINTS WERE inspired by twentieth-century cowboy literature, comic strips, movies, and TV shows. Though the theme was an early Hollywood staple, its stereotyped images rarely appeared on fabrics until the 1940s and 1950s. These printed textiles were designed almost entirely for children, with occasional patterns drawn from the regional culture and landscape of the West. They were at their peak of popularity during the postwar period, when America seemed at its strongest and most heroic, then declined during the 1960s, when the western also went out of fashion on TV and movie screens. In the 1980s, during the "Morning in America" years of the Reagan presidency, western prints reemerged, this time on luxury goods for the adult urban cowboy. (See also *Ethnic: American Indian Look,* page 363.)

1.

2.

3.

4.

ANIMALS

1. France, 1945, RP or SP rayon, AYG, 110%
2. France, c. 1920, RP cotton, AYG, 100%
3. France, 1886, RP cotton, AYG, 120%
4. France, c. 1960s, RP silk, AYG, 80%

ANIMALS APPEARED ON textiles as long ago as ancient Egypt, when their significance was mystical and symbolic. In nineteenth- and twentieth-century printed fabrics, the animal chosen is generally designed to look cute or cuddly, exotic or graceful. Until World War II, when farm life was still a reality or a recent memory for many people, prints of agricultural animals such as sheep, pigs, and cows were rare. Exceptions to this generalization are the late-eighteenth-century and early-nineteenth-century European scenic toiles, which were intended for use as home furnishings in upper-class homes, and in these prints, the pastoral images of shepherds and country life were deliberately romanticized. The first textiles printed with images of the fierce big cats were designed largely for export to colonial lands. Few nineteenth-century Western women would have associated themselves with creatures so savage. Today, in the search for "something different," more animal species have become acceptable subjects for prints, though it is still unusual to see a beast popularly considered ugly or scary in a design. Rhinoceroses and bats are almost nonexistent in Western textiles—poor risks in the marketplace.

1.

2.

3.

4.

ANIMAL SKINS

1. **France, 1842, RP cotton chintz, HFYG, 80%**
2. **France, c. 1820, gouache on paper, HF (carpet pattern), 100%**
3. **USA or France, c. 1900, RP cotton, AYG, 80%**
4. **USA or France, 20th C, gouache on paper, AYG, 100%**
5. **Italy, 1960s–70s, gouache on paper, AYG, 100%**

ANIMAL-SKIN PRINTS date from the early nineteenth century, when Napoleon brought back to Paris real hides collected on his expedition to North Africa. His campaign tent sported a faux leopardskin carpet. At first these images of exotic pelts appeared only as patterns on rugs and other home furnishings; to wear one would probably have been thought outrageous. In the twentieth century, however, animal skins began to appear on clothing, almost exclusively in fashions for women. The two most common kinds—big cats and snakes—have become perennial favorites. The look is primal, savage, and exotic, the message wild and sexy. More recently, with the increasing awareness of ecology and animal rights, many view the wearing of real fur as barbaric, and the fake has become even more fashionable.

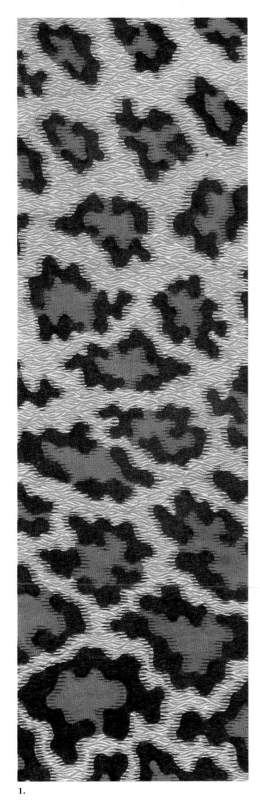

1.

2.

3.

4.

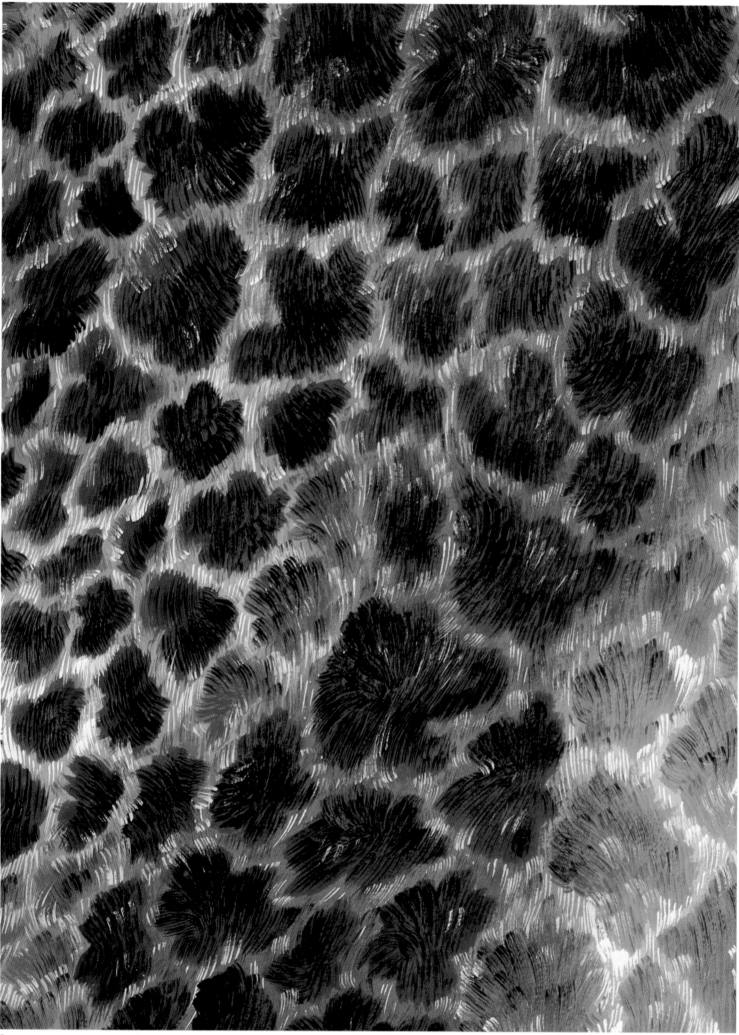

5.

ARCHITECTURAL

1. **France, c. 1900–1920, gouache on paper, A (scarf pattern), 25%**
2. **USA, 20th C, gouache on paper (after an American wallpaper, c. 1830–40), HFYG, 39%**
3. **France, c. 1860, RP cotton chintz, HFYG, 58%**
4. **France, c. 1880, gouache on paper, HFYG, 25%**

ARCHITECTURAL PATTERNS COVER a wide range of possibilities. They usually impart a sense of three-dimensional depth to an architectural motif, whether it is structural, such as the Gothic tracery in number 2, or ornamental, like the bas-relief escutcheon in number 4. Number 3 lacks this three-dimensional quality and instead gives the impression of an architect's rendering of an ornate ceiling decoration fit for a Renaissance palace.

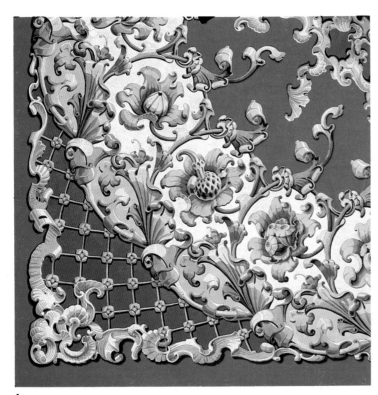

1.

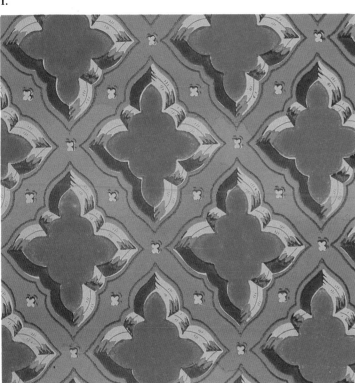

2.

3.

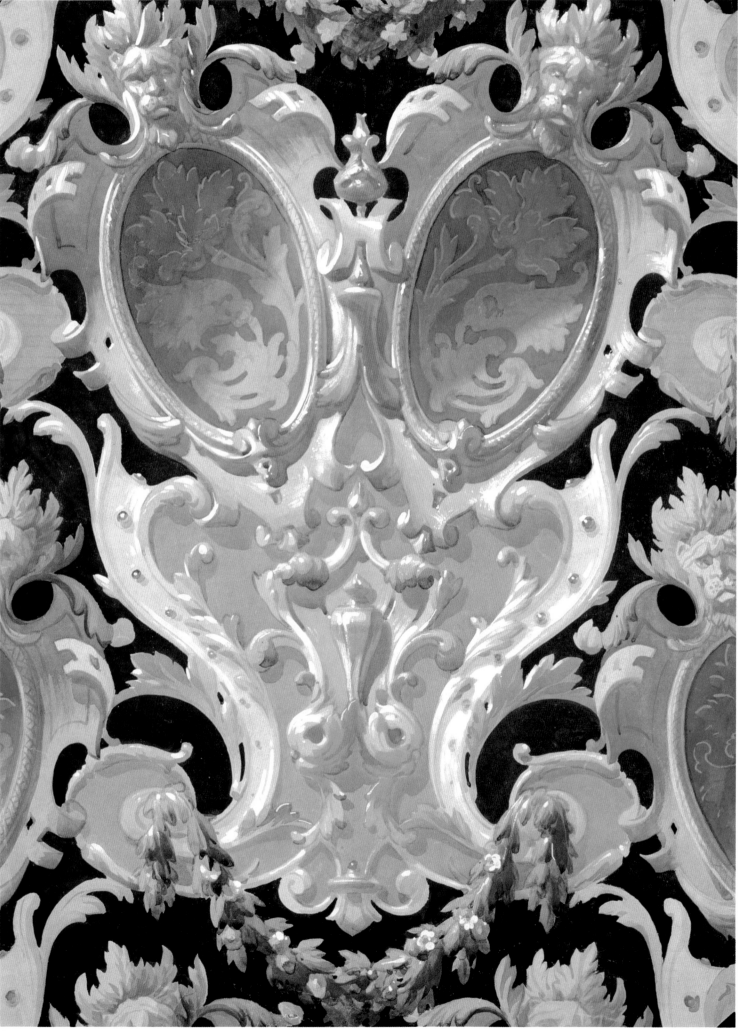

4.

BELTS, CHAINS, KNOTS, AND ROPES

1. France, 1887, RP wool challis, A (scarf border), 150%
2. France, c. 1850, gouache on paper, A (ribbon pattern), 100%
3. France, c. 1880–90, RP cotton, AYG, 100%
4. France, c. 1890, gouache on paper, AYG, 50%
5, 9. France, c. 1900, RP cotton, AYG, 100%
6. France, 1820, RP cotton, AYG, 100%
7. France, 1920s–30s, gouache on paper, AYG, 50%
8. France, c. 1880–90, gouache on paper, AYG, 90%
10. France, 1890, gouache on paper, AYG, 150%
11. France, c. 1910, gouache on paper, AYG, 150%
12. France, c. 1910–20, gouache on paper, AYG, 100%

HISTORICALLY SYMBOLIC OF bondage, entanglement, and eternity, some of these patterns are related to the mazelike knots of Celtic art, others to the intertwining lines of the Gothic style. They may strike a nautical note or, more commonly, make a trompe-l'oeil reference to the accessories and ornaments of clothing itself. Technically, these forms offer the designer a clever way to work out a repeat pattern, for they explicitly tie together the shapes that recur.

1.

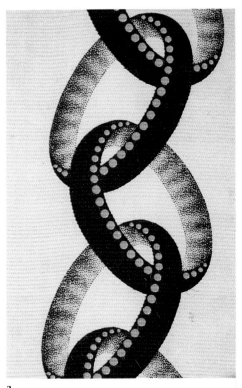

3.

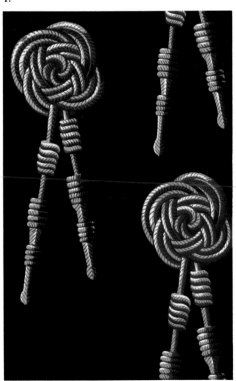

2.

4.

5.

6.

7.

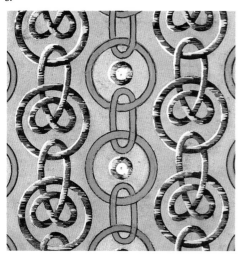

8.

9.

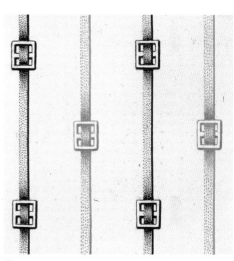

10.

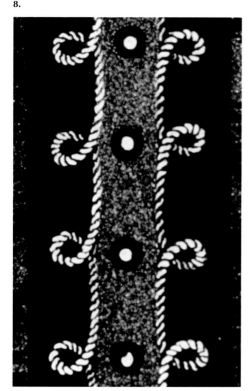

11.

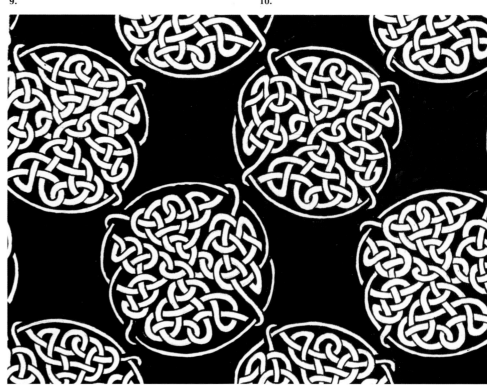

12.

BIRDS

1. **France, 1886, RP cotton, AYG, 90%**
2. **France, c. 1880–90, gouache on paper, AYG, 70%**
3. **France, c. 1880–90, gouache on paper, AYG, 25%**
4. **England, c. 1830, RP cotton chintz, HFYG, 50%**
5. **France, 1930s–40s, RP silk crepe, AYG, 80%**
6. **France, 1930s–40s, RP silk crepe, AYG, 50%**
7. **France, 1930s, RP silk crepe, AYG, 50%**
8. **England, c. 1830, RP cotton chintz, HFYG, 25%**

BIRDS HAVE BEEN a constant theme in fabric design since its beginnings. Small, brightly colored, and daintily formed, they are a convention of feminine imagery and often appear in patterns for spring women's wear. They have always been an important motif in home-furnishing patterns, where they add interest and elegance. A series of printed furnishing fabrics based on John James Audubon's *Birds of America,* which was published in London between 1827 and 1838, was printed in England in the early 1830s. The birds in number 8 may well have been inspired by Audubon's plates. The rooster in number 2 appears often in French textiles, as the cock is a national symbol of France. The larger game birds conjure up a more masculine image of the sporting life. In parts of eastern Europe, birds depicted on cloth are thought to bring bad luck—an idea perhaps stemming from the folkloric interpretation of the bird as symbolic of the soul. The superstition was imported to the American garment industry, where bird patterns were often shunned. In recent years, however, this taboo has begun to fade.

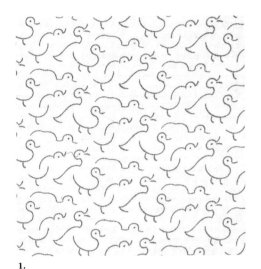

1.

2.

3.

4.

6.

7.

8.

BOWS AND RIBBONS

1. France, c. 1830, gouache on paper, AYG, 94%
2. France, c. 1880, RP cotton, AYG, 96%
3. France, c. 1840–50, BP wool challis, AYG, 60%
4. France, 1930s, gouache on paper, AYG, 66%
5. USA, 1934–40, gouache on paper, AYG, 55%
6. France, c. 1820–30, RP cotton, AYG, 94%
7. France, c. 1820–30, RP cotton, AYG, 100%
8. France, c. 1840–50, RP wool challis, AYG, 75%
9. France, 1940s, gouache on paper, AYG, 50%
10. USA, 1950s, RP cotton, AYG, 38%
11. USA, 1930s–40s, RP silk, A (handkerchief), 50%
12. France, 1930s–40s, gouache on paper, AYG, 66%

LIKE CHAIN AND knot designs, bows and ribbons provide innately repeatable, innately decorative patterns. Their graceful drapes and curves match the drapes of a dress or a curtain—they flow with the folds of the cloth. Bows and ribbons have never gone out of style, and when the fashion is for the romantic, they appear in full glory, either by themselves or entwined among garlands and bouquets.

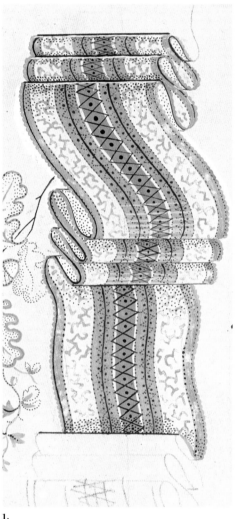

1.

2.

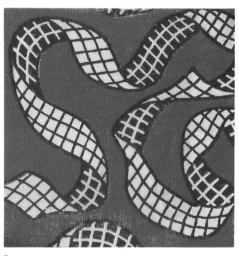

3.

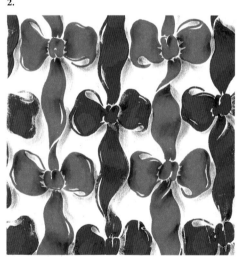

4.

5.

6.

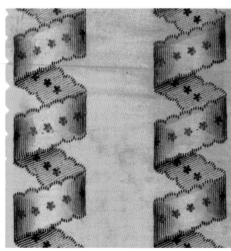

7.

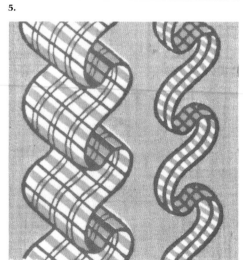

8.

9.

10.

11.

12.

BUBBLES AND SPHERES

1. France, 1883, RP cotton, AYG, 50%
2. France, 1890, gouache on paper, AYG, 112%
3. France, 1880–84, gouache on paper, AYG, 50%
4. France, 1950s–60s, gouache on paper, AYG, 75%

THE SOAP BUBBLE, a globe of empty air, is an evanescent illusion, and fashion is all illusion—an ephemeral skin temporarily locating the body in its time and place. The motif is unusual in textiles, and these elegant designs come from quite different, quite disparate periods—number 1 suggesting bubbles floating freely in space and number 4 air bubbles trapped underwater by pieces of floating seaweed. The sphere (numbers 2 and 3) is the solid equivalent of the circle, replete with symbolism. (See also *Geometric: Circles and Dots*, pages 156–57.)

1.

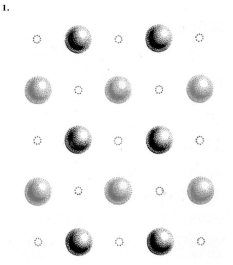

2.

3.

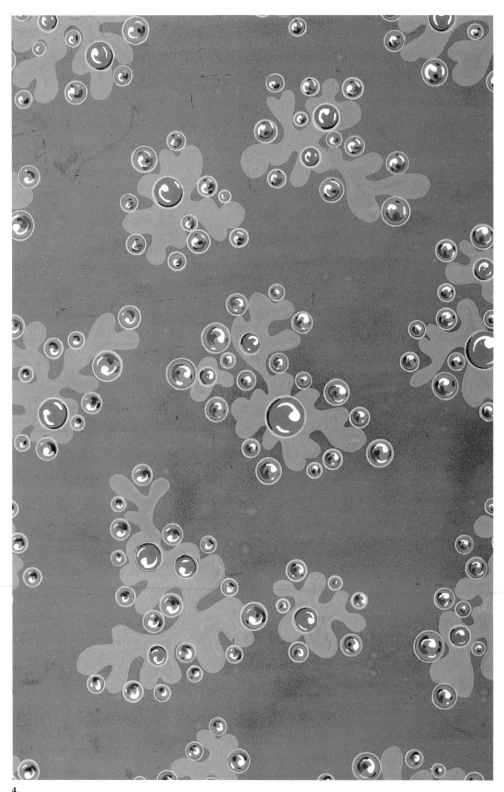

4.

BUILDINGS

1. USA, 2d quarter 20th C, RP cotton, AYG, 100%
2. France, c. 1880, RP cotton, AYG, 100%
3. USA, 1940s, SP rayon, AYG (tie pattern), 64%
4. France, 1890, RP cotton, AYG, 105%

As the main motif, buildings appear infrequently in printed textiles: they're often an awkward shape on a flowing piece of cloth, and the suggestion of hard surfaces is not always welcome. Toiles are an exception, as are commemorative prints like number 4, which displays an image of the Eiffel Tower, built in Paris for the Universal Exposition of 1889. And buildings do appear in prints from the Art Deco period, in which many familiar objects are stylized into straight angles and planes. Sometimes, a designer makes ingenious use of architecture's natural repetitions—in number 2, bricks and windows combine to make a subtle allover pattern.

1.

2.

3.

4.

BUTTERFLIES

1. France, c. 1860, gouache on paper, A (ribbon pattern), 100%
2. France, 1810–20, gouache on paper, AYG, 100%
3. France, c. 1810, gouache on paper, AYG, 110%
4. France, 1810–20, gouache on paper, AYG, 100%
5. France, c. 1860, gouache on paper, A (ribbon pattern), 100%
6. France, 1920s, gouache on paper, HFYG, 50%

THE BUTTERFLY, A symbol of joy, life, and the spirit, appears often in fabric designs. Like the bird, it is, when small in size, a naturally colorful, naturally delicate form and the poetic staple of a traditional feminine imagery. On the rare occasions when it is greatly enlarged, it can become a rather threatening insect. Number 6, a Fauvist example in which boldness of color and form is the statement, is reminiscent of the butterfly patterns in larger-than-life size published around 1920 in a portfolio of pochoir prints by the designer and naturalist E. A. Séguy.

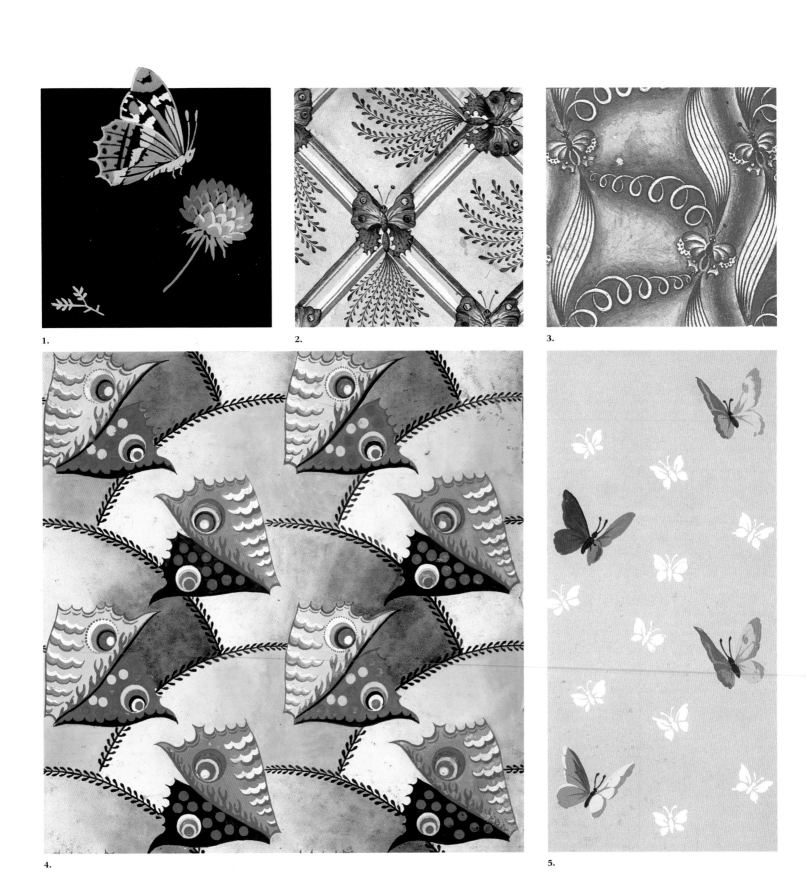

1.

2.

3.

4.

5.

6.

CAMOUFLAGE

1. "Woodland," USA, 1983, SP cotton, AYG, 45%
2. "Day Desert," USA, 1990, SP cotton, A (handkerchief), 45%
3. France, c. 1840, RP cotton, AYG, 100%
4. France, c. 1840, RP wool challis, AYG, 100%
5. USA, c. 1870–80, RP cotton, AYG, 100%

MILITARY PRINTED CAMOUFLAGE evolved with the use of airplanes in warfare, replacing such battle dress as the famously scarlet coats of earlier British armies. As the patterns here show, however, camouflage has ancestors in an older cloth and custom. At one time, only the wealthy could buy richly colored and patterned clothes. But with the arrival of industrially printed fabric, colorful designs became far more affordable, and upper- and middle-class families needed a new way to distinguish themselves from their employees. Thus the household help was often forced into the darks and drabs of fabrics that had the effect of "camouflaging" the wearer from the eyes of her superiors. They also hid dirt, a quality not lost on practical, hard-working women of both city and farm. In the 1980s, camouflage was endorsed by the fashion industry. Like prints of animal skins, it brought the jungle to city streets, along with a fading memory of aggressive war. But world events of 1990 suddenly turned those memories into another reality, Operation Desert Storm, and half a million people ditched the drab olive greens of "Woodland" for the spotted tans of "Desert" battle dress. Number 1 is cloth from a United States Army government-issue shirt; number 2 is an Army handkerchief.

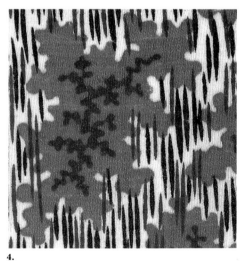

1.

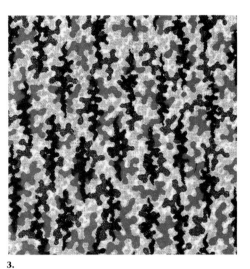

3.

4.

2.

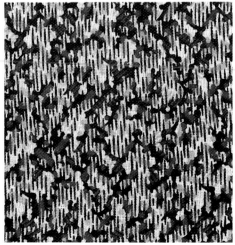

5.

CARTOONS

1. USA, c. 1950s–60s, SP cotton, A (handkerchief), 76%

MOST PATTERN MOTIFS have no known creator—the paisley and the polka dot are up for grabs—and appear in countless variations. But twentieth-century cartoon characters are trademarked, copyrighted, and licensed. They are the only devices an artist must pay to use, yet they have become the most lucrative to reproduce. (No one does PR for the polka dot or gives it a TV show.) Made to be photogenic, the graphic images of cartoons transfer easily to scarves, T-shirts, sheets, and curtains. Most were designed for children, but some, like Mickey, appeal to the child in all of us.

1.

CATS

CATS WERE A novelty theme in late-nineteenth-century patterns, when many newly prosperous urbanites were discovering that they could be kept as pets as well as mousers. Since then, despite their present wide popularity as images on paper products and hard goods, cats have largely retreated from cloth. Textile designers tend to avoid motifs that look subliminally uncomfortable—sharp, say, or scratchy. Perhaps cats connote claws and allergies. They remain favorites for children's wear, however, especially as soft cuddly kittens. The oversize jungle cats are in a class by themselves, replete with their special symbolism. (See also *Conversational: Animals,* page 249, and *Animal Skins,* page 250.)

1.

2.

3.

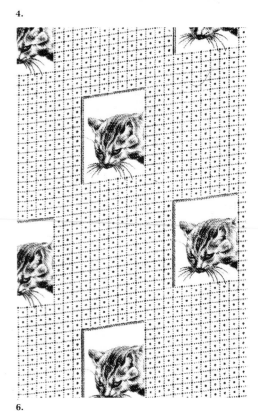

4.

5.

6.

7.

CELESTIAL: NINETEENTH-CENTURY

STARS, PLANETS, SUNS, moons, and comets, and, closer to home, clouds, rainbows, and lightning are all in the celestial family. From time immemorial, they have had a deep and powerful influence on humanity, which has worshiped them, feared them, and assigned countless mystical, magical, and spiritual meanings to them. Modern science says that stars aren't star-shaped, that the moon is not a crescent, that the sun is a white-hot ball of gas. But the old signs continue to convey a feeling of power, energy, and mystery.

1. France, c. 1880–1900, RP cotton, AYG, 120%
2. France, 1820–25, RP cotton, AYG, 110%
3. France, c. 1890, gouache on paper, AYG, 110%
4. France, 1820, gouache on paper, AYG, 100%
5. France, c. 1810–20, gouache on paper, AYG, 135%
6. France, c. 1890, RP cotton, AYG, 100%
7. France, 1890, gouache on paper, AYG, 130%
8. France, 1895, RP cotton, AYG, 100%
9. France, 1883, RP cotton, AYG, 135%
10. France, c. 1910, RP cotton, AYG, 105%
11. France, c. 1810–20, BP cotton, A (scarf pattern), 92%

1.

2.

3.

4.

5.

6.

7.

8.

9.

10.

11.

CELESTIAL: TWENTIETH-CENTURY

1. "Lunar Rocket," England, 1969, designed by
Eddie Squires for Warner Fabrics, SP cotton, HFYG
2. France, 1960s, gouache on paper, HYFG, 31%
3. USA, 1940s–50s, SP cotton, HFYG, 24%

WITH THE LAUNCHING of Sputnik 1, in October 1957, the sky had a new, mechanical kind of star. It had taken the universe eons to produce an artificial celestial object, but once satellites, rockets, and their orbiting relatives actually existed, no time was lost before they showed up in the galaxy of printed fabrics. What was the arrival of a completely different class of heavenly bodies above our heads if not a motif opportunity? Numbers 1 and 2 are commemorative prints, celebrating humanity's first ventures into outer space. Number 3 falls into an older tradition of picturing the night sky, but this is a sky full of wonders newly revealed by twentieth-century telescopes.

1.

2.

3.

CIRCUS AND CLOWNS

1. France, 1886, RP cotton, AYG, 135%
2. France, c. 1880–90, RP cotton, AYG, 92%
3. France, c. 1880–90, RP cotton, AYG, 72%
4. France, c. 1880–90, RP wool challis, AYG, 92%
5. France, 1896, RP cotton, AYG, 92%
6. France, 1927, RP cotton, AYG, 48%
7. France, c. 1895, RP cotton, AYG, 47%
8. France, c. 1895, RP cotton, AYG, 86%
9. France, 1880–90, RP cotton, AYG, 47%
10. France, 1883, RP cotton, AYG, 135%

PLAYFUL, HUMOROUS IMAGES of the circus have made appearances on cloth since the late 1800s—most often since the early twentieth century, when the marketing of prints especially for children began. The circus performer's antics can sneak slyly into everyday patterns, such as number 1, where the balls he juggles are also polka dots. Historically, the clown or buffoon was the court jester—the very antithesis of the king, and the humblest of his subjects, yet paradoxically above them all. He and only he could speak the truth, could point out in his own way the foibles of the court, the king, and the world. Today, passé in prints, clowns are replaced by cartoon and movie characters.

1.

2.

3.

4.

5.

6.

7.

8.

9.

10.

COMMEMORATIVE

1. **USA, 1892, RP cotton, HFYG, 36%**
2. **England, 1924, RP cotton, A (scarf), 13%**
3. **USA, 1876, RP cotton, AYG, 60%**

IN 1783 THE Montgolfier brothers launched the first hot-air balloon, and this aviation feat was soon celebrated in textiles depicting the event or the motif of the balloon itself. Commemorative prints have recorded the great events of politics, history, and anything else sufficiently public to be quickly capitalized on with a decorative design. Number 1 does double duty, honoring both Columbus's discovery of the Americas and the Chicago World's Columbian Exposition, four centuries later. Number 2 is a souvenir of the British Empire Exhibition held in Wembley, England, in 1924–25, and number 3 celebrates the United States Centennial of 1876. All the world's fairs of the nineteenth and twentieth centuries have spawned commemorative textiles, as have most of the American presidential campaigns since the late 1800s. In 1976 Jimmy Carter got a peanut print.

1.

2.

3.

CORAL AND SEAWEED

1. **France, c. 1880–90, gouache on paper, AYG, 80%**
2. **France, 1899, gouache on paper, AYG, 100%**
3. **France, 1899, gouache on paper, AYG, 100%**
4. **France, c. 1810–20, gouache on paper, A (scarf pattern), 68%**
5. **France, 1898, gouache on paper, AYG, 100%**
6. **France, 1825–30, RP cotton, AYG, 100%**
7. **France, c. 1820, gouache on paper, AYG, 100%**
8. **France, 1898, gouache on paper, AYG, 100%**
9. **France, 1825–30, RP cotton, AYG, 105%**

THESE MOTIFS WERE popular in the early 1800s, declined, and then reemerged in the last two decades of the century. A kind of organic version of the allover grid, they are also warm designs, evocative of tropical seas. The abstraction of the coral pattern may temper its exoticism; in any case, the colors and intricate shapes of coral have been used as decoration in the West since antiquity. Chaucer describes women wearing bracelets of coral, and from the seventeenth century onward coral appeared frequently in the *Wunderkammer*, or chamber full of natural and man-made curiosities, collected as an aristocratic hobby. Coral and seaweed patterns appear occasionally as twentieth-century home furnishings, but rarely in clothing. However, they are presently enjoying a resurgence as a fresh-looking, understated decorative chintz.

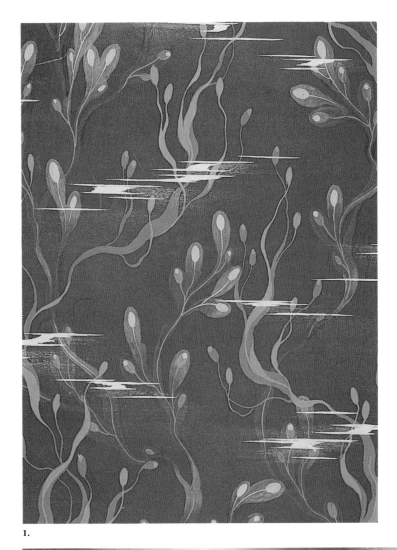

1.

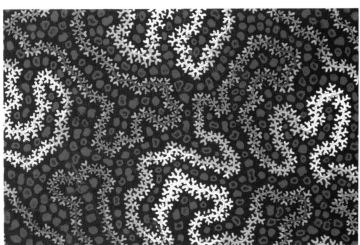

2.

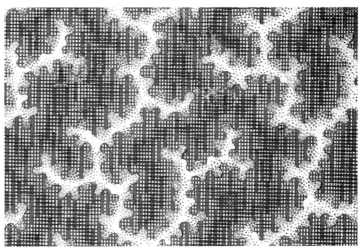

3.

4.

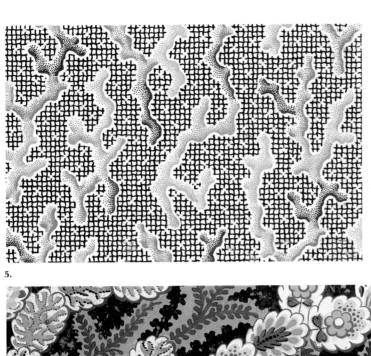

5.

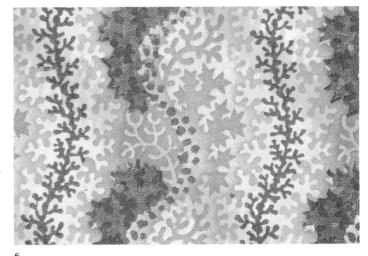

6.

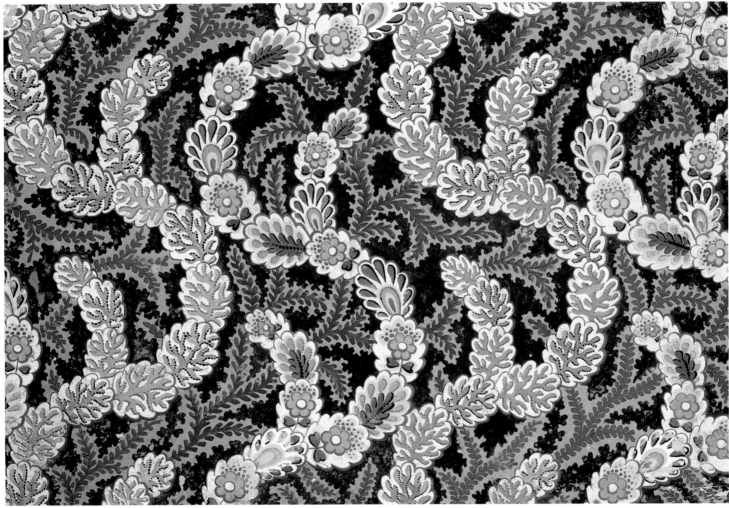

7.

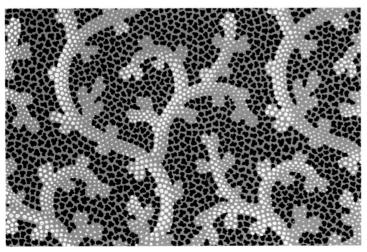

8.

9.

CORNUCOPIA

1. France, c. 1810, gouache on paper, A (scarf border), 100%

GREEK MYTH HAS it that the Titan Kronos, when he ruled the universe, feared that he would be superseded by one of his children and faced down his fear by eating them. (This was before the days of psychotherapy.) So Kronos's wife, Rhea, hid his last-born son, Zeus, in a cave on the island of Crete. There the baby was protected by the Curetes, a tribe of nymphs, who fed him the milk of the goat Amalthea. When the grateful Zeus grew up, he gave the goat's horn to the nymphs and promised that it would be a never-empty source of milk and honey—the ambrosia of the gods. This is the origin of the cornucopia, the horn of plenty. Its classical ancestry and its symbolism of a bountiful harvest make it a recurring motif in textile designs, but not a common one; it is a rather ungainly shape, with phallic undertones.

1.

DOGS

1. France, c. 1885, RP cotton, AYG, 125%
2. France, 1887, RP cotton, AYG, 135%
3. France, c. 1885, RP cotton, AYG, 82%
4. France, 1887, RP cotton, AYG, 88%
5. France, 1886, RP cotton, AYG, 150%
6. England or France, 3d quarter 19th C, gouache on paper, A (scarf pattern), 64%

DOG PATTERNS USUALLY show recognizable breeds of canine, rarely a mutt. Mutts can be cute and endearing, but their social station is uncertain, and that makes them a less reliable bet with the print-buying public than the pedigreed dog, which is identified with aristocracy and tradition. The exception to this rule, however, one of the best-known dogs in textile history, belonged to Jean-Baptiste Huet (1745–1811), the foremost designer for Christophe-Philippe Oberkampf. Huet depicted his favorite dog—of unknown ancestry—again and again in his masterfully drawn toiles de Jouy.

1.

2.

3.

4.

5.

6.

DRAPERY

1. England, c. 1820, RP cotton, HFYG, 41%
2. USA, 1940s, RP or SP cotton, HFYG, 39%
3. France, c. 1930s, gouache on paper, AYG, 50%
4. France, 1949, gouache on paper, AYG, 50%

AN IMAGE OF cloth printed on cloth, number 1 depicts a typical curtain arrangement of the Regency period. Number 2 gives a home-furnishing fabric of the 1940s a naive neoclassical look. Drapery effects often work like trompe l'oeil, making a flat cloth seem three-dimensional or intensifying the sense of weight and curving fold in a wall or window hanging. As in countless old-master paintings, the representation of drapery is also an opportunity for a demonstration of the artist's skill.

1.

2.

3.

4.

EYELET, LACE, AND NETTING

1. USA or France, mid-20th C, gouache on paper, AYG, 68%
2. Probably France, c. 1950s, RP or SP silk, AYG, 80%
3. France, c. 1920, gouache on paper, AYG, 82%
4. Probably France, c. 1850, RP wool challis, AYG, 135%
5. Probably mid-20th C, RP cotton, AYG, 96%
6. France, 1882, RP cotton, AYG, 100%
7. USA, late 19th C, RP cotton, AYG, 100%
8. Probably France, late 19th C, RP cotton, AYG, 80%
9. France, 1882, RP cotton, AYG, 100%

EXPENSIVE LACE ONCE decorated the costumes of both men and women, but in the nineteenth century men's wear fell under a long-lasting spell of simplicity and sobriety, and today lace is exclusively feminine finery. Lace patterns were emulated in wood-block prints of the eighteenth century, but these were incapable of very fine detail, and the look did not come into its own until the invention of the copperplate-printing technique. Even then, it waited in the wings until the late nineteenth century, when printers went to great lengths to create the most realistic of fakes. Eyelet (numbers 1 and 3) combines the look of lace with more solid areas of embroidery, while netting (numbers 2 and 4) is cleaner and more gridlike; it can create interesting trompe-l'oeil effects of folds and creases.

1.

2.

3.

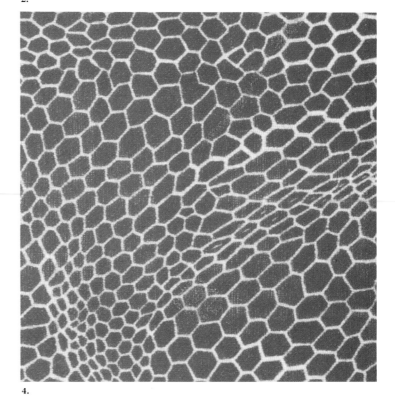

4.

5.

6.

7.

8.

9.

FAKES

1. Probably USA, c. 1890, RP cotton, AYG, 100%
2. France, 1895, RP cotton, AYG, 100%
3. Probably USA, c. 1890, RP cotton, AYG, 100%
4. Probably USA, c. 1890, RP silk velvet, AYG, 100%

PRINTED IMITATIONS OF more expensive woven cloths are common enough to have acquired a handful of aliases: fakes, shams, faux looks, pretenders. Those illustrated here are intended to stand in for plissés, moirés, and seersuckers. In 1850, the editor of the British trade publication *Journal of Design and Manufacturers* complained that "shams and imitations . . . placard the backs of the female population with a sort of material falsehood," making a habit of dishonesty and leading to a weakening of morals. He was fighting a losing battle: the only threat to the production of fakes occurs when a style of cloth, such as seersucker, becomes cheaper to weave than to copy in a print. But fashion can be manipulated in many ways, and today the cleverly produced fake can be more desirable than the real thing. (See also *Conversational: Trompe-l'Oeil,* page 351.)

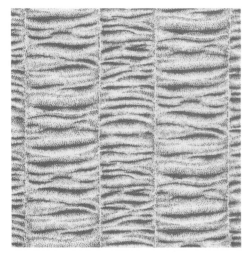

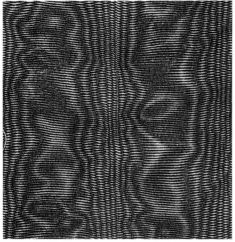

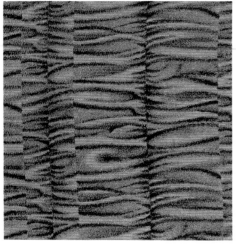

1.

2.

3.

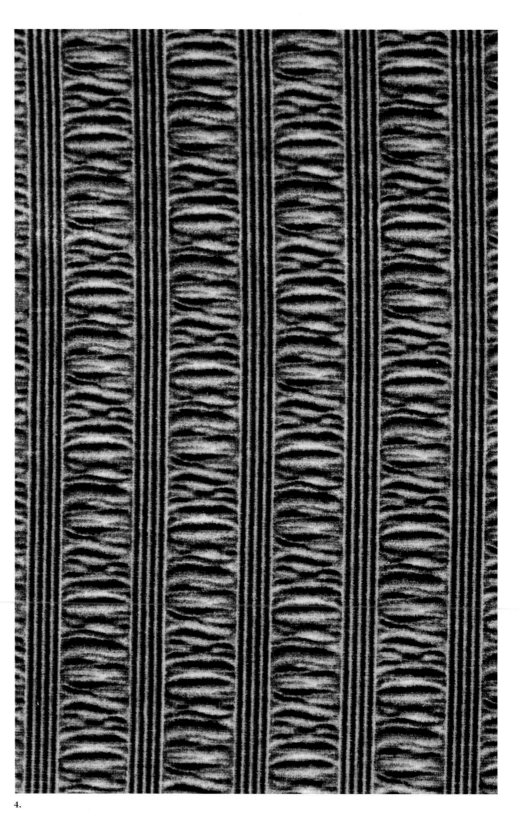

4.

FANS

1. France, c. 1880–1900, RP silk, AYG, 60%
2. France, c. 1915–20, gouache on paper, AYG, 90%
3. France, c. 1880–90, RP cotton, AYG, 86%
4. France, 1882, RP cotton, AYG, 90%
5. France, c. 1880, RP wool challis, A (scarf corner), 100%

THESE GRACEFUL ARCHING shapes appear in patterns throughout the nineteenth and twentieth centuries, though they are seen less often in contemporary fabrics, just as fans themselves are rarer now than before the spread of air-conditioning. The fan offers the opportunity for an economical combination of two sets of associations: it is a motif in itself, decorating the cloth; and it is an object to be decorated, with a flower pattern, perhaps, or filigree work. The typical Western fan is of the folding type, and classical symbolism associates it with the phases of the moon, which themselves are symbolic of femininity and changes of mood and physical state.

1.

2.

3.

4.

5.

FEATHERS

1. France, 1880–84, gouache on paper, AYG, 100%
2. France, 1880–84, gouache on paper, AYG, 90%
3. Probably France, c. 1860–80, RP cotton, AYG, 100%
4. France, c. 1920, paper impression, AYG, 80%
5. France, c. 1850, RP wool challis, AYG, 100%
6. France, c. 1810, gouache on paper, AYG, 96%
7. Germany, c. 1930s, gouache on paper, A (tie pattern), 110%
8. France, c. 1860–80, RP cotton, AYG, 90%
9. France, c. 1810, gouache on paper, AYG, 94%

IN CULTURES LIKE the Native American, feathers were worn not simply as adornment but as a way to connect people with the spirit of the bird whose feathers they wore, to endow them with the characteristics of that bird. Such feelings are not totally foreign to the wearers of machine-printed feathers. There is a regal aura about a velvet cloth bearing images of peacock feathers or formal plumes, and a sense of the genteel sporting life, the woodsy outdoors, in autumn-colored game-bird feathers scattered over a silk scarf or a soft wool-challis skirt.

1.

2.

3.

4.

5.

6.

7.

8.

9.

FLAGS

1. USA, c. 1900–1914, RP cotton felt, 47%
2. USA, c. 1900–1914, RP cotton felt, 32%
3. USA, c. 1900–1914, RP cotton felt, 32%
4. USA, c. 1900–1914, RP cotton felt, 32%
5. USA, c. 1900–1914, RP cotton felt, 28%
6. USA, c. 1900–1914, RP cotton felt, 47%
7. England, 2d half 19th C, RP silk, A (scarf), 50%

NATIONAL FLAGS ARE first cousins to heraldic motifs, the former identifying one with one's country, the latter with one's family. Sporting and nautical flags are less personal and are often used on casual clothing. Numbers 1–6 are tobacco premiums, printed felt or silk pieces that many turn-of-the-century tobacco companies gave away in pouches of their product as an incentive to buy their brand. These premiums were of varying sizes and subjects, including butterflies, Indian chiefs, baseball players, and Persian carpets. People collected them, sometimes sewing them together to make fanciful patchwork quilts.

1.

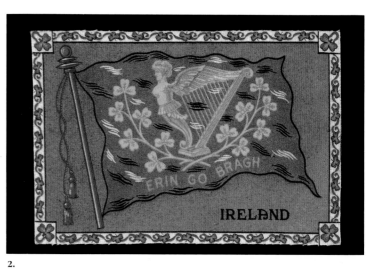

2.

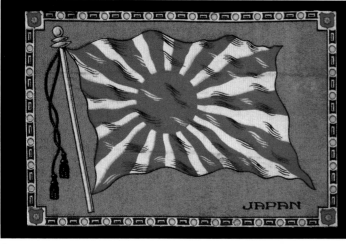

3.

4.

5.

6.

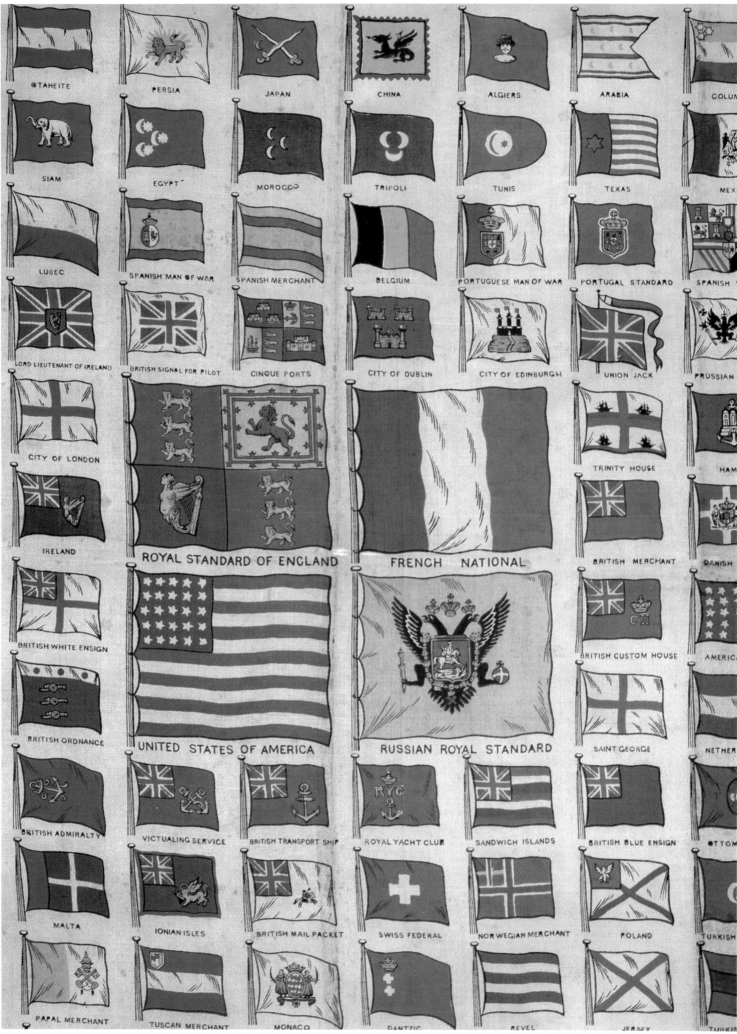

7.

FRUIT

1. France, c. 1920, gouache on paper, HFYG, 60%
2. France, c. 1912, RP cotton, AYG, 100%
3. England or France, late 19th C, RP cotton, AYG, 100%
4. France, c. 1800, BP cotton, A (scarf pattern), 58%
5. France, c. 1820–30, gouache on paper, AYG, 100%
6. USA, 1940s–50s, gouache and oil paint on paper, AYG, 90%
7. France, c. 1810, gouache on paper, A (scarf border), 54%

THE MOST COMMON fruit prints show cherries and strawberries—cheerful, brightly colored, sweet-flavored treats that come in convenient clusters and shapes. (Scattered on cloth, cherries are virtually polka dots.) Designers of home-furnishing fabrics tend to arrange them more formally than apparel artists do, going for presentation-basket styles instead of fruit salads. But both favor the familiar over the exotic species that the buyer may never have tasted. An exception is the pineapple, now known to all but a rare delicacy in 1800, about the time number 4 was printed. This tropical export to Europe was so expensive then that it was a gift of kings. It became a symbol of hospitality in both Europe and America, for the host who gave his dinner guests pineapple was entertaining them royally.

1.

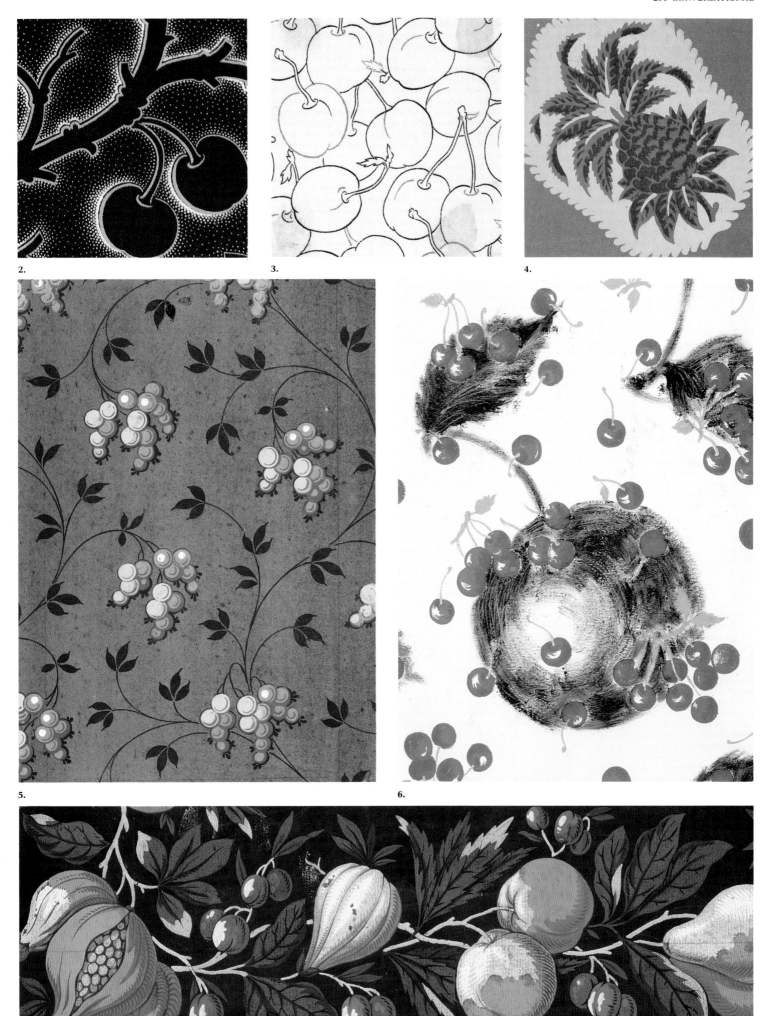

2.

3.

4.

5.

6.

7.

GAMES AND TOYS

1. France, 1888, RP cotton, AYG, 100%
2. France, 1880–84, gouache on paper, AYG, 80%
3. France, 1883, RP cotton, AYG, 100%
4. England or USA, 2d quarter 20th C, gouache on paper, AYG, 125%
5. France, 1930s, gouache on paper, AYG, 16%
6. France, 1886, gouache on paper, AYG, 150%
7. France, c. 1930s, gouache on paper, AYG, 100%
8. France, c. 1930s, gouache on paper, AYG, 115%
9. USA, c. 1930s, RP cotton, AYG, 115%
10. France, c. 1860, gouache on paper, A (ribbon pattern), 72%
11. France, c. 1930s, gouache on paper, AYG, 78%

EARLIER IN THE twentieth century, brightly colored toys were a novelty motif often used for children's wear (numbers 7, 9, and 11). Today, mothers are likely to identify with these old-fashioned prints more than their children, who have a culture of their own—one of robots, computer games, and creatures from outer space, all well promoted on television. Numbers 1, 4–6, 8, and 10, however, were intended for adults.

1.

2.

3.

4.

5.

6.

7.

8.

9.

10.

11.

GROTESQUES

1. France, c. 1880–90, RP cotton, AYG, 185%

FANTASTIC DECORATIONS WITH a slightly wicked air were popular in ancient Rome, then disappeared until their rediscovery by Renaissance lovers of all things classical. Giorgio Vasari, the great biographer of the Renaissance artists, describes the pleasure these designs inspired when they were unearthed, in the fifteenth century. Soon costly silk brocades appeared on the market with highly stylized grotesque animals as the main motifs, and for a period after that they were much copied and enjoyed. In the eighteenth century, however, when a purified version of neoclassicism was in the ascendant, grotesque ornament came to be seen as decadent, even repugnant. It is seldom seen on printed cloth. The example shown here is an exact copy of an early Renaissance brocade.

1.

HARDWARE AND TOOLS

1. **France, c. 1885, RP cotton, AYG, 90%**
2. **France, 1888, RP cotton, AYG, 100%**
3. **England or USA, 2d quarter 20th C, gouache on paper, AYG, 94%**
4. **France, 1886, RP cotton, AYG, 94%**
5. **France, 1885, RP cotton, AYG, 170%**

HARDWARE AND TOOLS have appeared most often in printed patterns during two distinct periods: the 1880s, when the designers of mill engravings like those below were turning out thousands of patterns a year and would seize on almost any possible motif; and the 1920s, a period of Constructivist influence. These fabric designs all reflect the ethos of industry, the mill engravings perhaps more playfully and less self-consciously than the Constructivist celebration of the machine.

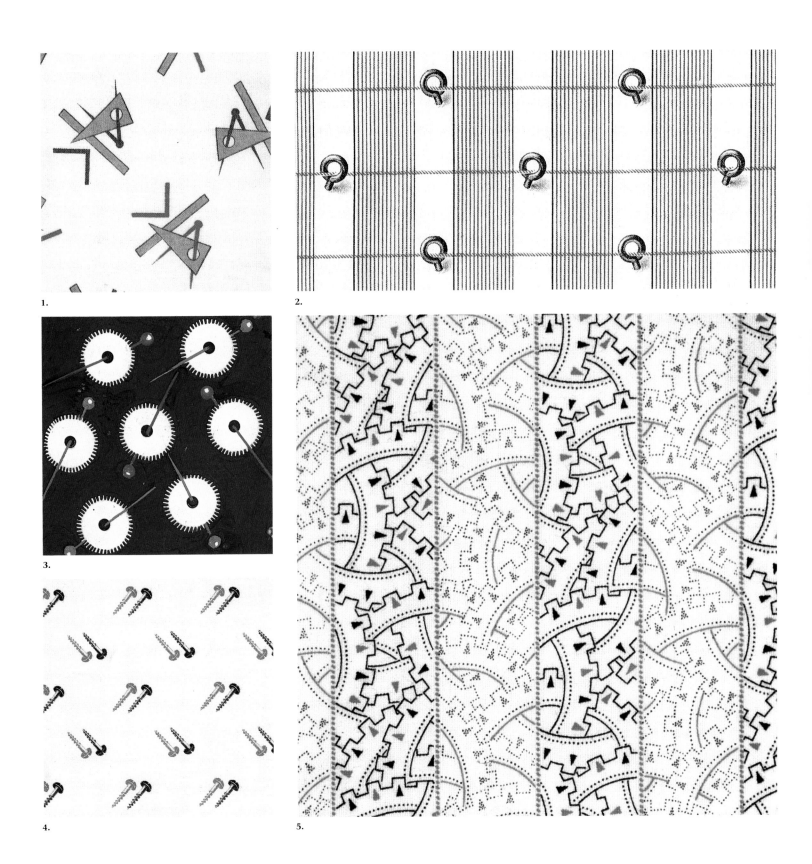

1.

2.

3.

4.

5.

HEARTS

1. **France, 1930s–40s, gouache on paper, AYG, 200%**
2. **France, c. 1850, paper impression, AYG, 100%**
3. **USA or France, c. 1885–90, RP cotton, AYG, 100%**
4. **USA, 1930s, gouache on paper, AYG, 110%**

IN THE MIDDLE AGES, as an emblem in Christian iconography, the human heart began to be symbolized by the stylized shape we know today. This may explain why the heart did not appear much in printed textiles until the present, secular, century. But it had been a motif in folk art all along, painted on dowry chests, embroidered on cloth, or carved into tree trunks, and its symbolism gradually broadened to include friendship, loyalty, warmth, and, of course, romantic love. For the manufacturers of printed textiles, a certain risk attaches to the heart motif because of its association with Saint Valentine's Day: there can be little market for a print worn once a year.

1.

2.

3.

4.

HERALDIC

1. France, c. 1890–1910, gouache on paper, HFYG, 47%
2. England, 1910–11, RP cotton, A (scarf), 30%
3. France, c. 1920, paper impression, AYG, 78%

THE MEDIEVAL EUROPEAN coat of arms was a sign that a family belonged to the nobility; it was a symbol of class. Heraldic devices, then, are literally a classy motif. They have greater vogue in the United States than in Europe, which takes its nobility with the grain of salt born of familiarity. The coats of arms that appear on printed fabric are often completely made up. As a result, they have lost their association with a particular family and have become merely decorative motifs with an uncertain cachet.

1.

2.

3.

HOLIDAY MOTIFS

1. Late 19th C–early 20th C, RP cotton, A (handkerchief), 70%
2. France, c. 1930s, gouache on paper, AYG, 170%
3. USA, c. 1950s, gouache on paper, AYG, 90%
4. USA, 1940s–50s, gouache on paper, AYG, 88%
5. USA, c. 1950s, RP or SP cotton, YG, 100%
6. USA, c. 1950s, SP cotton, A (handkerchief), 48%

EVERY HOLIDAY HAS its equipment: red hearts for Saint Valentine's Day; bunnies, eggs, and chicks for Easter; pumpkins, black cats, witches, and bats for Halloween; reindeer, Santas, angels, sleighs, stockings, candy canes, snowflakes, the colors red and green, and so on for Christmas. The market for most of these prints is limited, as the holiday lasts only one day. But Christmas is a whole season unto itself, and textile designers have been generous in coming up with motifs that celebrate it.

1.

2.

3.

4.

5.

6.

HORSES

1. France, 1928, RP or SP silk, AYG, 115%
2. France, c. 1885, RP cotton, AYG, 145%
3. France, 1887, RP cotton, AYG, 105%
4. France, 1940s, SP rayon, AYG, 135%
5. England, 2d quarter 19th C, RP cotton chintz, HFYG, 32%

LARGER, STRONGER, AND faster than humans, horses have symbolized power through more than three thousand years of art history; yet the power always seems to attach not so much to the animals themselves as to the people who command them. Even today, when their work is done by the internal-combustion engine, horses remain an aristocratic motif. Art Deco artists often used stylized horses as an image of speed.

1.

2.

3.

4.

5.

HORSESHOES

1. France, 1890, gouache on paper, AYG, 110%
2. France, 1886, RP cotton, AYG, 100%
3. France, 1887, RP cotton, AYG, 105%
4. France, 1887, RP cotton, AYG, 86%
5. France, 1890, gouache on paper, AYG, 82%
6, 7. France, 1890, gouache on paper, AYG, 120%
8. France, 1886, RP cotton, AYG, 80%
9. France, 1890, gouache on paper, AYG, 94%

HUNTING

1. England or USA, c. 1920s, SP linen, HFYG, 31%

THERE IS A legend that Dunstan, a tenth-century archbishop of Canterbury and the patron saint of blacksmiths, once tried to horseshoe Satan, putting the devil in such pain that he swore never to go near one of those arcs of iron again. Horseshoes have been considered good luck ever since, even by people who don't believe in them—for they are found often in printed fabrics from the late nineteenth century to the present, and surely not all those designers and customers were superstitious. Horseshoes appear far more often than horses do, in fact—which makes some kind of sense, since every horse had four.

HUNTING SCENES ARRIVED on printed fabrics in the late eighteenth century with French and English toiles, and in the late nineteenth century with large-scale scenes imitating woven tapestries. Emblems of the chase have been popular ever since, originally as designs for furnishings but more recently on clothing as well. The type of hunting shown is never the subsistence kind or the American, deer-strapped-to-the-hood-of-the-truck sort; it is the landed-gentry style: patrician, expensive, leisured.

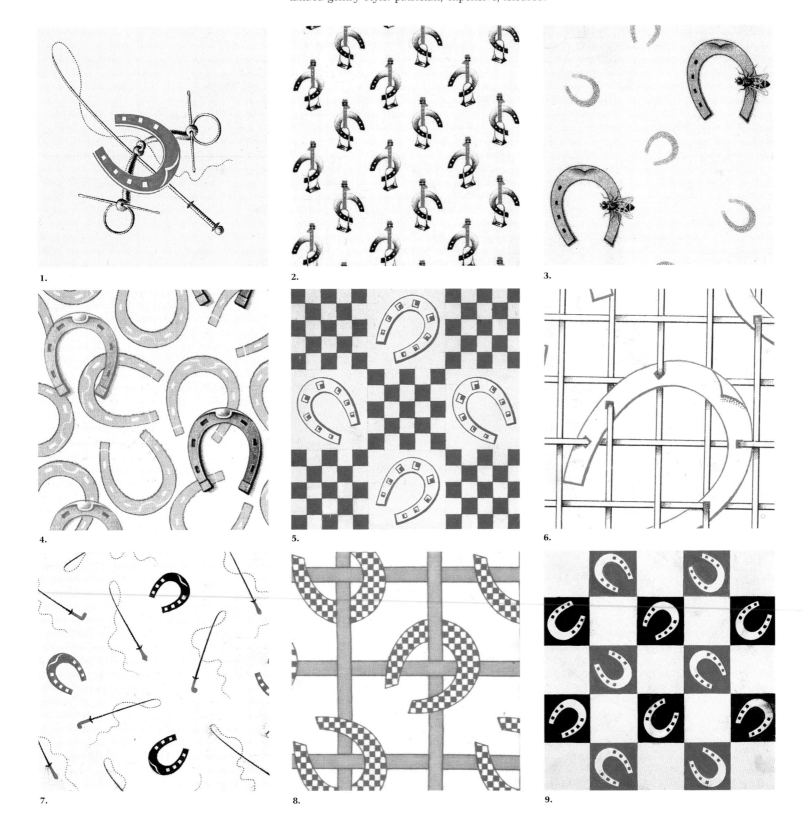

1.

2.

3.

4.

5.

6.

7.

8.

9.

1.

INSECTS

1. France, 1880, gouache on paper, AYG, 70%
2. USA, c. 1930s, RP cotton, AYG, 70%
3. France, c. 1810, gouache on paper, AYG, 70%
4. France, 1944, paper impression, AYG, 80%

LADYBUGS ARE CUTE, butterflies are pretty, but with the exception of the Napoleonic bee, other insects rarely decorate a piece of cloth—at least in this century. Designers in the 1800s were more adventurous entomologically. Back then, it was not unusual to make short runs of a print, maybe a hundred yards or so, and a risk could be taken on a beetle or a fly. A short run today is five thousand yards, and a print must have a good chance of selling that much to be produced. So creepy-crawlies are swatted away—"too buggy." If there is any economic latitude left for experimentation, it is for the most part at the upper end of the market, where customers pay prices steep enough to justify limited runs. Number 4 is just such an example; from a fine Lyonnais establishment, it was intended for haute-couture silk. Number 2, however, extends the luxury of the insect print to humbler cloth: it was destined to be made up into sacks for chicken feed and given away. Cheap cloth of this type was printed in patterns with a wide variety of motifs, including spiders. (See also *Floral: Sackcloth,* page 116.)

1.

2.

3.

4.

IRONWORK

1. France, 1920s, paper impression, AYG, 100%

ALSO KNOWN BY the French word *ferronnerie,* the ironwork motif has not been a favorite with the public since it went out of style with the last suit of armor. As with the imitation stone and brick of printed building patterns, make-believe iron is too hard and stiff to complement the suppleness of cloth. But some of the ornate grilles of the ironwork look are finely filigreed and scrolled, and even the somewhat forbidding example here would have been softened when printed on the cloth for which it was intended, a rich silk cut-velvet.

1.

JEWELS

1. France, 1930s, gouache on paper, AYG, 33%
2. France, 1930s–40s, gouache on paper, AYG, 140%
3. France, 1930s–40s, gouache on paper, AYG, 140%
4. France, c. 1920, gouache on paper, AYG, 100%
5. France, 1930s, gouache on paper, AYG, 70%

PRINTED JEWELS—FROM free-floating pearls and gemstones to ornate jewelry—have ornamented fabrics since the mid-nineteenth century, playing on the practice of studding garments with real gems. Art Deco designers in particular took advantage of the faceted sparkle and crystalline solidity of jewels. In symbolic terms, jewels represent spiritual truths. Gems hidden away in dark rooms or caves are analogous to intuitive knowledge buried in the unconscious. Treasures guarded by monsters symbolize the difficulties in the quest for self-awareness.

1.

2.

3.

4.

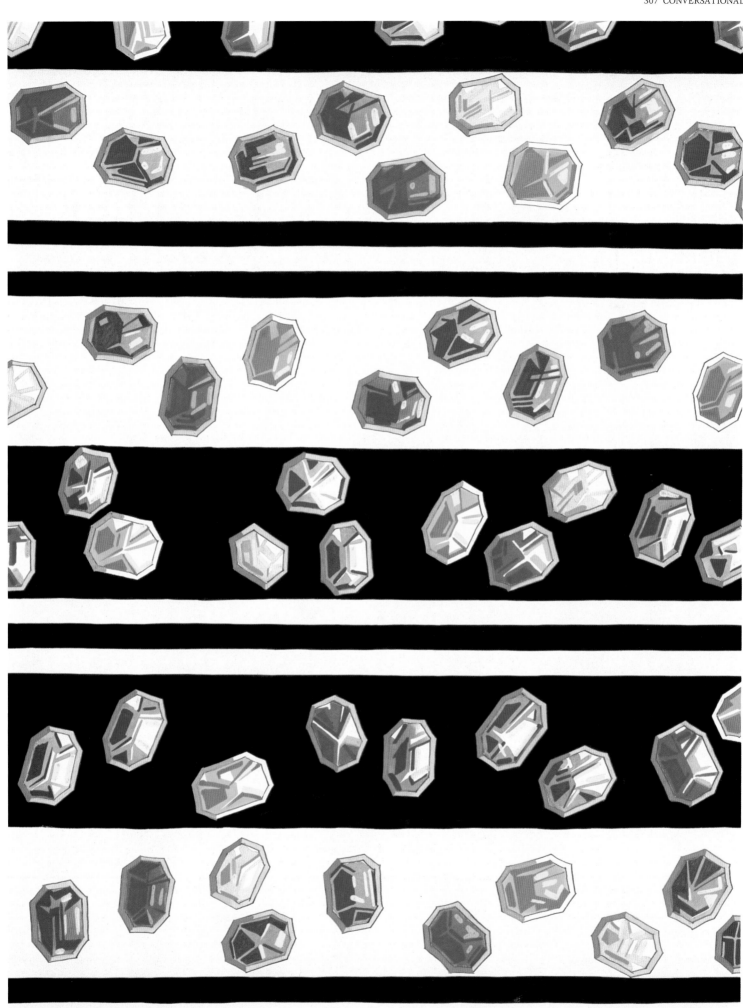

5.

JUNGLE

1. England or France, 2d half 19th C, gouache on paper, A (scarf corner), 90%
2. France, c. 1930s, gouache on paper, AYG, 40%
3. England, 2d quarter 19th C, RP cotton, HFYG, 40%

JUNGLE GREENERY, WITH its attendant wild beasts and brilliantly colored birds, began to appear on fabrics during the mid-nineteenth century. Like the animal-skin look, this type of design was at first thought too exotic and florid to wear and was used only for home-furnishing goods—with the exception of apparel yard goods exported to hot countries, where this particular wildlife was local and familiar. (For authenticity's sake, in fact, some of the larger French mills maintained greenhouses full of tropical flowers for their artists to copy.) Jungle prints only became fashionable for clothing in the twentieth century. In the 1980s a new term entered the garment-industry vocabulary—"safari"—and with it came a transfer of the jungle look from lush rain forest to bush and savannah and an expansion of landed-gentry imagery from mere foxes and pheasants to big game. But the 1990s are bringing an end to "safari," with its associations of hunting. The new term is "ecology," or "preservation," which brings us back to rain forests and jungle.

1.

2.

3.

JUVENILE

1. France, 1927, RP cotton, AYG, 84%
2. France, 1882, RP cotton, AYG, 76%
3. Probably USA, 1920s–30s, gouache on paper, AYG, 100%
4. France, 1880s, RP cotton, AYG, 84%
5. France, 1920s, RP cotton, AYG, 90%
6. France, 1920s, RP cotton, AYG, 82%
7. France, first half 20th C, gouache and watercolor on paper, A (handkerchief pattern). 66%

"JUVENILES"—A SOMEWHAT archaic term for patterns designed specifically for children— weren't seen much until the end of the nineteenth century and became an industry unto themselves only after World War I. But the English artist Kate Greenaway, whose illustrations of Victorian children at play are nearly as popular today as they were in the late nineteenth century, was responsible for a surge in the textile industry of Kate Greenaway look-alikes. Number 2 is based on a Greenaway image. It was mainly in the days when parents selected their offspring's clothes that children were made to wear idealized pictures of children. Today they have more say and tend to choose bright colors and cartoon characters.

1.

2.

3.

4.

5.

6.

7.

LETTERS AND NUMBERS

1. France, 1886, RP cotton, AYG, 85%
2. Probably USA, mid-20th C, RP or SP rayon, AYG, 88%
3. USA or France, 1950s–60s, SP cotton, AYG, 110%
4. France, 1940s–50s, RP rayon, AYG, 100%

CONCRETE POETRY FROM the brush of the textile designer is relatively unsuccessful with the public, except when used to spell out some direct and popular message. The alternative is to make the letters abstract, as are, to all intents and purposes, the Chinese ideograms of number 2 for the Western customer, who may or may not choose to wonder what they mean.

1.

2.

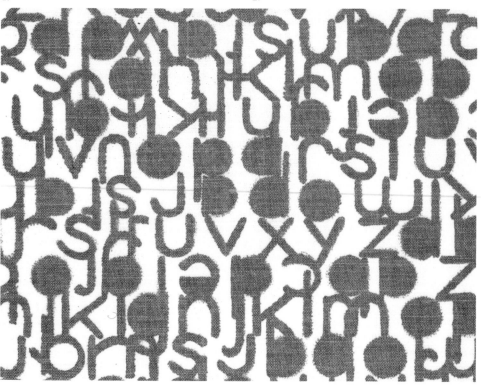

3.

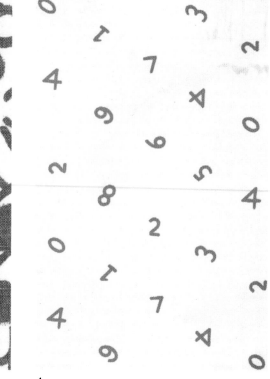

4.

MARINE LIFE

1. France, 1950s, RP cotton sateen, AYG, 100%
2. France, 1950s, RP or SP blend, AYG, 50%
3. France, 1890s, gouache on paper, AYG, 64%
4. England, 2d half 19th C, gouache on paper, AYG, 50%

THE CREATURES OF the sea bring nature to cloth in the same way that birds do and offer as much variety of color and form, but they have never been as popular—people may think they're too clammy, too reptilian, too, well, fishy. On a small scale, however—as a shoal of glittering shapes in the depth of the sea—they can be an elegant motif. With the proliferation of leisure clothing—sport, beach, cruise, and resort wear—in the second half of the twentieth century, marine imagery has been liberated from the shower curtain and is more accepted now than ever before. (See also *Conversational: Shells,* page 336.)

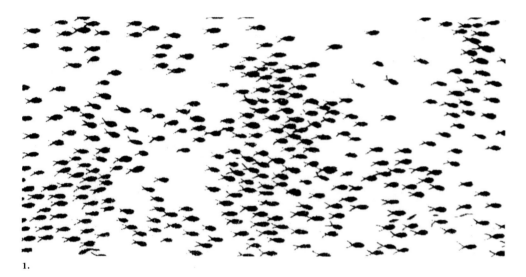

1.

2.

3.

4.

MILITARY AND WEAPONRY

1. **France, 1893, RP cotton, AYG, 100%**
2. **France, 1930s, RP or SP silk, AYG, 100%**
3. **France, 1890, RP cotton, AYG, 115%**
4. **France, 1930s–40s, RP or SP silk, AYG, 70%**
5. **England, 1914–18, RP cotton, A (scarf), 37%**
6. **France, 2d half 19th C, gouache on paper, AYG, 27%**
7. **France, 1882, RP cotton, AYG, 60%**

EVERY CULTURE HAS attached deep significance to its weapons and to the weapons of its gods and heroes. Zeus had his thunderbolt, Thor his hammer, Moses his rod, Saint George his dragon-slaying spear, and Prince Valiant the singing sword. For centuries, weapons represented the triumph of good over evil, in a spiritual as well as a physical sense. They appear regularly in trophies and heraldry and as main motifs in prints of the nineteenth century, when even a military debacle like the famous Charge of the Light Brigade could be called "noble" by as thoughtful a writer as Tennyson. It was probably World War I that ended many such ideas about military glory; after that, the spiritual symbolism of weaponry was replaced by a feeling of revulsion. Weapons are taboo for twentieth-century designers, unless their bearers are harmless and cute, like the tin soldier, or unless their threat is explicit, as in the "punk" look.

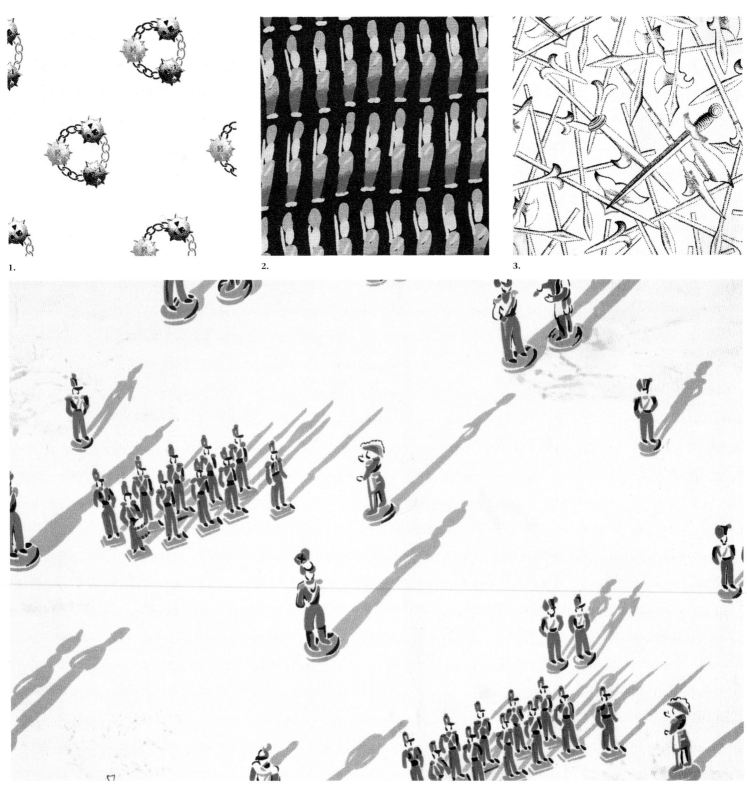

1.

2.

3.

4.

5.

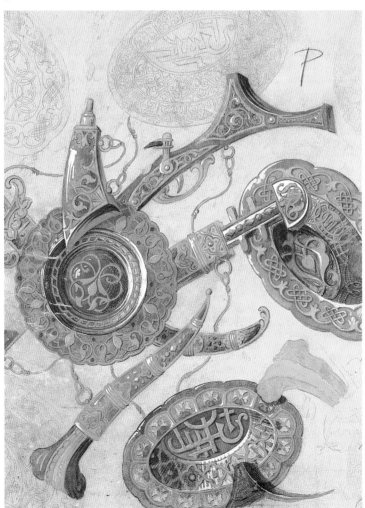

6.

7.

MILL ENGRAVINGS

1. France, 1886, RP cotton, AYG, 120%
2. France, 1889, RP cotton, AYG, 110%
3. France, 1882, RP cotton, AYG, 100%
4. France, 1887, RP cotton, AYG, 100%
5. France, c. 1885, gouache on paper, AYG, 100%
6. France, c. 1885, RP cotton, AYG, 100%
7. France, 1886, RP cotton, AYG, 100%
8. France, 1890, gouache on paper, AYG, 135%
9. France, 1886, RP cotton, AYG, 100%

MILL ENGRAVINGS—PRINTS made with copper rollers, themselves engraved with a design transferred from a small steel roller called a "mill"—were extremely popular on both sides of the Atlantic in the last quarter of the nineteenth century. Usually printed on shirting-weight white cotton, these designs decorated women's aprons and blouses, boy's shirts, children's garments, and patchwork quilts. A factory might produce several hundred mill engravings a season, forcing designers to throw in almost any motif not out-and-out tasteless in their search for variety. The results, often simple spaced layouts printed in no more than two colors (usually black and red), could be strange and whimsical, as the examples here show. Anything went—even something as prosaic, for the textile worker at any rate, as the bunch of fabric swatches in number 7. Whatever the image, it was likely to be distinguished by the fine detail and line that the technique made possible. This effect is largely lost today, when most cloth printing is done by silk screen. (See also *Floral: Mill Engravings*, pages 90–91.)

1.

2.

3.

4.

5.

6.

7.

8.

9.

MUSICAL INSTRUMENTS

1. France, 1950s, gouache on paper, AYG, 50%
2. France, 1880s, RP cotton, AYG, 68%
3. USA, 1960s, dyes on paper, AYG, 70%

MUSICAL INSTRUMENTS APPEAR regularly in textile designs. Lutes, bagpipes, horns, tambourines, and lyres are often included in nineteenth-century designs for trophies (number 2)—clusters of objects used as a decorative device since the Renaissance to celebrate some victory or achievement. But they also sound less refined and romantic notes, as the wonderfully vulgar number 1 shows.

2.

1.

3.

MYTHOLOGICAL

1. **France, 1920s, paper impression, AYG, 43%**
2. **France, 1880–85, gouache on paper, HFYG, 50%**
3. **England, c. 1890, BP linen, HF (table mat), 38%**
4. **France, c. 1900, gouache on paper, HFYG, 60%**

PRINTED CLOTH IS inhabited by countless creatures from mythology, as if it were a common heaven where cupids, unicorns, dragons, satyrs, and angels all coexisted (though probably not in the same design). Cupid is the most ubiquitous mythological motif. Cute, inoffensive, romantic, he might have been relegated to Saint Valentine's Day but for his place in the pantheon of neoclassicism, with its ethos of an antique, graceful, and aristocratic culture. More unusual are centaurs and satyrs, who appear in Art Nouveau and Art Deco prints; angels, fairies, and dragons find a home in the designs of the Arts and Crafts movement. The unicorn was a favored motif in medieval tapestries, the dragon in Chinese embroideries, and both appear in printed imitations of those fabrics.

1.

2.

3.

4.

NAUTICAL

1. USA, mid-20th C, gouache and dyes on paper, AYG, 86%
2. USA, 1940s–60s, RP or SP cotton, AYG, 80%
3. USA, 1930s, RP cotton, AYG, 84%
4. USA, 1930s, RP cotton, AYG, 100%
5. USA, 1940s–50s, RP cotton, AYG, 84%

NAUTICAL MOTIFS APPEAR in nineteenth-century prints but become a fashion classic in the twentieth century, particularly with the rise of resort clothes and sportswear. Like heraldic imagery, flags with a maritime aspect convey a rather patrician image—the wearer no doubt identifying with the ship's captain rather than the deckhand. They can also be crisp and fresh as a sea breeze, conjuring up the sporting outdoor life. Red, navy blue, and white are the characteristic colors.

1.

2.

3.

4.

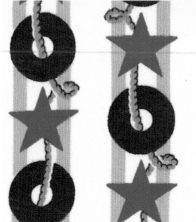

5.

NUTS AND PINECONES

1. France, 1883, RP cotton, AYG, 105%
2. France, 1886, RP cotton, AYG, 94%
3. France, 1886, RP cotton, AYG, 100%
4. France, c. 1910–20, gouache on paper, AYG, 96%
5. France, c. 1880–85, RP cotton, AYG, 90%

A SIMPLY SHAPED nut, such as a hazelnut, makes a polka dot into a recognizable, three-dimensional, and flavorsome object. More complicated nuts demand fine detail and are somewhat more unusual now, in the era of silk-screen printing, than in the copper-roller days of the last century. (An insufficiently walnut-like walnut can look uncomfortably like a brain.) Pinecones are too seasonal to be a common motif—they have a particular association with Christmas. Being part of an evergreen tree, they are symbolic of immortality and fertility.

1.

2.

3.

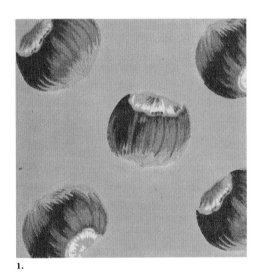

4.

5.

OBJECTS

1. France, 1930s, gouache on paper, AYG, 120%
2. France, 1940s, RP rayon, AYG, 80%
3. France, 1950s, gouache on paper, AYG, 28%
4. France, 1930s, gouache on paper, AYG, 60%

ANYTHING THE DESIGNER fancies can go into a print—beach balls, crockery, candy, and even ashtrays. A motif must prove its popularity, though, before a designer will repeat it. Innumerable objects show up here and there in printed textiles without appearing often enough to become a genre. When Andy Warhol turned the Campbell's soup can into an allover repeating pattern, he was doing on canvas what textile designers had been doing for centuries—removing an everyday object from its usual context, isolating its image on cloth, and putting it in repeat—making a statement beyond mere description of utilitarian function.

1.

2.

3.

4.

PATCHWORK

1. USA, 1880s, RP cotton, HFYG, 41%

A NECESSITY OF the traditional patchwork quilt is, of course, the patch—the small piece of fabric sewn painstakingly together with many other pieces to make a continuous pattern. Printed patchwork offers the look without the time-consuming labor, which is why it was also called "cheater cloth." In the late nineteenth century, when more quilts were made by hand in America than ever before, cheater cloth was a yard-goods staple. Often two joined lengths of it were used for the backing of an otherwise genuine quilt, but sometimes quilts were made entirely of simulated patchwork. Since the quilting had to be done anyway—the stitching together of the quilt top and backing to the inner padding to prevent it from shifting—there was still a lot of work to do; and so these cheater-cloth quilts are rather puzzling. Maybe their makers simply preferred the look of the cheater cloth to the real thing . . . or maybe by circumventing the piecing process they really were cheating . . . well, half cheating.

1.

PEOPLE

1. USA, 1920s, gouache on paper, AYG, 100%
2. USA, 1920s, gouache on paper, AYG, 100%
3. USA, 1920s, gouache on paper, AYG, 125%
4. USA, 1920s, gouache on paper, AYG, 115%
5. USA, 1920s, gouache on paper, AYG, 135%
6. USA, 1920s, gouache on paper, AYG, 110%
7. USA, 1920s, gouache on paper, AYG, 115%
8. USA, 1920s, gouache on paper, AYG, 110%
9. USA, 1920s, gouache on paper, AYG, 115%
10. France, c. 1880, RP cotton, AYG, 400%

PEOPLE APPEAR OFTEN in scenic prints such as the toiles de Jouy. Except in mill engravings and juvenile designs, however, it's unusual for them to make up a pattern on their own. Perhaps we consider it dehumanizing for human figures to be reduced to a motif in a layout; perhaps we would feel dehumanized ourselves, one among a crowd, by wearing such a throng. And would we sit on them if they upholstered a couch?

1.

2.

3.

4.

5.

6.

7.

8.

9.

PHOTOPRINTS

1. USA, c. 1939, cotton, YG, 50%
2. USA, 1939, cotton, YG, 50%

A TECHNIQUE FOR printing photographs on cloth was perfected in the 1930s, and since then souvenir and commemorative items have often carried exact likenesses of people and places—though a scene's sense of space can become confusing when it is fractured into a repeat pattern. Number 2 shows the Trylon and Perisphere of the 1939 World's Fair in New York—or it claims to. Actually, since the cloth had to be ready to go on sale as a souvenir when the fair opened, the printer seems to have photographed a maquette of the buildings rather than waiting for construction to be finished. Number 1 is a view of New York City. The Chrysler and Empire State buildings as well as the Brooklyn Bridge still stand, but the original, columned Port Authority Building is gone. Most often, photoprints like these were made into men's sport shirts, which were sold as tourist items.

1.

2.

PILLAR PRINTS

1. England, c. 1820, RP and BP cotton chintz, HFYG, 27%

POPULAR FOR CURTAINS and bedcovers in England from around 1815 to 1830, pillar prints make a wide stripe pattern representational by relating it to architecture, giving it the joints, depth, and decoration of the neoclassical column. The pillar is never straight and unbroken; here, for example, it is softened with flowers. While they never caught on in the rest of Europe, imported pillar prints sold well in America and were often turned into whole-cloth quilts.

1.

PLAYING-CARD MOTIFS

DESIGNERS OF THE 1880s liked to play with these motifs, which, in their colors of black and red, were a natural for mill engraving. The deck of cards we use today originated in the medieval tarot pack.

1. France, 1883, RP cotton, AYG, 145%
2. France, 1880–90, RP cotton, AYG, 80%
3. France, 1887, RP cotton, AYG, 80%
4. France, 1887, RP cotton, AYG, 100%
5. France, 1880, gouache on paper, AYG, 80%

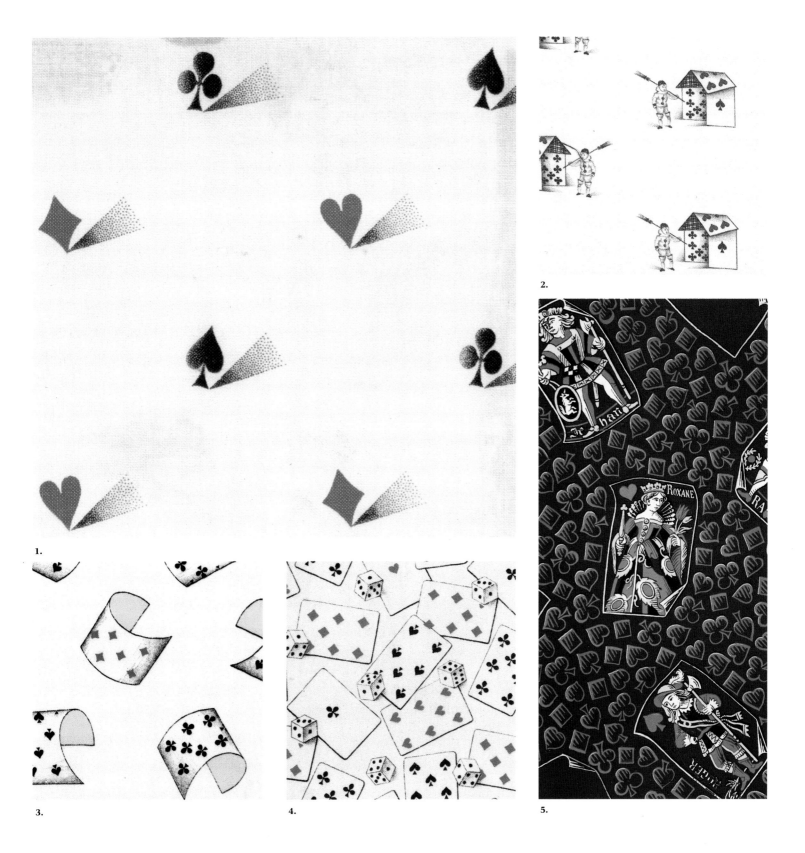

1.

2.

3.

4.

5.

REPTILES

1. England or France, 2d half 19th C, RP cotton, AYG, 92%
2. France, 1880s, gouache on paper, AYG, 80%
3. Germany, 1930s, gouache on paper, AYG (tie pattern), 100%
4. France, 1880s, gouache on paper, AYG, 70%
5. France, 1949, RP rayon, AYG, 210%

LIKE INSECTS, REPTILES were more acceptable subjects for a print in the nineteenth century than they are now. The salamander in number 2 coexisted with the enameled salamander pins that were all the rage in the 1880s. Turtles have a pleasing shape, and their pretty shells hide their reptilian skin; frogs, too, can be made to look endearing, as long as they're not too toadlike. Both appear in modern textiles. The snake throttling the panther in number 1 is not a design that would have been sold in the West, even in the nineteenth century, when it was made. It was intended for export to one of the colonies. Snakes are usually allowed only when their serpentine shapes have been flattened into the textured allover pattern of their skins.

1.

2.

3.

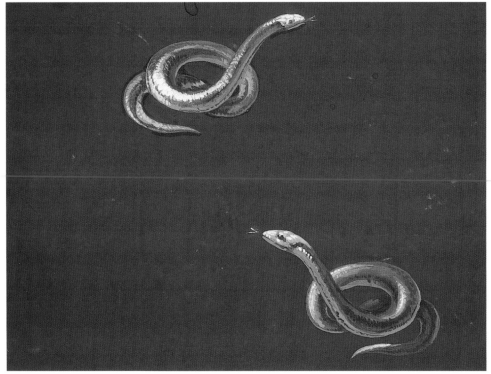

4.

5.

RUFFLES

1. **Probably France, c. 1860–70, gouache on paper, AYG, 160%**
2. **France, c. 1900, gouache on paper, AYG, 140%**
3. **France, 1873, RP cotton, AYG, 200%**

THIS PATTERN IS also known as ruching, particularly in nineteenth-century terminology. Number 3 was designed to be cut into bands and used as a border. The others are clever allover designs, giving cloth the illusion of—more cloth. Today, ruffles are used mainly in sleepwear patterns and alongside floral motifs in home-furnishing chintzes.

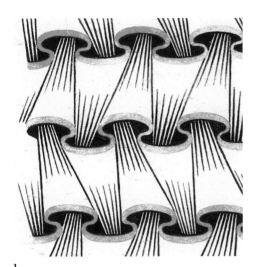

1.

2.

3.

SCENIC LANDSCAPE

1. **France, 1920s, gouache on paper, HFYG, 40%**
2. **France, 1900–1920, gouache on paper, HFYG, 50%**

THE EIGHTEENTH-CENTURY English and French toiles were the first scenic prints, inspired by the fine-art engravings of their time. The prints illustrated here also follow fine art— number 1 imitating a Fauvist look, for example. Scenic images appear more often in furnishing fabrics than in apparel. In a wall hanging or on a curtain, they suggest a whole space to be looked into, as if through a window; that space becomes confusing when it wraps a human body. (See also *Conversational: Toiles,* pages 342–45.)

1.

2.

SCENIC PICTORIAL

1. "Sleeping Beauty," France, 1882, designed by
Atelier Martin, gouache on paper, HFYG, 36%
2. France, c. 1880, designed by Atelier Martin,
gouache on paper, HFYG, 35%

TO THE PASTORAL beauty of the scenic landscape, the scenic pictorial adds human figures and the hint of a story. Number 1 shows a version of the legend of the Sleeping Beauty—complete with princess, prince, good and bad fairies, and spinning wheel. Number 2 illustrates a party of elegantly dressed eighteenth-century aristocrats enjoying the simple pleasures of the country. Intricate scenes such as these were popular in late-nineteenth-century furnishing fabrics, and the printed textile was remarkably true to the original painted design. "Sleeping Beauty" has eighteen colors and was roller-printed on a finely ribbed cotton called "Gobelin" by its manufacturer.

1.

2.

SHELLS

1. **France, c. 1810, gouache on paper, AYG (scarf pattern), 76%**
2. **France, 1883, RP cotton, AYG, 100%**
3. **France, 1880s, RP cotton, AYG, 86%**
4. **France, 1880s, RP cotton, A (scarf border), 78%**

SHELLS HAVE BEEN a motif in textile printing since the beginning of the industry, though never a very common one until the growth of the resort-wear business after World War II. The most widely used shell is the scallop, with its flat, symmetrical, fanlike shape, both abstract and referential at the same time. In the Middle Ages, the sea off Compostela, an important Spanish pilgrimage site, was rich in scallops, and the pilgrim would set a shell in his hat to show he'd been there. The Crusaders wore them too, and the scallop became a symbol of Christianity. The contemporary designer who puts these shells on a resort-wear shirt may not be aware of their long association with Western clothing.

2.

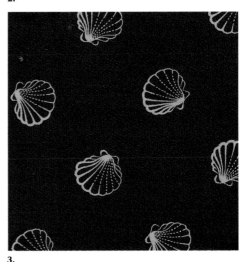

3.

1.

4.

SILHOUETTES

1. **France, 1880, gouache on paper, AYG, 100%**
2. **France, 1880, gouache on paper, AYG, 100%**
3. **France, 1880, gouache on paper, AYG, 100%**
4. **France, 1880, gouache on paper, AYG, 100%**

ETIENNE DE SILHOUETTE was the French minister of finance for a short period in 1759. In the battle between the would-be cloth printing industry and the established textile weavers, he was instrumental in having a ban on printed textiles repealed in September 1759. His opponents circulated caricatures of him cut out of black paper. Whether because of this or because of the penny-pinching economies he introduced, silhouettes—which are far easier, quicker, and therefore cheaper to produce than a painted portrait—have been called by his name ever since. (More charitably, it is also said that he made them as a hobby.) They were a ladies' handicraft and pastime in the nineteenth century, and Victorians could have their silhouettes made as we now may sit for a photograph. The patterns here were popular in the 1880s, when this technique was in vogue.

1.

2.

3.

4.

SPORTS

1. USA or France, mid-20th C, gouache on paper, AYG, 62%
2. France, 1890, gouache on paper, AYG, 370%
3. France, 1893, RP cotton, AYG, 82%
4. USA, 1940s, RP silk, AYG (tie pattern), 70%
5. France, 1870–80, RP wool challis, AYG, 86%
6. France, 1882, RP cotton, AYG, 175%
7. France, 1890, gouache on paper, AYG, 120%
8. England or USA, 2d quarter 20th C, gouache on paper, AYG, 225%
9. USA, 1945, watercolor on paper, AYG, 80%

SPORTING MOTIFS ARE seen occasionally in late-nineteenth-century printed designs, but more as an incidental motif, like the jockeys in mill engravings, than as the emblems of a whole ethos. Since World War I, however, with the growth of the leisure industry and of big-business sports, they have become a way for many men to state their identity.

1.

2.

3.

4.

5.

6.

7.

8.

9.

STAINED-GLASS LOOK

1. USA, 1930s–40s, roller-printed rayon, AYG, 76%
2. Probably France, c. 1900, roller-printed cotton, 74%

STAINED GLASS IS a rather uncommon theme in textiles, perhaps because of its religious and architectural associations. When they use it today, designers are more concerned with capturing the luminescent, jewel-like colors of the stained glass and the bold graphic outlines of the leaded pieces than the actual image of the window itself.

1.

2.

TAPESTRY LOOK

1. France, c. 1880, block-printed cotton canvas, HFYG, 25%

TAPESTRY-LOOK PRINTS often imitate medieval tapestries in style and subject, and their colors are usually in the subdued tones of the now-faded originals. The designer of this particular pattern used more than two dozen wood blocks on a cloth whose weave closely resembles the tapestry stitch. It is difficult to distinguish it from the real thing unless the fabric is viewed from close up.

1.

TOILES: ALLEGORICAL, HISTORICAL, AND MONUMENTAL

1. England, c. 1800, CP cotton, HFYG, 35%
2. "Jeanne d'Arc," France, c. 1815, CP cotton, HFYG, 25%
3. "Les Monuments de Paris," France, 1816–18, RP or CP cotton, HFYG, 25%

TOILES ARE USED for home furnishings, most often coverlets, bed hangings, and draperies. Originally "toile" meant simply a cotton or linen cloth, but since the mid-eighteenth century the word has also referred to the large-scale, engraved scenic designs that decorate these fabrics. Copperplate- or roller-printed in one color (most commonly red, sepia, black, puce, or blue), these designs can be grouped in several categories. Number 1, an allegorical toile, seems to satirize personalities of the period and may also refer to the legendary Masque of the Red Death. Number 2 is a historical toile showing the burning of Joan of Arc at the stake. There was also a monumental genre: number 3, a toile with a view of the Louvre, was designed by Hypolite Le Bas and engraved by Leisnier for Christophe-Philippe Oberkampf.

1.

2.

3.

TOILES: MYTHOLOGICAL, PASTORAL, AND ROMANTIC

1. "Psyché et l'Amour," France, c. 1810, CP cotton, HFYG, 43%
2. "Scènes Flamandes," France, c. 1797, CP cotton, HFYG, 18%
3. France, 1927, RP cotton, HFYG, 28%

THE FIRST COPPERPLATE-PRINTED toiles were made in Ireland, by Francis Nixon of Drumcondra, in 1752. They rapidly grew popular—and both Benjamin Franklin and George Washington, among others, imported toiles for use in their homes. In fact, the images of Franklin and Washington appeared on post–Revolutionary War English toiles in homage to these American patriots and with an eye to the American market. The French soon learned the printing technique, and the best-known toiles became the toiles de Jouy, named for the famous Oberkampf mill in Jouy, near Versailles, where they were produced from 1783 on. (The original furnishings of the President's House in Washington, D.C., included toiles de Jouy.) Oberkampf hired the best artists of the time to design these prints. Provincial florals made his fortune, but the toiles made his name—they were what today would be called his luxury line. Number 1, in the mythological genre of toile, and the pastoral number 2 are both Oberkampf toiles designed by Jean-Baptiste Huet. Number 3, a romantic scene, was printed in 1927—in the style of a Nantes toile of 1785.

1.

2.

3.

TRANSPORTATION

1. France, 1887, RP wool challis, A (scarf corner), 54%
2. USA, c. 1920s, RP rayon jacquard, AYG, 88%
3. France, c. 1885, RP cotton, AYG, 84%
4. France, 1887, RP cotton, AYG, 96%
5. France, c. 1890, gouache on paper, AYG, 72%
6. "Design Overseas," USA, late 1930s–early 1940s, RP cotton chintz, HFYG, 50%

TRANSPORT MOTIFS WERE used as themes in themselves primarily by Art Deco designers who wanted to capture the sense of speed conveyed by cars, planes, and trains. Number 6 was intended for a boy's room, most likely for curtains. The theme of number 1 was as unusual then as it is today: a train chugging its way around the border of a woman's scarf.

1.

2.

3.

4.

5.

6.

TREES

1. France, 1810, gouache on paper, AYG, 78%
2. France, 1920s, RP cotton, AYG, 110%
3. France, c. 1900, gouache on paper, HFYG, 30%
4. England, c. 1810, BP cotton, HFYG, 70%

ONE-DIRECTIONAL, GENERALLY heavy in shape, and potentially awkward to work into a repeat pattern, trees are not a staple subject for designers, though they often show up modified as branches in arborescent prints, or in the background of a jungle or a scenic print. Number 3 is an Art Nouveau border print—a linear design, with the trees forming horizontal rows instead of an allover pattern. The palm trees in number 4 reflect a vogue in British chintzes of about 1815, where they often appeared incongruously with such English game birds as the pheasant. Some trees have symbolic meanings, though these old associations tend to be played down in modern textiles. The oak stands for longevity, strength, and steadfastness, but the trees themselves are seen less often than their leaves and acorns. The weeping willow is a symbol of bereavement, and in the eighteenth and nineteenth centuries a widow might have included a willow in her embroidery; but there is no willow-patterned mourning cloth as such.

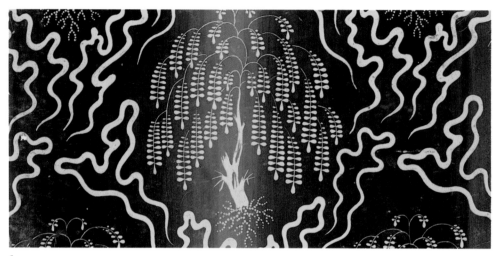

1.

2.

3.

4.

TRIMMING

1. USA, c. 1880, RP cotton, AYG, 105%
2. France, 1873, RP cotton, AYG, 94%
3. France, 1870–80, RP cotton, A (scarf border), 100%

LIKE CERTAIN BORDER prints—the floral chintz borders, for example—most of these images of fringes and braiding were sold as yard goods and designed to be cut into strips. They served as an inexpensive substitute for the real thing, or perhaps, as they do today, provided a certain wry spoof. But the tassels in number 3 are the trompe-l'oeil border of a cotton scarf.

1.

2.

3.

TROMPE-L'OEIL

1. **USA, c. 1940s, RP cotton, HFYG, 80%**
2. **France, c. 1880, RP cotton, AYG, 100%**
3. **Probably France, late 19th C, RP silk velvet, AYG, 90%**
4. **France, c. 1880, RP cotton, AYG, 100%**

TROMPE-L'OEIL EFFECTS carry to an extreme the ability to make printed cloth look three-dimensional, but unlike many designs that aim to make a cheap fabric resemble an expensive one, they get away with an obvious display of their own fakery. Often, they have a tongue-in-cheek edge: thus the needles apparently left behind by the tailor (number 2) or the Japanese beetles tethered to someone's shirt with pins and thread (number 4). (In the 1960s, there was a brief vogue for a literal version of this look, featuring live beetles.) Number 1 is more sincerely phony, a print pretending to be a satin patchwork, though it is more successful as an imitation of the vinyl that upholstered 1950s diner banquettes. Number 3 is a genuine but luxurious pretender, a printed version of passementerie embroidery reproduced on expensive silk velvet.

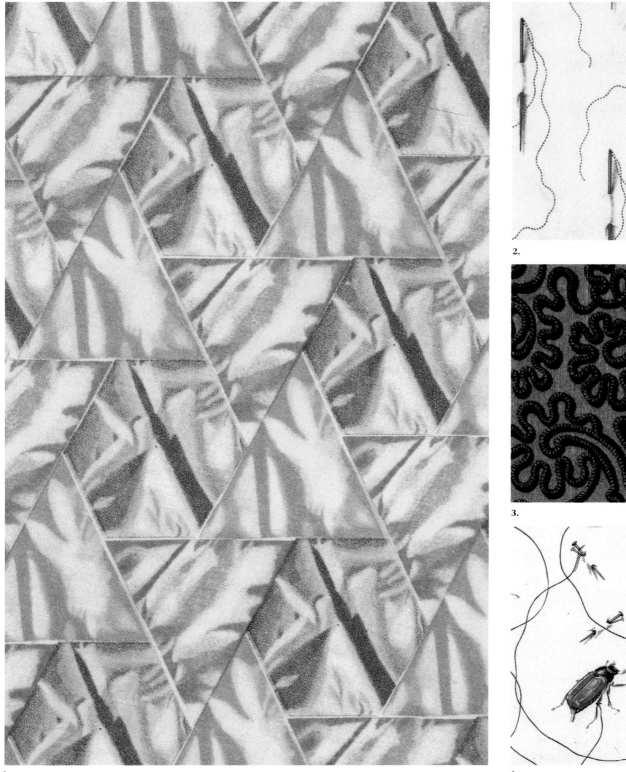

1.

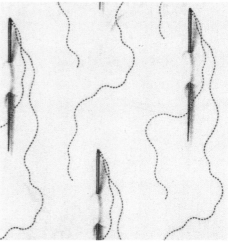

2.

3.

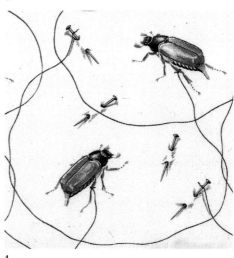

4.

TROPHIES

1. France, 1870s, RP cotton, HFYG, 50%
2. France, 1870s, RP cotton, HFYG, 80%
3. France, 1890, RP cotton, HFYG, 50%

FOR THE ANCIENT Greeks and Romans, a trophy was a collection of arms and other spoils of war, mounted on a tree or pillar on the battlefield or elsewhere, to commemorate victory and honor the gods who had bestowed it. By the fourteenth century, the trophy had become a formal but graceful decorative device, transforming the swords, pikes, and helmets of some successful Renaissance campaign into a wall ornament or painting, or celebrating a peacetime achievement such as a hunt by depicting rabbits and game birds hanging by their feet. Fabric designers have preferred gentler subjects still in trophies, composing them out of garlands, musical instruments, and pastoral accouterments. The victory here seems to be the achievement of a harmonious and leisured civility.

1.

2.

3.

TROPICAL

1. France, 1883, RP cotton, HFYG, 31%

A CLOSE RELATIVE of the jungle print—but minus the wild animals—the tropical print conveys a Caribbean- or Pacific-island mood, filled with exotic flowers and birds, lush foliage and fruit, palm trees, and the summer sea. Although number 1 is a nineteenth-century design, tropical prints are really a twentieth-century genre, an outgrowth of booming tourist travel to sunny places and of the demand for cruise and resort wear.

1.

VEGETABLES

1. France, c. 1950s, SP silk, AYG, 50%
2. France, c. 1860, RP cotton, AYG, 90%
3. France, c. 1800, paper impression, AYG, 70%
4. France, c. 1880, RP cotton, AYG, 80%

LESS DELICATELY SHAPED and perfumed than flowers, less sweet-tasting than fruit, vegetables have lost out in textile design to more favored plant life. The Welsh may sometimes sport leeks, their national emblem, in their hats, but soup greens would be considered an oddity as decoration for the body in most of the West. In the 1950s there was a vegetable vogue in American goods for the kitchen—tablecloths, curtains, and aprons. And throughout the history of printed textiles, vegetables have been cultivated on and off for their symbolism of harvest and the riches of the earth. In general, though, fruit salad beats ratatouille and blossom beats brussels sprout. The turnip pattern of number 3 (for an Oberkampf fabric) would be an unlikely design today because of an association of turnip roots with soil that might too easily translate into an impression of soiled cloth.

1.

2.

3.

4.

WATER AND WAVE PATTERNS

1. France, 1920s, paper impression, AYG, 70%
2. Probably France, 1940s, RP or SP silk crepe, AYG, 140%
3. Probably USA, c. 1900, RP silk, AYG, 100%
4. France, 1899, RP cotton, AYG, 100%

THESE ORIENTAL-LOOKING motifs appeared with the Western craze for all things Japanese in the latter half of the nineteenth century. Wave patterns are classic in Japanese art and decoration—so common, in fact, that the different styles of presenting them have developed their own vocabulary, each having its own name. But they have never been numerous in the West. Certain fabric designs stay more or less permanently in style, but anything with a hint of ethnicity may go in and out of vogue quite rapidly; this season's ethnic trend looks stale next year. And water and wave patterns are evocative enough of Japan that they have never become fixtures in the European and American markets. On a psychological level, water is fraught with symbolism. A force of both creation and destruction, it represents the unconscious, the unfathomable. It can be contained and yet never contained. It is at once disturbing and soothing.

1.

2.

3.

4.

WICKERWORK

1. France, 1950s–60s, gouache on paper, HFYG, 66%

2. France, 1950s–60s, gouache on paper, HFYG, 42%

WICKER CAN BE woven out of a wide variety of stout reedlike plants, but the traditional material is rattan, an Oriental grass that was bundled up and used as ballast in nineteenth-century American clippers on the voyage back from trading in the East. Jettisoned as waste on Boston quaysides, the bundles were picked up for furniture material by local makers. The technique itself is ancient everywhere, however, and doesn't necessarily connote the Orient—though wicker's suitability in hot climates (because of its light-colored, ventilating surface) evokes feelings of summer warmth. Although wicker prints appear less often on sun-porch and beach furnishings than their cousins the bamboo prints, both designs soften geometric line work by building it of literally organic lines.

1.

2.

ZODIAC

1. France, 1940s–50s, RP or SP cotton chintz, HFYG, 40%

THE ZODIAC AS we know it dates at least from the sixth century B.C., when it appeared on a tablet of the Persian king Cambyses, but it is probably far older, being anticipated in the Babylonian empire of Hammurabi, of the eighteenth century B.C., and in relics of the Sumerian king Sargon of Akkad, from about 2340 B.C. The symbolism of the cyclic wheel of the seasons, or the wheel (the Greek *diakos*) of life (*zōē*), is actually prehistoric. Since Galileo, no one has believed that the twelve annual phases of the sun have any influence on human life and character—or rather no one and everyone, since the number of Westerners unable to name their birth sign at the drop of a hat is certainly small. Still, the zodiacal symbols don't appear often in printed textiles. We may not mind wearing our own personality on our sleeves, but not eleven others. The design illustrated here is in the style of Jean Cocteau, the French *littérateur*, artist, and filmmaker, who at one point created some designs for textiles.

1.

4. Ethnic

EUROPEAN TRADE WITH countries now called the Third World long predates the invention of mechanical printing, and cloth was always a staple of that exchange. But the industrial revolution dramatically changed the balance of the old relationship. Not only did it equip the West with ever more powerful weapons of war, but it created an insatiable demand for raw materials to be turned into marketable goods. As European factories grew in number and efficiency, turning out ever greater quantities of products, they also created a demand for new markets. Whether willingly or not, the nonindustrialized world supplied both the markets and the raw materials.

Nineteenth-century colonialism depended on this technological imbalance. But if the West held the cards in the new relationship, it also had to produce goods that the colonized peoples would buy. Hence some of the patterns in this chapter: Western interpretations of designs taken from different parts of the world, made to be sold back to the people in the countries where they originated. The results are often a fascinating stylistic mélange, for a European version of an Indian motif, say, looks neither quite Indian nor quite European. Yet such was the power of the industrial system that some of these prints saturated the markets for which they were intended to the point where they now seem indigenous. A visitor to a contemporary African city may notice a lot of Western-style clothing worn on the street and may lament the passing of more traditional dress; but that traditional dress was itself very likely made of cloth manufactured and printed in the West.

Most of the patterns illustrated in this chapter, however, were produced not for the overseas market but for the domestic one. Ethnic fashions—meaning, in textile vocabulary, any pattern or style with a foreign or exotic feeling—come and go in Western design. Their associations vary with the culture they imitate, but a common implicit theme is a withdrawal from our own technological world through an embrace of the forms of some older, often simpler (supposedly), and certainly less industrialized society. Many of these designs simulate regional motifs and techniques, but they are always Western interpretations of those local styles. The prints in this chapter are ethnic "looks," designed not by ethnics but by their imitators. They can even be offensive to the people whose style they claim to copy: many Mexicans, for example, may see the Mexican-look sombrero prints in this chapter as a distortion of their culture, and the Dutch may be similarly annoyed by the Netherlandish look, with its obligatory wooden clogs. That such distortions appear in European countries and the United States as well as the Third World has nothing to do with democratic fair play and everything to do with the market.

The ethnic styles have their day in Western design and then submerge, to reappear whenever someone senses that the time is right for a "new" twist on the constant demand for a folkloric pattern. Like conversationals such as the commemoratives, however, ethnic looks tend to be self-limiting. With the exception of the paisley, which has been popular long enough to be completely assimilated into Western fashion, their vogue usually doesn't last more than one season—as if there's only so much playing around with the exotic we're prepared to do before we head for home.

AFRICAN LOOK

1. **France, 1st half 20th C, gouache on paper, AYG, 50%**
2. **France, 1st half 20th C, gouache on paper, AYG, 50%**
3. **France, 1st half 20th C, gouache on paper, AYG, 50%**
4. **France, 1st half 20th C, gouache on paper, AYG, 50%**
5. **France, 1st half 20th C, gouache on paper, AYG, 50%**
6. **France, 1st half 20th C, gouache on paper, AYG, 50%**

PRINTS LIKE THESE are today part of a traditional African look, not only in Africa but also in the West, where some people wear them as a sign of pride in their heritage and others wear them to the beach. The origins of these textiles, however, are European. From the eighteenth century on, European mills sold fabric to the countries we now call the Third World. As the colonial system developed, creating vast markets in underdeveloped countries for the cheaply produced goods of the industrial West, whole firms could survive solely by making cloth for export. Scouts in the colonies would relay information home about the regional tastes and fads. Thus the patterns below are a peculiar hybrid—part a European designer's conception of what the people of a country he or she had almost certainly never visited would like, part the result of a rough but effective form of market research. By the middle of this century, the export-to-Africa industry was all but dead in Europe (though the Dutch have managed to maintain it on a reduced scale). African independence movements opened the continent's markets to goods from other sources, such as India and the Far East, and many Africans now wear Western-style clothes.

1.

2.

3.

4.

5.

6.

AMERICANA

1. USA, 1940s–50s, SP cotton, HFYG, 50%

OFTEN MODELED ON naive paintings like those of Grandma Moses, Americana prints show rural landscapes of peaceful prosperity—the good life of the farm and small town. They were popular in the late 1940s and 1950s, when thousands of American soldiers were returning home after World War II and starting a new life. It was the time of the Early American look in home furnishings, and colonial motifs, American eagles, and scenes such as this covered many an easy chair, sofa, and window.

1.

AMERICAN INDIAN LOOK

1. France, c. 1880, RP cotton, AYG, 86%
2. USA, mid-20th C, dyes on paper, AYG, 105%
3. USA, c. 1900–1915, RP cotton felt, 50%
4. France, 1930s, RP silk, AYG, 66%

NATIVE AMERICANS HAVE no tradition of printing cloth, but the sophisticated patterns of their woven textiles have inspired a genre of earth-toned designs often based on zigzags, diamonds, and other angular shapes. Like American West conversational prints, these designs are a phenomenon of the twentieth century, when actual conflicts between cowboys and Indians were safely in the past, or, as in number 1, safely out of sight on cloth intended for the French market. These designs now tend to look a little quaint and nostalgic, if not downright corny. But all fashion is cyclical, and as this book goes to press, Indians and cowboys are reappearing on pajamas for men, to capitalize on precisely that nostalgia. Native-American–inspired geometric patterns, being abstract, are less explicit and seem to be on their way to becoming a fashion classic—called the "Santa Fe," or "desert," look.

1.

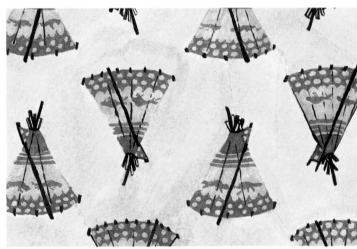

2.

3.

4.

BANDANNAS

1. USA, c. 1880, RP cotton, A, 33%
2. France, c. 1880, RP cotton, A, 50%
3. USA, c. 1880, RP cotton, A, 50%
4. France, 1880, RP cotton, A, 50%
5. USA, 1912, RP cotton, A, 50%

THE WORD "BANDANNA" comes from the Hindustani *bandhnu* (tie-dye), suggesting that these oversize men's handkerchiefs once bore the soft-edged abstract patterns that distinguish that old hand-dyeing technique. But by the nineteenth century the bandanna had become a field for all kinds of machine-made designs—geometric, floral, and conversational. Notable among the latter were the commemorative prints, such as number 5, run off as souvenirs of political campaigns and other historic events. Teddy Roosevelt liked bandannas and wore one when he led his Rough Riders in the Spanish-American War of 1898–99 (number 5 was printed by the National Kerchief Company for his Bull Moose party campaign). Their association with the cowboy, who used them to protect his neck from the sun and his mouth and nose from the dust of the trail, give bandannas a special place in masculine affections. Whatever the design, the classic color combination is red and white, with blue and white running second.

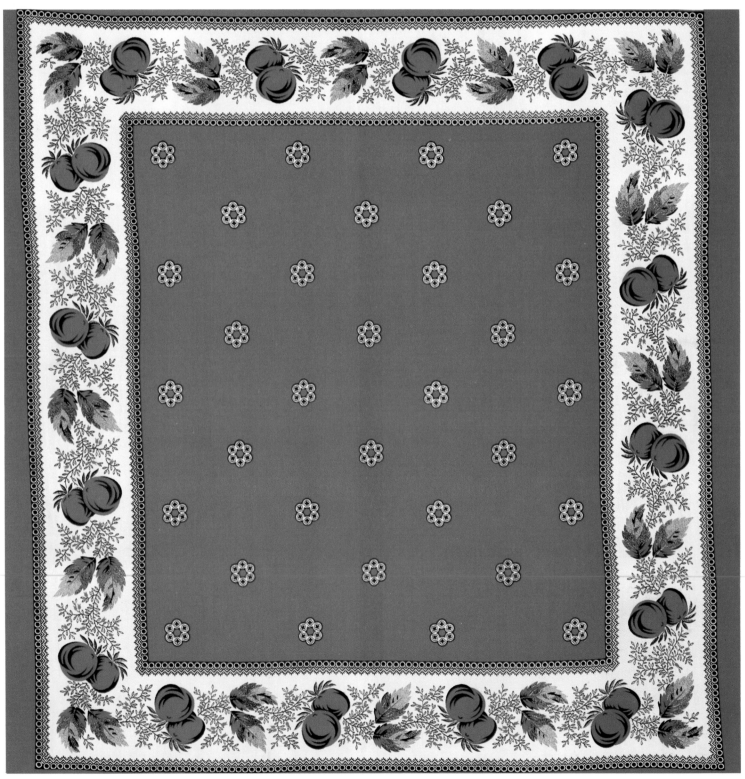

1.

2.

3.

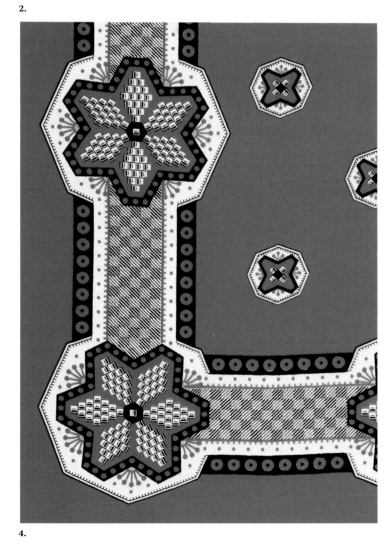

4.

5.

BATIK AND INDONESIAN LOOK

1. **England, mid-19th C, RP cotton, AYG, 100%**
2. **France, 1888, RP and BP cotton, AYG, 100%**
3. **European, early 19th C, BP cotton, AYG, 40%**
4. **Probably England, early 20th C, RP cotton, AYG, 40%**
5. **Switzerland, 1903, RP cotton, AYG, 70%**

THE TRADITIONAL INDONESIAN batik artist draws a pattern directly on the cloth, using a tool called a *tjanting* to apply a resist of melted wax. The cloth is dyed and the wax removed, leaving relatively color-free designs in the areas it has covered. To speed the process, the wax can be stamped on with a *tjap* (a wooden block in which copper strips are inserted)—or a Western designer can try to approximate the look in a conventional print. The examples shown here were made in Europe for export to the Far East, a trade that flourished from the mid-nineteenth century until World War II. (As with the African look, the Dutch have managed to preserve a share of this business as well, exporting to the rest of Europe, Africa, and America mechanically printed batik made with a wax-resist process.) Number 1, designed for the Surabaya market, is not imitating batik; instead it uses Indonesian shadow puppets as its theme.

1.

2.

3.

4.

5.

CARPET PATTERNS

1. France, 1898, RP cotton velvet, HFYG, 37%
2. France, 1892, RP cotton rep, HFYG, 44%
3. France, last quarter 19th C, RP silk satin, HFYG, 50%
4. France, 1898, RP cotton velvet, HFYG, 47%
5. France, c. 1890, gouache on paper, HFYG, 50%

THE PATTERNS OF Near Eastern carpets inspired Western home-furnishing prints throughout the nineteenth century, particularly during the last quarter, when Egypt, Turkey, and Persia became regular stops on the grand tour, now traveled by the expanding upper-middle class as well as by the aristocracy. The Turkish-boudoir look eventually developed into a classic Victorian interior style, replete with ottomans and hassocks upholstered in faux-Oriental carpets like those illustrated here. Back then, these designs were usually printed on fabrics (often velvet) woven to simulate the texture of a carpet. Today, on lighter-weight material, they have made the transition from home furnishings to apparel.

1.

2.

3.

4.

5.

CHINOISERIE

1. England, c. 1810, BP cotton chintz, HFYG, 100%
2. France, 1928, gouache on paper, HFYG, 70%
3. France, c. 1880, gouache on paper, HFYG, 58%

"CHINOISERIE" IS A French term that is applied in textiles to a Western interpretation of Chinese motifs. The West has been fascinated by Oriental design since Marco Polo's return to Venice from the court of Kublai Khan in 1295. But chinoiserie as such did not appear until the eighteenth century, when its great popularizers were the French court painter Jean Baptiste Pillement and Madame de Pompadour. According to Ernst Flemming's *Encyclopedia of Textiles,* Madame de Pompadour was a major shareholder in the Compagnie des Indes and as such favored Chinese and Indian textiles, whose motifs were consequently copied by French manufacturers. Chinoiserie remains a classic and widely used theme particularly in home furnishings and still, after nearly a century of intermittent civil war and revolution in China, perpetuates the Western romantic fantasy of paper lanterns, pagodas, dragons, and mandarin court scenes.

1.

2.

3.

EGYPTIAN LOOK

1. France, c. 1880, RP cotton, AYG, 100%
2. France, 1920s, RP silk chiffon, AYG, 100%
3. England or France, c. 1850, gouache on paper, AYG, 100%
4. France, 1881, RP cotton, HFYG, 66%

ANCIENT EGYPTIAN DEVICES began to appear in printed textiles after Napoleon's 1798–99 campaigns in North Africa. They grew more common as the nineteenth century advanced and as more Europeans visited Egypt, but their real popularity came after 1923, when Howard Carter and the earl of Carnarvon excavated the tomb of Tutankhamen, exposing its exotic relics to the modern air. The repercussions were profound for the sciences of archaeology and women's fashion. Egyptian art and hieroglyphs are based on flat forms that transfer well to cloth. Neither schematic nor coldly rational, their strong sense of order is enriched by the mysteries of their symbolism. When the famous exhibition of objects from King Tut's tomb began to tour in the mid-1970s, a resurgence of Egyptian-look fashions was expected. But it never arrived, probably because the hostile political climate in the Middle East took precedence over the aesthetic appeal of Egyptian art when it came to dollars-and-cents manufacturing decisions.

1.

2.

3.

4.

EXPORT GOODS— ENGLAND TO INDIA

1. **England, 2d half 19th C, RP cotton, AYG, 120%**
2. **England, 2d half 19th C, RP cotton, AYG, 100%**
3. **England, 2d half 19th C, RP cotton, AYG, 100%**
4. **England, 1896, gouache on paper, AYG, 60%**
5. **England, 2d half 19th C, RP cotton, AYG, 100%**
6. **England, 2d half 19th C, RP cotton, AYG, 52%**

WITH THE INTRODUCTION of mechanized mills in the early nineteenth century, the cost of producing cloth was drastically reduced. Cotton imported raw from the colonies to Europe, where it was woven and printed, and then shipped back to the colonies, was actually cheaper in those foreign markets than the local stuff made by hand. Manchester cotton exports to colonial India were inexpensive enough to clothe millions. The designs combined Indian and Western motifs. Even when India developed its own industrial mills, British law restricted their manufacturers from competing in their own market. Many Indian mill owners actively supported the independence movement led by Mahatma Gandhi, who after World War I began to organize a boycott of British cottons. In 1931, on a visit to Manchester, the heart of the English cotton-printing industry, Gandhi assured the city's workers he meant them no ill. He also remarked later, and more pointedly, "I'm no mechanic, but I've seen enough up here in three days to show me that the English are using antiquated machinery. It probably explains their inability to compete with other countries. The machinery in the Bombay and Ahmedabad mills is one hundred percent more efficient." Whether that was true or not, the proclamation of India's independence in 1947 was a serious blow to the already declining textile-printing industry in Great Britain.

1.

2.

3.

4.

5.

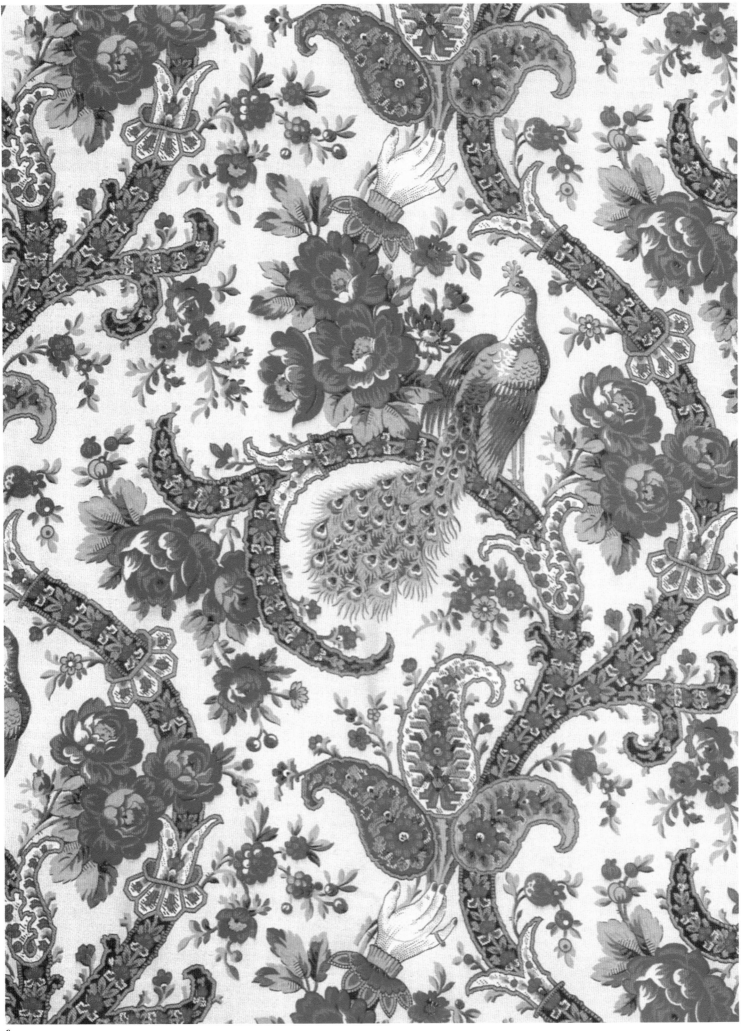

6.

EXPORT GOODS— FRANCE TO AFRICA

1. **France, late 18th C, wood-block impression on paper, A (scarf border), 100%**
2. **France, late 18th C, wood-block impression on paper, A (scarf border), 50%**
3. **France, late 18th C, wood-block impression on paper, A (scarf border), 50%**
4. **France, late 18th C, wood-block impression on paper, A (scarf border), 100%**

THESE INDIENNES DE TRAITE (trade indiennes), as they were called, were produced in eighteenth-century France for export to Africa, where they were traded for slaves. In France itself the possession of human beings was illegal, but French merchants were free to ship slaves across the Atlantic to sell in the Americas—from where in turn cotton was sold to Europe for, among many other uses, *indiennes de traite.* The system had a self-sustaining logic, then, particularly when one remembers that the cotton was raised and harvested by slave labor. Many of the motifs on this cloth were made explicitly African, to suit the tribal chiefs for whom it was intended; red-and-black was a particularly popular color combination. All the examples below—by Petitpierre et Favre of Nantes—were printed on paper as sample proofs; on cloth, the colors would have been deeper and brighter. (See also *Ethnic: African Look,* pages 360–61.)

1.

2.

3.

4.

EXPORT GOODS— ENGLAND TO THE MIDDLE EAST

1. England, 2d half 19th C, RP cotton, A (scarf), 53%

THIS COTTON SCARF, or bandanna, dyed Turkey red and printed in Manchester, must have been intended for the Middle Eastern market—there was no domestic trade in motifs like this one. The complete scarf was printed twice, selvage to selvage, on cloth thirty-six inches wide, and continuously repeated through the length of the bolt. It was in this form that it was sold from the mill. Occasionally an English quilt will turn up with a backing made of two joined lengths of this type of export cloth. Since it was not sold domestically, one can only speculate as to how it made its way from the mill to the cottage where it was sewn up.

1.

EXPORT GOODS— RUSSIA TO AFGHANISTAN AND UZBEKISTAN

1. Russia, 1st half 20th C, RP cotton, AYG, 50%
2. Russia, late 19th C, RP cotton, AYG, 50%
3. Russia, 2d half 19th C, RP cotton, AYG, 29%
4. Russia, 2d half 19th C, RP cotton, AYG, 36%

RUSSIA, TOO, PRODUCED inexpensive cottons to be bartered in trade with its "colonies"—the outlying lands not ethnically Russian but either within or adjoining the country's borders— and with the nomadic peoples who wandered the trade routes between Afghanistan and Persia. Export of these prints began in the nineteenth century and has continued through the twentieth. Often florals, paisleys, or imitations of embroidery, they are designed as bright-colored folk or peasant looks of no particular sophistication. Bold reds, pinks, yellows, and greens are the usual palette. The cloth is made into everyday garments, but not fine wear; an Afghan silk ikat coat, for example, often has a cheap Russian print as its inner lining.

1.

2.

3.

4.

EXPORT GOODS— ENGLAND TO PORTUGAL, SHANGHAI, AND SURABAYA

IN THEIR MANUFACTURING heyday, the Western industrial countries sold cloth wherever they could find a profitable market, and they made it a practice to modify their prints to the local taste. Number 1, with its characteristic cobalt blue background, wide-stripe layout, and vase of flowers, was part of a genre of designs so commonly sold to Portugal that they are now thought of generically as Portuguese. The Chinese-style motif of number 2 was intended for a Shanghai buyer, and number 3, with its Indonesian look, was to go to Surabaya.

1. **England, mid-19th C, RP cotton, HFYG, 39%**
2. **England, c. 1927, RP cotton, AYG, 60%**
3. **England, c. 1927, RP cotton, AYG, 64%**

1.

2.

3.

FOLKLORIC

1. France, c. 1945, RP silk, AYG, 84%
2. USA, c. 1940s, RP cotton, AYG, 84%
3. France, 1941–45, paper impression, AYG, 94%

"FOLKLORIC" IS A catchall market term for the folk designs and motifs of Europe's past, whether eastern European, Slavic, Nordic, or unplaceable. It is not in fact intended so much to suggest a particular ethnic group as to evoke a colorful, faintly exotic time and place, unsophisticated yet not primitive—the European equivalent of the Americana look, as though the premodern peasantry really had life good. (See also *Ethnic: Tyrolean Look,* page 405.)

1.

2.

3.

GREEK LOOK

1. France, 1938, watercolor on paper, 70%
2. France, 1860–80, paper impression, A (scarf border), 75%

THE EIGHTEENTH-CENTURY beginnings of the printing industry coincided with the great revival of classical antiquity in European culture, and ancient Greek motifs have appeared on printed cloth throughout its modern history. Number 1, a rare pictorial pattern, depicts Iphigenia, daughter of Agamemnon, king of Mycenae, and Clytemnestra. In one version of the story, the goddess Artemis demanded Iphigenia's death as a sacrifice if Agamemnon were ever to reach Troy, which he planned to besiege, and he was obliged to kill his daughter after her own gift to the gods, perhaps the box she holds in her hand, failed to please them. Subsequently Clytemnestra killed Agamemnon, and Iphigenia's brother Orestes killed Clytemnestra and then went mad. Such is Greek tragedy—far more popular with playwrights than with textile designers. However, the Greek key, the classical fretwork device in number 2, is a widely used border motif. It is a symbol of eternity, for it has no beginning and no end.

1.

2.

HAWAIIAN

1. USA (Hawaii), 1940s, SP rayon, AYG, 50%
2. USA (Hawaii), 1950s, SP rayon, AYG, 50%

TRADITIONAL HAWAIIAN DRESS does not include shirts; they didn't arrive until the nineteenth century, when Christian missionaries decided they had a moral imperative to improve upon the local nakedness. By the 1920s, shirtmaking was a regional industry supported in part by the thousands of United States military personnel stationed there. Patterns were often adapted from old designs on tapa cloth, the indigenous fabric made from the bark of the *wauke* plant, and at first they had symbolic meaning, at least for the native people who knew their history. Yet they also appealed to the increasing numbers of visitors to the islands. By the mid-1930s, the souvenir-shirt business was large enough to require factories of its own, and Hawaiian shirts only grew more popular as armies of Americans passed through the islands during and after World War II. The style has continued its appeal with the growth of the leisure-wear industry. The patterns have long since been commercially designed; they no longer have their old Polynesian symbolism, but the fact that their splashy color and bold designs have been introduced into the casual wardrobes of American men does say something about changes in taste and in the attitudes that underlie it.

1.

2.

JAPONISME

1. France, c. 1900, gouache on paper, HFYG, 50%
2. France, 1882, RP polished cotton, HFYG, 50%
3. France, 1879, RP cotton jacquard, HFYG, 50%

JAPAN REFUSED MOST contact with the West until 1853, when Commodore Matthew Perry sailed an American naval squadron into Kurihama harbor with a letter from President Millard Fillmore demanding the opening of trade. Nine years later, a display of objects bought in Japanese shops and bazaars by the first British ambassador to Japan, Sir Rutherford Alcock, was displayed in the "Japanese Court" at the International Exhibition in South Kensington, London. In 1867 the shogun, whose dynasty was to be abolished the following year, tried to raise funds by sending some of his own possessions to a similar exhibition in Paris. This was the European public's first exposure to real masterpieces of Japanese art. By the 1870s, as Sir Ernst Gombrich writes in *The Sense of Order,* Westerners thought of the Japanese as artists to rival the ancient Greeks, whose works were considered the epitome of classical art. The new imports from the East were tremendously influential for artists and designers. The stylized but fluid renderings of nature and the asymmetrical spacing seemed to fulfill a need that European artists had sensed but had not met.

1.

2.

3.

MEXICAN, PRE-COLUMBIAN, AND SOUTH AMERICAN LOOKS

THE HAPPY PEASANT woman, the tequila bottle, the pistol, guitar, siesta, spurs, and sombrero: such is Mexico, at least as Western textile designers used to depict it. (Today, the public's heightened social consciousness would probably keep such stereotypes from making it to the marketplace.) Numbers 5, 7, and 8 adopt motifs from classic pre-Columbian art; number 6 imitates a *mola,* a cotton cloth of layered appliqués made by the Cuna people of the San Blas Islands, off the north coast of Panama.

1. USA, 1930s–40s, RP cotton, AYG, 70%
2. USA, 1950s, SP cotton, HF (dish towel), 50%
3. USA, 1950s, SP cotton, AYG, 40%
4. USA, 1950s, SP cotton, HF (tablecloth), 50%
5. France, 1920s–30s, RP or SP silk crepe, AYG, 72%
6. France, 1960s, gouache on paper, AYG, 30%
7. France, 1920s–30s, paper impression, AYG, 40%
8. France, 1960s, dyes on paper, AYG, 50%

1.

2.

3.

4.

5.

6.

7.

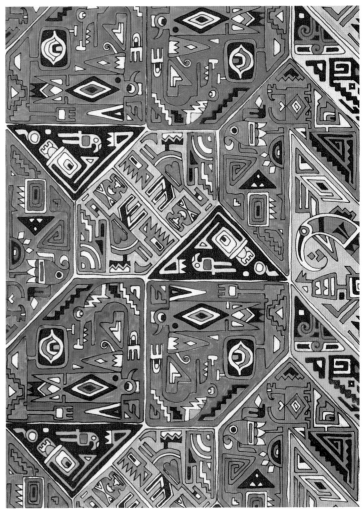

8.

NETHERLANDISH LOOK

WOODEN CLOGS, WHITE caps, windmills, and tulips are usually found in prints with a Dutch theme, which most often are intended for children's wear. Holland, like Mexico, has been reduced on cloth to a group of stereotyped motifs, not particularly appreciated by natives of these countries.

1. USA, 1920s–30s, RP cotton, AYG, 110%
2. France, c. 1890, RP cotton, AYG, 86%
3. Probably Europe, c. 1900, RP cotton, A (handkerchief), 45%
4. Probably Europe, c. 1900, RP cotton, A (handkerchief), 88%
5. Probably France, c. 1920, RP cotton, AYG, 50%

1. Scotland or England, mid-19th C, BP wool, A (shawl), 27%

1.

2.

3.

4.

5.

OTTOMAN LOOK

1. **France, 1920s–30s, RP or SP silk velvet, AYG, 56%**
2. **Probably USA, c. 1950s, RP synthetic, AYG, 90%**
3. **Probably France, 1930s, RP silk, AYG, 100%**
4. **c. 1960s, SP cotton blend, AYG, 60%**

THE OTTOMAN COURT was rich in sumptuous silks and velvets, often with woven-in or embroidered patterns of stylized carnations, such as those in numbers 1, 2, and 3. These prints are Western versions of the Turkish designs. Early Ottoman brocades sometimes display bold, highly sophisticated abstract shapes that strike today's viewer as extremely contemporary, yet it is the more traditional, familiar floral patterns that nineteenth- and twentieth-century designers have drawn upon for reproduction.

1.

2.

3.

4.

PAISLEY: ALLOVER

1. **France, c. 1870–80, RP wool challis, AYG, 70%**
2. **France, 1920s, gouache on paper, AYG, 50%**
3. **France, 2d half 19th C, RP wool challis, AYG, 60%**
4. **France, c. 1920s, gouache on paper, AYG, 56%**
5. **France, c. 1850, gouache on paper, A (shawl pattern), 66%**

THE PAISLEY MOTIF (also known as the pine) has become the subject of a great deal of sometimes argumentative scholarship. It is generally agreed, however, that the paisley's characteristic teardrop shape evolved out of a stylized plant form—stem, drooping flower head, and bulbous root system—that is found woven into seventeenth- and eighteenth-century Indian cashmere shawls. These shawls arrived in Europe during the eighteenth century, to the delight of those who could afford them. By the early 1800s, they had become a fashion necessity of the very wealthy. A fine shawl, which might take an Indian weaver up to five years to make, cost as much as a London town house. In order to make an even stronger appeal to the tastes of the European market, Western designers were hired to develop patterns; these were then sent to India, where they were reinterpreted by Indian weavers. The resulting shawls, a mixture of East and West, met with rapid success, and the paisley shape and pattern became more and more elaborate as the decades went by. By 1850, a writer in the London *Journal of Design* could write that any manufacturer producing this "fine form" "is sure of the patronage of large numbers out of pure regard for the old friendly shape."

2.

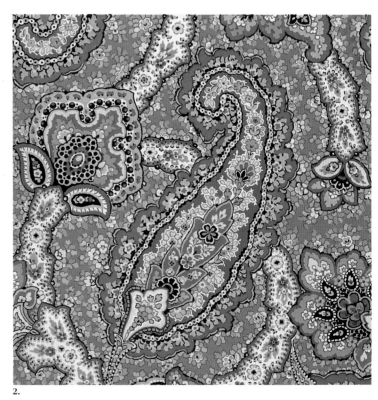

4.

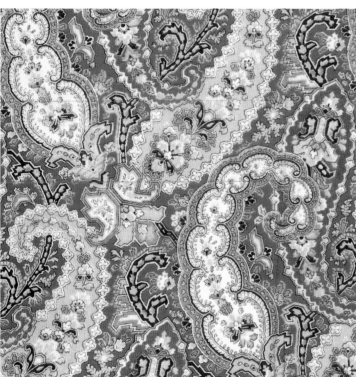

1.

3.

5.

PAISLEY: BOTEH

1. **France, c. 1800–1810, gouache on paper, A (scarf border), 105%**
2. **France, c. 1800–1810, gouache on paper, A (scarf border), 100%**
3. **France, c. 1800–1810, gouache on paper, A (scarf border), 48%**
4. **France, c. 1820–30, gouache on paper, A (scarf border), 76%**
5. **France, c. 1820, gouache on paper, A (scarf field), 100%**
6. **France, c. 1800–1810, gouache on paper, A (scarf border), 86%**

THE BOTEH IS the large paisley form found in the borders of an Indian cashmere shawl, where it was a handwoven motif; Western designers of the early nineteenth century adapted it in far less expensive prints. But by the 1830s this particular style of paisley had gone out of fashion. The boteh—the name is Anglicized from the Hindi *buta,* or flower—is usually found in set and spaced layouts, or as the motif in a row along a border. Among the Western contributions to paisley design was a preference for allover layouts in which the forms flow around each other in elaborate profusion, and these rich designs quickly replaced orderly boteh patterns in the public's taste. It is rare nowadays to see a simple paisley, except in foulard prints.

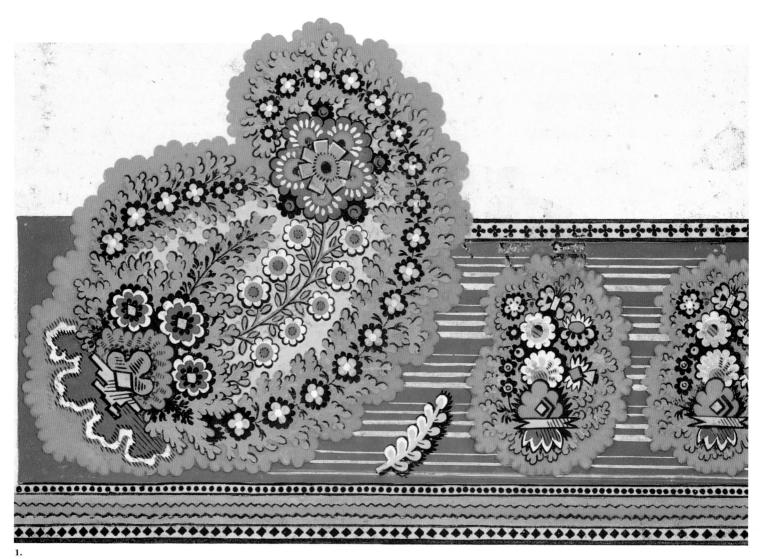

1.

2.

3.

4.

5.

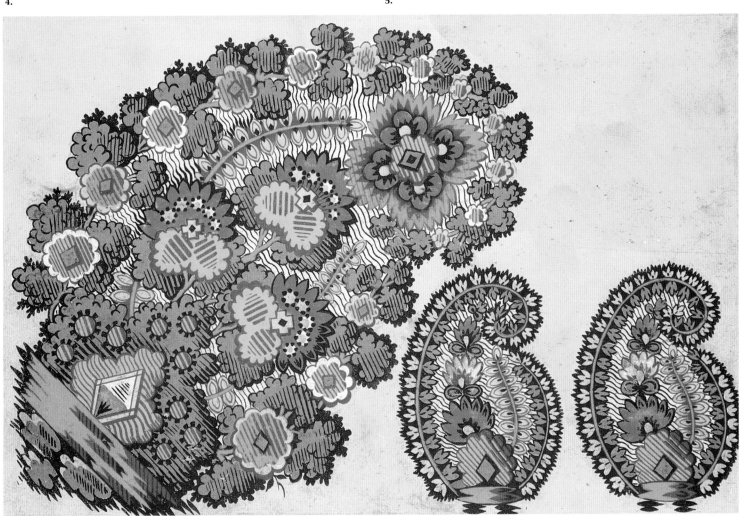

6.

PAISLEY: BUTI

1, 7, 24, 29, 31, 40. France, c. 1830–40, gouache on paper, AYG, 100%

2, 20. France, c. 1810–20, BP cotton, AYG, 100%

3, 4, 6, 8–10, 12, 15–19. France, c. 1810–20, gouache on paper, AYG, 100%

5. France, 1890, gouache on paper, AYG, 110%

11. France, 20th C, gouache on paper, AYG, 100%

13. France, c. 1860, gouache on paper, AYG, 100%

14. France, 1825–30, BP cotton, AYG, 100%

21, 23, 25–28, 30, 32–34, 36, 38, 39. France, c. 1810–20, gouache on paper, AYG, 100%

22. France, c. 1820–40, RP and BP cotton, AYG, 100%

35. France, c. 1910–20, RP silk, AYG, 100%

37. France, c. 1840–50, RP wool challis, AYG, 100%

"Buti" is the Hindi word for small flower, and this smaller abstraction of the boteh was a filler pattern in Indian woven shawls. It unobtrusively filled out the field of the shawl, taking second place to the more dominant boteh border. Common on Western printed yard goods throughout the first half of the nineteenth century, butis were often designed with hatching to simulate their woven models, and they usually became the main motif in small-scale repetitive patterns. Although the buti's slightly exotic, stylized flower form is capable of fine sophistication and endless variation, it has all but disappeared from twentieth-century textile prints—a motif waiting to be rediscovered.

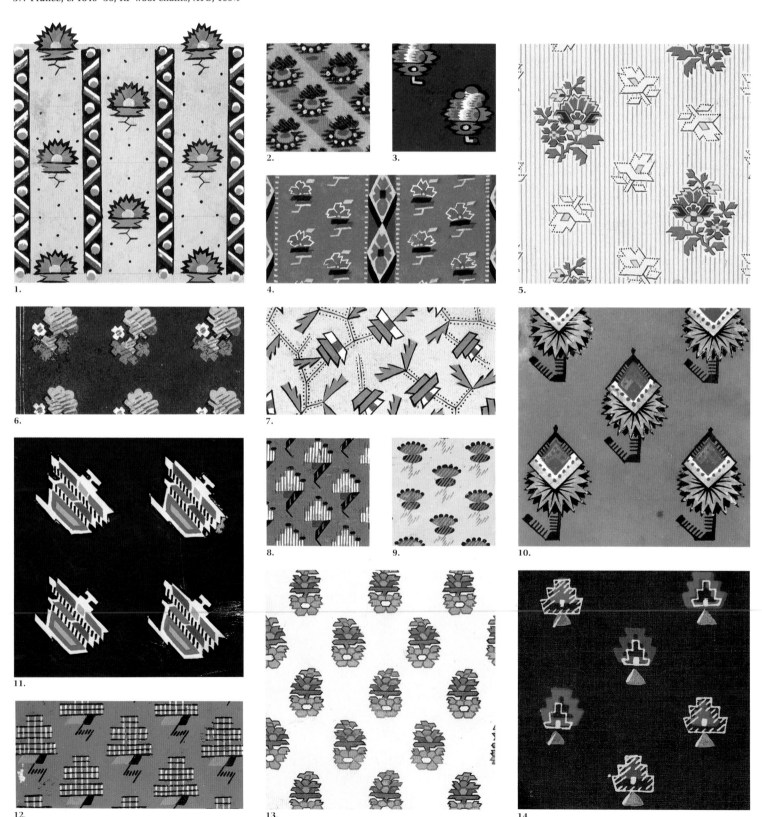

1.
2.
3.
4.
5.
6.
7.
8.
9.
10.
11.
12.
13.
14.

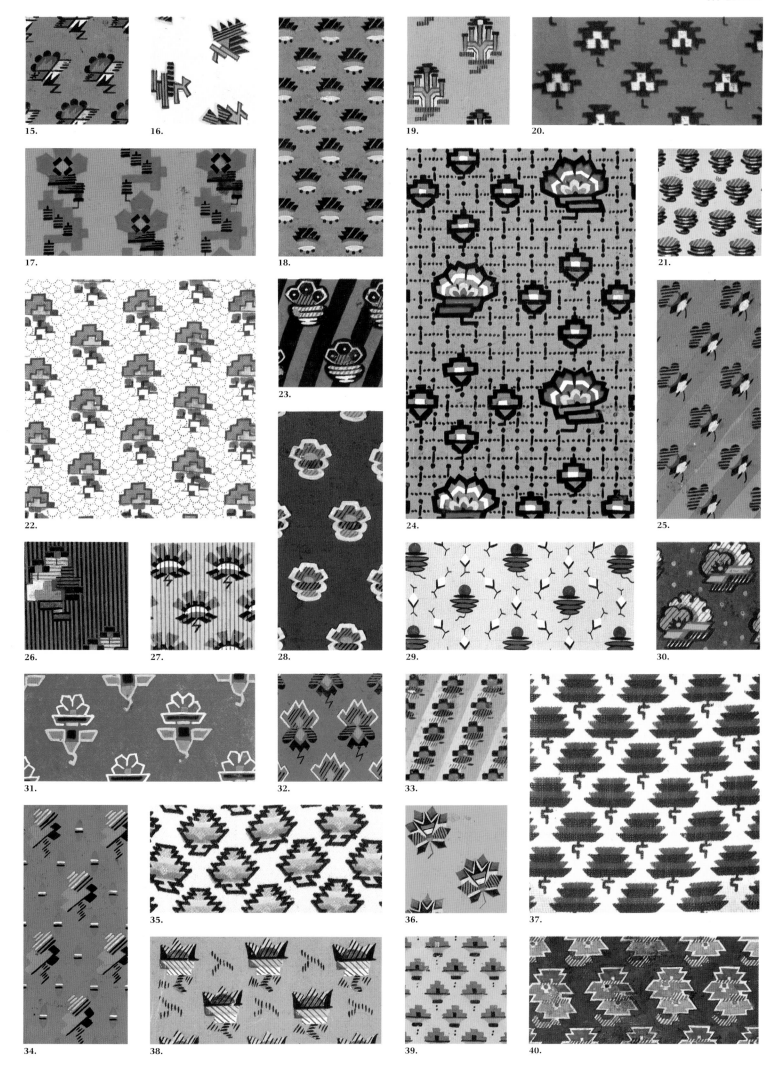

15.

16.

17.

18.

19.

20.

21.

22.

23.

24.

25.

26.

27.

28.

29.

30.

31.

32.

33.

34.

35.

36.

37.

38.

39.

40.

PAISLEY: FOULARDS

SMALL-SCALE PAISLEYS have become a staple foulard pattern—an exception to that genre's customary geometric motifs. For the man who is a very conservative dresser, paisley foulard ties provide an acceptable dash of color and design.

1. **Probably England, 20th C, BP silk, A (tie pattern), 100%**
2. **Probably England, 20th C, BP silk, A (tie pattern), 100%**
3. **Probably England, 20th C, RP or SP silk, A (tie pattern), 100%**
4. **Probably England, 20th C, RP or SP silk, A (tie pattern), 100%**
5. **England, 20th C, BP silk, A (tie pattern), 100%**
6. **England, 20th C, BP silk, A (tie pattern), 100%**
7. **Probably England, 20th C, RP or SP silk, A (tie pattern), 100%**
8. **England, 20th C, BP silk, A (tie pattern), 100%**
9. **England, 20th C, RP or SP silk, A (tie pattern), 100%**

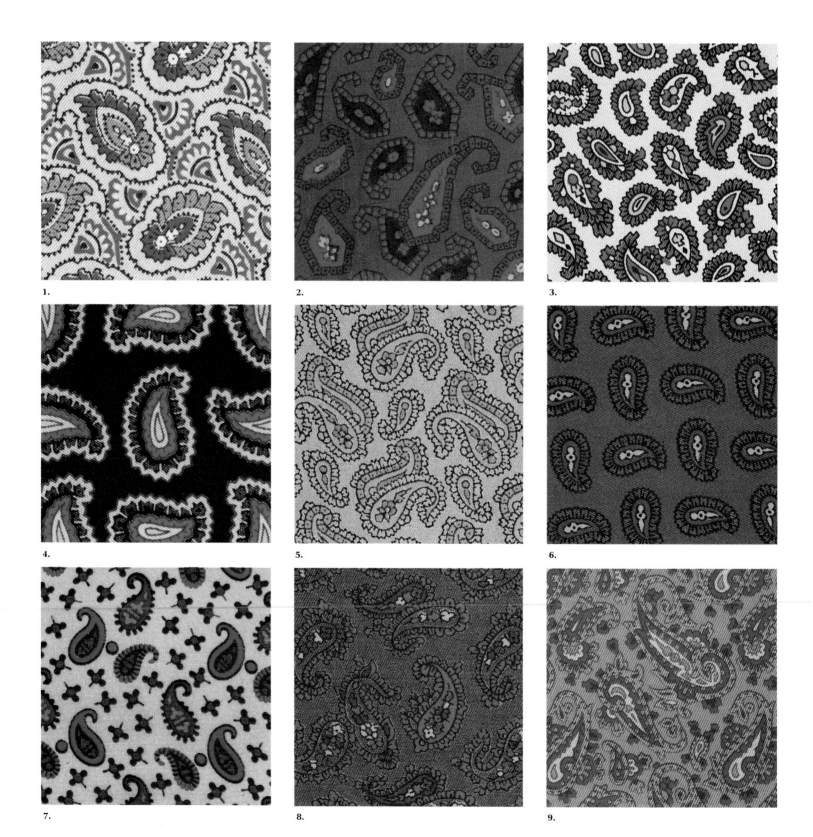

1.

2.

3.

4.

5.

6.

7.

8.

9.

PAISLEY: SHAWLS

1. Scotland or England, mid-19th C, BP wool, A (shawl), 27%

THE ORIGINAL CASHMERE shawls from which the paisley pattern derived were remarkable garments and extraordinarily expensive. Although the English had access to them first, through the East India Company, it is said that the craze for the shawls was sparked when Napoleon gave one to Josephine (who amassed more than sixty of them). Anything as desirable as this was bound to be reproduced in more affordable forms. The paisley motif, in fact, gets its name from the town of Paisley, in Scotland, where the enterprising mill owners of the early nineteenth century began to copy the Indian shawls on mechanical jacquard looms that could weave cloth into a pattern in a fraction of the time it took to weave a shawl by hand. The wraps they produced were handsome and relatively inexpensive, but printed paisleys were even cheaper. By the late 1860s any serving maid could afford a printed shawl for a few shillings. That in itself was enough to make her mistress stop wearing paisley shawls, but the coup de grâce was the introduction of the bustle in 1869, a dress accessory that interfered with the drape of the shawl. An entire industry perished. In India, whole villages had done nothing but weave cashmere shawls for two hundred years. With a change of fashion in the West coinciding with famine in India, thousands of these villagers died. But their shawls survived, cherished as heirlooms and museum pieces.

1.

PAISLEY: STRIPES

THE PAISLEY MOTIF was also arranged in a stripe layout—not nearly as popular a format as the lavish allovers, though in the mid-nineteenth century a striped paisley shawl called a zebra was briefly in fashion.

1. France, mid-19th C, BP paper impression, AYG, 50%

1.

PAISLEY: TURKEY REDS

AMONG THE MOST riotous designs of the nineteenth century were the Turkey reds—a suitable partner for the ever-wilder paisley. The combination was particularly favored in Russian export fabrics, French provincial scarves, and English and Scottish Turkey-red yard goods. (See also *Floral: Turkey Reds,* pages 130–31.)

1. France, c. 1820, BP cotton, A (scarf border), 58%
2. France, c. 1820, gouache on paper, AYG, 60%
3. England or Scotland, 2d half 19th C, RP cotton, HFYG, 45%

1.

2.

3.

PERSIAN LOOK

1. France, c. 1880, gouache on paper, HFYG, 50%

THIS PATTERN WAS almost certainly copied directly from a Persian carpet or brocade, as it would be unusual for a French designer to depict the hunted animals' wounds so graphically. The design's existence probably reflects the popularity of Near Eastern patterns toward the end of the nineteenth century. Today, and perhaps even then, the goriness of the painted design would be toned down before the final rendering was approved for printing.

1.

POMPEIIAN LOOK

1. France, 1883, gouache on paper, HFYG, 25%

POMPEII WAS A fashionable resort for classical Romans: the town was near the sea, and its Hellenic past gave it a graceful style. On August 24, A.D. 79, it was buried deep under a shower of pumice and ash from the erupting Mount Vesuvius. Nothing more happened in the history of Pompeii until 1748, when a man digging a well uncovered some of its relics, setting off a series of exploratory excavations. Exposed to the light of day, the city's buildings, furniture, and frescoes were highly influential in eighteenth-century decorative art and architecture. The Louis XV style in France was decisively affected by them, and the Scotsman Robert Adam, later the court architect to George III, on visiting the Pompeiian ruins in 1756, was inspired by their "Greco-Roman" combination of symmetry and spirit. By 1800 the palette of the city's frescoes—their earthy reds, mustard yellows, and blacks—was familiar enough in England to have earned its own adjective, "Pompeiian"—although on home-furnishing fabrics it was usually only the coloring that bore any resemblance to the architectural decorations at Pompeii. The design below, however, incorporates both the motifs and the colors of those ancient paintings, though in characteristic French fashion, it is more ornate.

1.

RUSSIAN LOOK

1. 1950–60s, SP wool challis, A (scarf), 86%
2. France, c. 1880, gouache on paper, AYG, 74%
3. France or England, 2d half 19th C, RP cotton, AYG, 115%
4. France, c. 1820, gouache on paper, A (scarf border), 50%

THE ARISTOCRACY OF czarist Russia tended to look to Europe for its fashions, dressing as if the court were in Paris. (A number of nineteenth-century Alsatian printers, in fact, set up mills in Russia for the production of French-style designs.) But it was a genre of prints for the common folk that came to be regarded by Western Europeans as an ethnic Russian look: full-blown pink and red flowers with bright green leaves, usually on dark grounds of black or red challis, though sometimes on fields of white. Number 1 might still be worn by an old-fashioned *babushka* today. Numbers 2, 3, and 4 resemble the cotton cloth Russia used to export to its various outlying ethnic regions, but in fact they are all French designs. (See also *Ethnic: Export Goods—Russia to Afghanistan and Uzbekistan,* page 378.)

1.

2.

3.

4.

TIE-DYE LOOK

1. England, 2d half 19th C, RP cotton, AYG, 88%
2. Probably Europe, 20th C, RP cotton, AYG, 100%
3. France, c. 1890–1900, RP wool challis, AYG, 52%
4. Probably Europe, 20th C, SP silk, AYG, 50%

CALLED SHIBORI IN Japan, *plangi* in Indonesia, and *bandhana* in India, tie-dyeing is an ancient hand-dyeing technique traditional in many parts of Asia and Africa. The bare cloth is pulled into bunches and tied tightly according to the type of pattern desired. After it is dipped in dye and then untied, ornamental patterns are left where the layering of the fabric has prevented or slowed the color's penetration. Or, alternatively, the look can be approximated in a machine-made print. Number 1 imitates an Indian pattern and was probably intended for export to India; numbers 2 and 3 are Western copies of Japanese tie-dye. The style goes in and out of vogue along with the particular ethnic look it conjures up. Its association with 1960s hippie T-shirts produced a backlash in the 1970s and 1980s, but in 1990, with the 1960s back in fashion, so is tie-dye—in the American hippie look.

1.

2.

3.

4.

TYROLEAN LOOK

1. USA, 2d quarter 20th C, RP cotton, AYG, 90%
2. USA, c. 1940s, SP rayon crepe, AYG, 105%
3. Probably USA, 2d quarter 20th C, SP cotton, AYG, 90%
4. Probably Switzerland, 2d half 19th C, BP cotton, A (scarf), 36%

THIS SPECIALIZED FOLKLORIC look features motifs associated with the Tyrol, the Austrian and Italian regions of the Alps bordering Switzerland—hearts and naive flowers, young men in lederhosen and women in long aproned dirndls, chalets, and cows wearing bells. The folkloric look in general is a perennial, sometimes more and sometimes less popular but never completely absent from the fashion scene.

1.

2.

3.

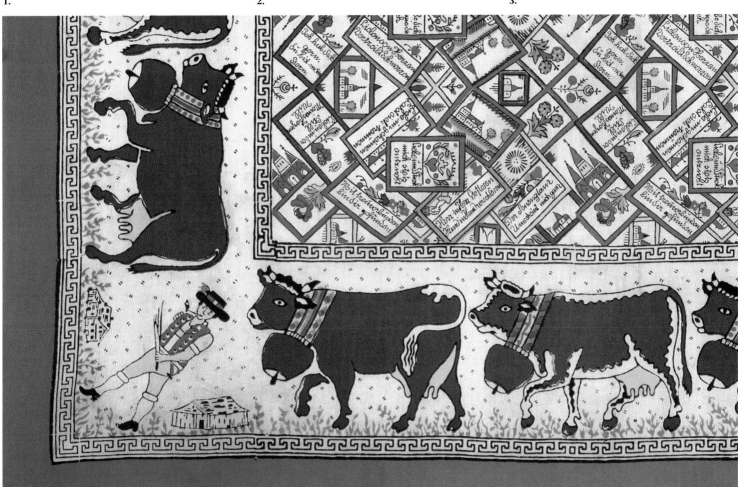

4.

5. Art Movements and Period Styles

THE DESIGN ARTS of the West change incessantly, generating new looks whose names eventually become familiar—Arts and Crafts, Belle Epoque, and so on. All these styles are reflected in printed cloth. Sometimes the fabric is designed by people consciously seeking to shape the look of their time, by ambitious artists such as Frank Lloyd Wright and William Morris or the more fashion-oriented Paul Poiret and Mario Fortuny. Designers like these are often the links between cloth and the fine arts—they are part of the art movements and ideas of the age, and are moved to carry them through in textiles. Styles like Biedermeier or psychedelic, on the other hand, have no notable figures associated with them but reflect a kind of consensus of the taste or zeitgeist of a period. That taste can be vernacular and street (as in punk) or educated and refined (as in Art Nouveau). And the period may last just a few years before it begins to look outdated, or, like Biedermeier, it can become a home-furnishing staple, manufactured so consistently since its initial appearance that it eventually connotes no particular time at all.

Styles that outlive their first life inevitably come to coexist with other patterns quite different in origin. Though a period may have a dominant look—making it possible, say, to talk of 1960s as opposed to 1950s fashions, or of Victorian as opposed to Modern—it and every other era will be well stocked with hints of what is to come and reproductions of what came before. Sometimes the throwbacks go back a long way. Thus alongside the styles that actually do belong to the two hundred years of fabric printing, this chapter includes patterns that re-create the look of the more distant past—of the Renaissance, say, or of the Middle Ages, or of the Jacobean period. A medieval pattern designed in the nineteenth century cannot really be called a medieval pattern; we would call it a medieval look.

Textile design, like any other art, or, indeed, any kind of creation at all, cannot help but reflect its time. To find a market, or even to be made in the first place, a pattern must somehow reflect the contemporary mood—even while it plays its part in creating that mood. Though a Renaissance-look print made in 1900 is certainly an impostor, it is no less genuine a response to the needs of its time than, say, an Art Nouveau print made in the same year. In fact, "look" patterns like these embody the elements of wish fulfillment that fabric printing very democratically makes possible: pick your fantasy, from virtually any point in history, and textile designers will meet it, usually most affordably. In this sense, the fabric designs of an era are like a gigantic book of dreams waiting for their Freud.

Art-movement patterns are no less revealing; if anything, their fantasy is the easier to comprehend because it is more explicitly articulated, not only in the print itself but in the prose explanations that art of ambitious intentions tends to attract. The creators of such prints are something of an anomaly in this book, for they are far better known than the average, usually anonymous, textile designer. Having boasted of the democratic nature of printed cloth, however, one must include the nobs and toffs along with the everyday hard workers. Their designs, on the whole, are really quite good.

AESTHETIC AND ARTS AND CRAFTS

1. "Compton," England, 1896, designed by John Henry Dearle for Morris and Co., BP cotton, HFYG
2. England, c. 1895, designed by C. F. A. Voysey for Liberty's, RP cotton velvet, HFYG
3. England, 1884, designed by Arthur Silver for Liberty's, RP cotton, HFYG
4. "The Four Seasons," England, 1893, designed by Walter Crane for Liberty's, RP silk

THE SOCIAL CONTEXT of the Aesthetic and Arts and Crafts movements was the industrial revolution; when its novel machinery spewed goods in unprecedented quantity into store and home, far-reaching questions were raised about the social role of the worker and, more generally, about the character of everyday life. A number of artists and authors—William Morris, John Ruskin, Oscar Wilde, and others—tried to reassert the value of beauty in this brave new world. A love of beauty, however, can take many forms, and the movements included both elitist young dandies who espoused an exaggerated doctrine of art for art's sake and serious artists trying to revive a medieval-guild or cottage-craft kind of workplace. The Aesthetic Movement peaked in the 1870s, but its attempt to bring together good design and modern technology was carried on by the Arts and Crafts Exhibition Society, founded in England in 1887 to promote the decorative arts, whose worth the Royal Academy had refused to recognize. Fundamental to both movements was a Ruskinesque reverence for nature—sunflowers, lilies, and peacocks were favorite motifs—in a palette of soft browns and terra-cottas, moss greens, and yellows. It was Morris's desire to restore the dignity of the worker, to unite the craftsman and the artist. Many of his designs were produced by hand. Ironically, this made most of them too expensive for the ordinary worker to buy.

1.

2.

3.

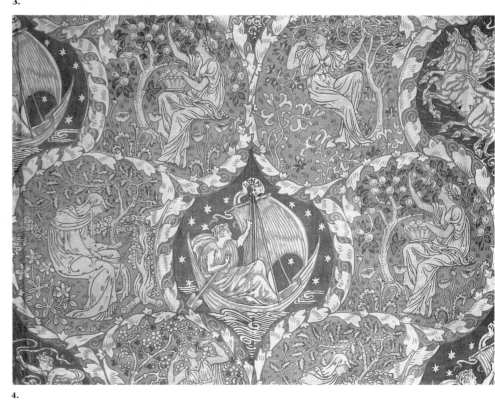

4.

ART DECO: CONVERSATIONAL

1. **France, 1925, designed by Mme. de Andrada for Paul Dumas, SP cotton, HFYG, 40%**
2. **France, 1920s, designed by Auguste H. Thomas, from *Formes et Couleurs*, 16%**
3. **"Antelopes," France, 1930, designed by Paul Poiret for F. Schumacher & Co., SP cotton percale, HFYG**
4. **France, 1920s, designed by Auguste H. Thomas, from *Formes et Couleurs*, 16%**

ART DECO, OR Art Moderne, was one of the dominant design modes of the years between the world wars, emerging in the early 1920s and crystallizing as a movement with the Paris "Exposition Internationale des Arts Décoratifs et Industriels Modernes," in 1925. (Though the term Art Deco abbreviates the *Arts Décoratifs* of the exposition's title, it was not coined until the 1960s, which saw a revival of interest in the style.) Pattern number 1 was exhibited in the show. Numbers 2 and 4 are from a portfolio of pochoir plates, a kind of reference book for designers. Number 3 was created by the couturier Paul Poiret. Poiret's career began well before the Art Deco period; he opened his first shop in Paris in 1903. Tremendously influential, he is credited with freeing twentieth-century women from the Victorian corset, designing clothes to follow rather than force the lines of the body. He was also, as the founder of the Atelier Martine, responsible for a wide variety of handsome household furnishings. The organizers of the 1925 exposition told the press, "It is possible to hold this event only because of the impetus that Paul Poiret has given to modern decorative arts." Yet in 1913, a visitor to an Atelier Martine show had exclaimed, "If we accept rugs like that, we might just as well hang Cézanne in the Louvre."

1.

2.

3.

4.

ART DECO: FLORAL

1. **France, 1920s–30s, pencil on paper, HFYG, 50%**
2. **France, 1930s, gouache on paper, A (scarf pattern), 50%**
3. **France, 1922, RP cotton sateen, HFYG, 50%**
4. **France, 1930, RP cotton sateen, HFYG, 50%**

ART DECO GATHERED influences from the preceding two decades of modern art, combining the geometric planes of Cubism, Futurism's celebration of speed and machine technology, the Constructivists' love of industrial materials and usable objects, and a Fauvist or Ballets Russes feeling for color and simple, flattened shapes. The Poiret-like roses of number 3, for example, have a primitivist simplicity and boldness that would not seem out of place in certain kinds of traditional folk costume, particularly as interpreted by the Ballets Russes. But the fractured roses and triangles of number 4 look distinctly Cubist and twentieth century.

1.

2.

3.

4.

ART DECO: GEOMETRIC

1. France, 1930s, gouache on paper, A (scarf pattern), 40%
2. France, 1933, paper impression, AYG, 50%
3. Germany, 1930s, gouache on paper, AYG (tie pattern), 70%
4. France, 1924, gouache on paper, AYG, 100%
5, 6. Germany, 1930s, gouache on paper, AYG (tie pattern), 100%
7. France, 1920s, SP cotton, AYG, 70%
8. Germany, 1930s, gouache on paper, AYG (tie pattern), 85%
9. Germany, 1930s, gouache on paper, AYG (tie pattern), 90%
10. USA, 1920s–30s, gouache on paper, AYG, 100%
11. USA, 1920s–30s, RP silk, AYG, 70%

ART DECO HAS been divided into three periods: the "zigzag moderne" of the 1920s, exemplified by the angled lines of the Chrysler Building in New York and by sharp-edged motifs of sunbursts and stylized animals; the "streamlined moderne" of the early 1930s, when straight lines and points were smoothed and curved as if swept by the wind; and the "classical moderne" associated with the years of the Depression, a more austere look based on modern stylizations of neoclassical forms. Though most of the patterns shown here are European, the United States produced much work of high quality in the Art Deco style. Yet when the French invited the United States to participate in the 1925 "Exposition Internationale des Arts Décoratifs et Industriels Modernes," Herbert Hoover, then secretary of commerce, declined, remarking that the country had nothing modern to show.

1.

2.

3.

4.

5.

6.

7.

8.

9.

10.

11.

ART NOUVEAU: CONVERSATIONAL

1. France, 1898, designed by Alphonse Mucha, RP cotton velvet, HFYG, 32%
2. France, 1895, designed by M. P. Verneuil, from *L'Animal dans la Décoration*, 105%
3. France, 1895, designed by M. P. Verneuil, from *L'Animal dans la Décoration*, 64%
4. France, 1895, designed by M. P. Verneuil, from *L'Animal dans la Décoration*, 64%
5. France, 1895, designed by M. P. Verneuil, from *L'Animal dans la Décoration*, 64%

THE PERIOD OF Art Nouveau lasted from the late 1880s to about 1910; it was a fin-de-siècle style, although its very name, "new art," showed a desire to abandon the past and to embrace the future. The movement began in Britain but spread quickly through Europe, called *stile Liberty* in Italy (after Liberty's, the trend-setting London department store), *Jugendstil* in Germany, *Sezessionstil* in Austria, *Modernista* in Spain, and *style moderne* in France. Number 1 was designed by Alphonse Mucha, the Parisian expatriate Czech artist particularly remembered today for his posters. Mucha was so closely associated with Art Nouveau that the Parisian art critic Edmond Goncourt referred to it as "style Mucha." The snails in number 5 illustrate the decorative power of Art Nouveau: most fabric designers would have avoided them altogether because of their suggestion of sliminess, but here their silver trails become positively elegant.

1.

2.

3.

4.

5.

ART NOUVEAU: FLORAL

1. France, 1897, designed by Félix Aubert, RP cotton velvet, HFYG, 26%
2. France, 1904, RP cotton velvet, HFYG, 38%
3. France, 1901, RP cotton velvet, HFYG, 38%
4. France, 1898, RP cotton velvet, HFYG, 40%
5. France, 1904, RP cotton velvet, HFYG, 40%

ART NOUVEAU DESIGNERS favored motifs from nature, but they did not espouse social causes or argue aesthetic doctrine. The idealists of the Arts and Crafts group considered Art Nouveau a decadent style: Walter Crane is said to have described it as "that strange decorative disease," and C. F. A. Voysey believed that it was "out of character with our national character and climate." Ironically, these sinuous-lined designs are perhaps the truer realization of the Aesthetic Movement's "art for art's sake." Art Nouveau textiles and decorative objects—often produced in rich, luxurious materials for the upper end of the market—never caught on with a wide public and unlike Art Deco have never been the subject of a popular revival. The distortions of Art Nouveau's motifs, its complexly intertwining shapes, and its sophisticated color palette may have proved vaguely disquieting to many potential customers.

1.

2.

4.

3.

5.

BAROQUE AND ROCOCO LOOKS

1. France, 1893, RP cotton velvet, HFYG, 43%
2. France, c. 1880, gouache on paper, HFYG, 39%

THE TERM "BAROQUE" describes a long period in European art, from the late sixteenth century until the mid-eighteenth century. The Rococo style, which grew out of the Baroque, developed in France during the first half of the eighteenth century, and reflects the cult of sensuousness prevalent in the reign of Louis XV. The original English meaning of the word "baroque" was "odd" or "grotesque"; it seems to have originated as a Portuguese jeweler's term for a misshapen pearl. To the authors of *The Oxford Companion to the Decorative Arts,* the Baroque is characterized by "floridity, grandiloquence, and exuberance." The *Oxford English Dictionary,* meanwhile, defines "Rococo" as "conventional shell- and scrollwork and meaningless decoration; excessively or tastelessly florid or ornate." (Number 1 shows the typical *rocaille,* or shell shape, that gave the Rococo its name.) What seems to have earned these styles their derogatory handles is their horror of empty space, which they tended to fill with a multitude of curlicues and arabesques. Yet many textiles in these modes are rich and elegant, finding harmony in their abundance—like the Baroque-look number 2. And their echoes of the ancien régime make them attractive to the modern aristo manqué.

1.

2.

BELLE EPOQUE

1. **France, 1898, RP cotton velvet, HFYG, 45%**
2. **France, 1899, RP cotton velvet, HFYG, 39%**
3. **France, 1896, RP cotton velvet, HFYG, 27%**

BELLE EPOQUE DESIGNS epitomize high Victorian style, evoking the stuffy parlors of the 1890s—every surface covered with pattern, none of it matching. Fabrics were heavy and colors cloying—fleshy salmon pinks, acid greens, poisonous blues. These were the interiors that were swept away by the bare walls of Modernist architecture.

1.

2.

3.

BIEDERMEIER LOOK

1. France, 1906, RP cotton, HFYG, 48%
2. Germany, c. 1900–15, RP cotton, HFYG, 44%
3. France, 1898, RP cotton, HFYG, 50%
4. France, c. 1900, RP cotton, HFYG, 40%

GOTTLIEB BIEDERMEIER WAS a fictional character, an archetype up for grabs by any writer out to satirize the safe lives of the Austrian and German bourgeoisie in the years between the fall of Napoleon, in 1815, and Europe's year of revolutions, 1848. The decor to which Biedermeier gave his name is characterized by its safeness, the colors neither too bright nor too pale, the motifs neither small nor large, the layouts predictably regular; everything right down the middle. There is always a market for conservative prints, and the Biedermeier look is still produced, though it is seldom called by that name. None of the patterns below, in fact, is a genuine Biedermeier; all are later additions to the genre. Numbers 1, 3, and 4 were made in Alsace for the German market during the period after the Franco-Prussian War when the province was a German possession. Number 2 is a direct Biedermeier descendant.

1.

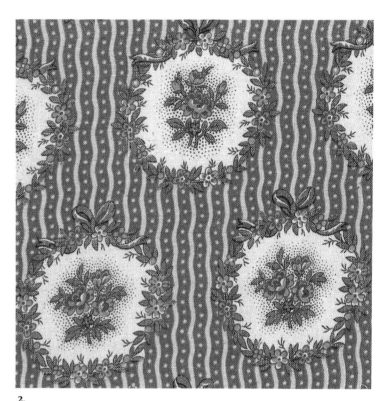

2.

3.

4.

EMPIRE

1. France, c. 1810–15, BP cotton, border pattern, 80%
2. France, c. 1810–15, gouache on paper, border pattern, 100%
3. France, c. 1810–15, BP cotton, border pattern, 80%

ON MAY 18, 1804, Napoleon promoted himself from first consul of France to emperor. (Later in the year Pope Pius VII came to Paris to perform the coronation but, as the story goes, was too slow for the great general, who snatched the crown from the pontiff's hands in the middle of the ceremony and put it on himself.) The style named for the period when France was an empire had begun to emerge a little earlier: it was essentially neoclassical, featuring literal copies of ancient furniture and decorative motifs. In textiles, the colors appropriate to an imperial power were popular—gold, crimson, purple, royal blue. The laurel wreath, symbol of victory, and the oak leaf or acorn, emblematic of strength, were common motifs. Dolphins, swans, acanthus leaves, and formal medallions were also favorites, and of course, the Napoleonic bee—which Napoleon appropriated from Egyptian hieroglyphics and made his personal emblem.

1.

2.

3.

FAUVE LOOK

1. **France, c. 1920, designed by Raoul Dufy for Bianchini-Férier, gouache on paper, AYG**
2. **France, 1920s, designed by E. A. Séguy, from** *Bouquets et Frondaisons,* **70%**
3. **France, 1925, paper impression, AYG, 25%**
4. **France, 1920s, designed by E. A. Séguy, from** *Bouquets et Frondaisons,* **70%**
5. **France, 1920s, SP silk satin, AYG, 70%**

AT THE PARIS Salon d'Automne of 1905, the critic Louis Vauxcelles, finding a Renaissance-style statue surrounded by walls of modern paintings, exclaimed loudly, "Donatello au milieu des fauves!" (Donatello among the wild beasts). Purely by accident, Vauxcelles had named an art movement, led by Henri Matisse and distinguished by vivid and surprising color. Fabric patterns like these were certainly influenced by the Fauves, but they relate even more closely to Sergei Diaghilev's Ballets Russes, which made their first appearance in Paris in 1909. Like the Fauves, Léon Bakst, designer of sets and costumes for Diaghilev, used intense clashing colors and bold motifs, starting a fashion trend. Right through the 1920s and into the 1930s women wore turbans, harem pants, Persian jackets, and slave bracelets inspired by the exotic, sensual costumes of the Ballets Russes. The motifs were highly stylized, flat, and almost primitive, but the result was extremely sophisticated. Number 1 was painted by a genuine Fauve, Raoul Dufy, one of the few artists who have achieved success as both painter and textile designer.

1.

2.

3.

4.

5.

GOTHIC REVIVAL

1. **France, c. 1830–40, RP cotton, HFYG, 50%**
2. **USA, c. 1840, RP cotton, AYG, 98%**
3. **France, c. 1830–40, gouache on paper, AYG, 60%**
4. **Probably France, c. 1840–50, RP wool challis, AYG, 145%**

GOTHIC REVIVAL was one of the dominant styles in British architecture from shortly after 1800 until the early twentieth century, and it was also popular on the Continent and in America. Like Pre-Raphaelite painting and the medieval tendencies of the Aesthetic and Arts and Crafts movements, it reflected a longing for a time before the industrial revolution, a time when beautiful churches could be built by hand through the collaboration of whole communities, in an ennobling kind of labor far removed from the dehumanizing factories of the Victorian age. Gothic Revival textiles were produced simultaneously with the resurgences of interest in the Gothic.

1.

2.

3.

4.

GRAFFITI

1. USA, 1988, designed by Keith Haring for Stephen Sprouse, SP cotton, AYG, 22%
2. USA, 1988, designed by Keith Haring for Stephen Sprouse, SP polyester, AYG, 23%

GRAFFITI HAVE BEEN found in the ruins of ancient Pompeii and Rome, but the style shown here has its roots in the American inner cities, and particularly New York, of the 1970s, when an unusually pictorial kind of graffiti began to appear on walls, subway trains, and, eventually, in photo spreads in books and magazines and on canvases in art galleries. Unlike most of the graffitists who made "tags"—pictorial versions of their own signatures—the late Keith Haring had an art-school education and made actual pictures—of people, dogs, babies, mutating TV sets. But it was surely graffiti that alerted him to the possibility of working in public spaces, and there was a great deal of exchange between him and the graffitists, as well as mutual respect. Haring's early-1980s chalk drawings in the New York subways became so popular that the posters he drew on were often stolen as soon as he'd finished with them. This was one reason he began to make more formal artworks. But Haring was a genuine populist and never gave up his love of outdoor murals and of cheap goods such as T-shirts, buttons, and fabrics like these—the same pattern printed in two different color schemes.

1.

2.

JACOBEAN LOOK

1. France, c. 1920s, BP linen, HFYG, 25%

KING JAMES I of England gave the Latin form of his name, Jacobus, to the Jacobean age and to a style of seventeenth-century decor distinguished by elaborate carving, heavy oak furniture, fine tapestries, and crewel embroidery with flowing arborescent designs. It is this crewelwork that is imitated in later, Jacobean-look prints. The original patterns seem to have had two principal sources: Flemish verdure tapestries, imported by the British on a grand scale in the seventeenth century and themselves derived from older Gothic designs; and Indian palampores, also a popular imported textile. (The English East India Company had been founded to trade with the East in 1600, three years before James came to the throne.) Both the tapestries and the palampores featured acanthus-like leaves filled in with allover patterns. But the palampore flowering trees were not purely Indian inventions: like modern Jacobean-look prints, many contained motifs modified from English crewelwork, sent to Indian craftsmen by British merchants to copy for the home market. This kind of recirculation of influences is commonplace in the hybrid world of fabric design.

1.

MEDIEVAL LOOK

1. France, 1885, RP cotton, HFYG, 54%
2. France, 1883, RP cotton, AYG, 70%
3. France, c. 1850–60, RP cotton chintz, HFYG, 50%

VARIOUS KINDS OF medieval ornament appear from time to time on printed fabrics, reproduced by methods their original makers could not have imagined. Number 2 is inspired by a tapestry, number 3 by an illuminated manuscript. Number 1 combines numerous motifs of medieval culture—the mosaic, the griffin, and Gothic tracery—probably all taken from a nineteenth-century reference book such as Auguste Racinet's *L'Ornement Polychrome* or Owen Jones's *The Grammar of Ornament*.

2.

3.

1.

MEMPHIS

1. "Congo," Italy, 1982, designed by Nathalie Du Pasquier, SP fabric, HFYG
2. "Kenya," Italy, 1982, designed by Nathalie Du Pasquier, SP chintz, HFYG
3. "Gabon," Italy, 1982, designed by Nathalie Du Pasquier, SP chintz, HFYG
4. "Rete," Italy, 1983, designed by Ettore Sottsass, SP fabric, HFYG
5. "Letraset," Italy, 1983, designed by Ettore Sottsass, SP fabric, HFYG
6. "Zambia," Italy, 1982, designed by Nathalie Du Pasquier, SP chintz, HFYG
7. "Zaire," Italy, 1982, designed by Nathalie Du Pasquier, SP chintz, HFYG
8. "Triangolo," Italy, 1983, designed by Ettore Sottsass, SP fabric, HFYG

FOUNDED IN 1981 by a group of Milanese architects and designers, among whom Ettore Sottsass was the best known, the Memphis company represented a reaction against classic Modernist interior design, with its neutral chrome and glass, its strict geometries, its logic of severity. Memphis objects and textiles would offer unfamiliar shapes, with a luxury of uncalled-for curves and angles; their colors would cover the bright primaries and everything in between, including overpowering purples and pinks and clashing uncomplementaries. This was attention-getting stuff, a wild child's version of design. When you enter a room of Memphis decor, everything in it stands up and says hello.

1.

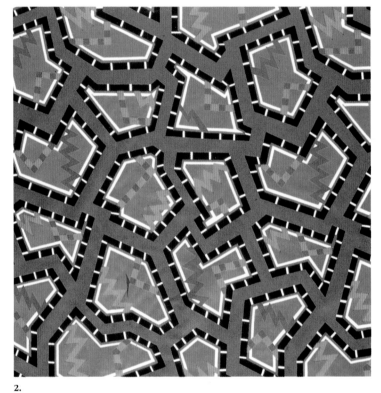

2.

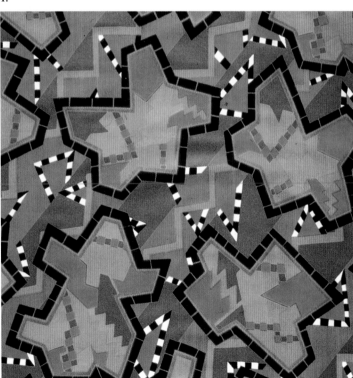

3.

4.

5.

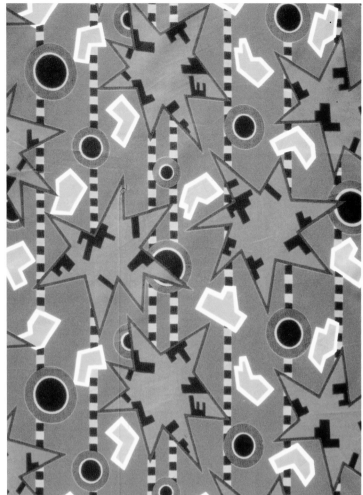

6.

7.

8.

MODERNISM

1. USA, 1955, designed by Frank Lloyd Wright for F. Schumacher & Co., SP linen, HFYG
2. USA, 1957, designed by Frank Lloyd Wright for F. Schumacher & Co., SP cotton, HFYG

THE MODERNIST SENSE of the twentieth century as unlike any preceding era could invest the everyday household object with a whole aesthetic and social philosophy. The designer of these prints, the architect Frank Lloyd Wright, wanted to shape not only the buildings that would shelter modern living but every interior detail of furnishings and fabrics, and he also tried to control the way the structure related to its surroundings. Wright's house-as-total-environment was just one of Modernism's many utopian visions. Two decades earlier, across the Atlantic in Germany, the Bauhaus designers also produced coordinated architecture, fabrics, and furnishings—but no prints. The Modernist tenet that form should follow function actually discriminates against prints, which as purely surface decoration create patterns that in no way relate to the weave. Wright designed number 1, a spin-off from one of his stained-glass windows, for F. Schumacher & Company's "Taliesin Line" of wallpapers and fabrics, which was inaugurated in 1955. He was paid $10,000 to begin the line, then $1,000 per pattern, plus a 25-cent royalty per yard sold. The fabrics ranged in price from $3.40 to $15.50 a yard. Patterns were added and dropped from the line until it was discontinued, in 1972.

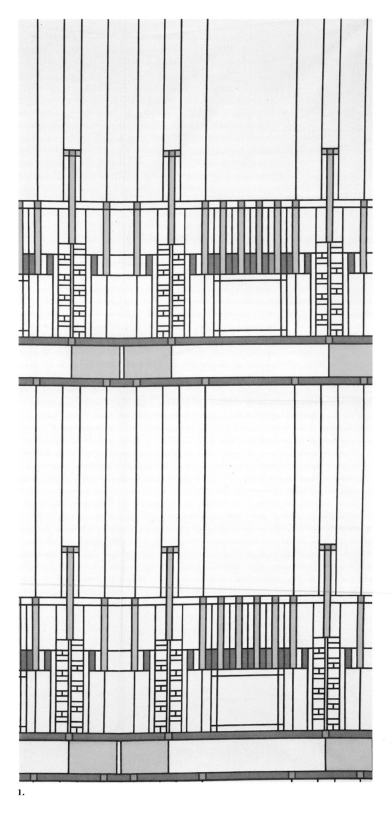

1.

2.

NEOCLASSICAL

1. France, c. 1815, gouache on paper, HF (carpet pattern), 76%
2. France, c. 1815, gouache on paper, HF (carpet pattern), 76%
3. "Allégorie à l'Amour," France, c. 1815, RP cotton, HFYG, 35%

THOUGH ANCIENT GREECE and Rome have been a source of inspiration for European artists since the Renaissance, the term "neoclassical" usually refers to an imitation of classical style that began in the mid-eighteenth century. A return to a simpler, more austere mode after the exuberant ornament of the Rococo, the movement was sparked in part by the discovery in 1748 of the ruins of Pompeii, a relatively small town of a graceful domesticity far more endearing than the imposing monuments of imperial Rome. Yet neoclassicism's urns, arabesques, and medallions quickly became a rather stuffy formal style, suitable for grand houses and occasions of state. Number 3 is an allegorical toile in the neoclassical taste of the day, by Favre Petitpierre et Cie of Nantes. (See also *Art Movements and Period Styles: Empire,* page 425.)

1.

2.

3.

PSYCHEDELIC

1. USA, 1960s, gouache on paper, AYG, 54%
2. France, 1960s, dyes on paper, AYG, 50%

TRADITIONALLY, FASHION HAS filtered down from the upper echelons of society to the lower ones. But in a reversal of that process, 1960s fashions emerged from the street, defying social conformity. Psychedelics were one such vogue. Their swirling shapes and neon colors seemed to capture on cloth the hallucinations of an acid trip, which is exactly what their name implies. This was no subtle message; it was a shrill scream of awakening. Psychedelic patterns were associated with a youth culture's dawning self-awareness and with a whole package of ideas about society, politics, and pleasure. Almost twenty-five years later, in 1990, the fashion world resurrected the psychedelic look. Another generation of youth is wearing it, but the social statement of the 1960s was so powerful that the neon seems dim without it.

1.

2.

PUNK

1. France, 1980s, gouache on acetate, AYG, 58%
2. France, 1980s, gouache on acetate, AYG, 58%

PUNK DRESS WAS the ultimate glorification of street fashion: aggressive, pulled together by the people who wore it, a nose-thumb to all conventional style. The youths of late-1970s punkdom may have had to buy their T-shirts and jeans, but they could rip them and stain them until the clothes were more their own creation than the manufacturers'. The new look was immediately interesting to the entrepreneurs of the garment business, which began to produce punk fashions; however, the very idea of mass-produced nihilist clothing is contradictory. The wearer of a garment-industry–designed punk print is announcing loudly, "I tried to come up with my own look, but I failed."

1.

2.

RENAISSANCE LOOK

1. Italy, early 20th C, designed by Mario Fortuny, stenciled silk velvet, HFYG
2. Italy, early 20th C, designed by Mario Fortuny, stenciled cotton, HFYG

THE RENAISSANCE LOOK is a genre of patterns inspired by the sumptuous handwoven fabrics of the old European aristocracy. The printed designs try to capture the richness of cut velvet, silk damasks, and brocades woven with gold and silver threads. Numbers 1 and 2 are by Mario Fortuny, the Italian designer whose couture was an expensive fashion from before World War I until his death, in 1949. Fortuny favored minimally constructed dresses that took their shape from the lines of the body. They were made in beautiful silks, velvets, and cottons, sometimes decorated with beads of Venetian glass, sometimes finely pleated by a patented process of Fortuny's invention and stenciled with classical designs. The color range was distinguished by its subtle metallics. Since the designer's home was Venice, the Italian Renaissance was the primary source of his pattern inspiration.

1.

2.

RUSSIAN CONSTRUCTIVIST

1. USSR, 1930, designed by S. Burylin, RP cotton
2. USSR, 1924, designed by Varvara Stepanova, gouache on paper
3. "Mechanization of the Red Army," USSR, 1933, designed by L. Raitser, RP cotton sateen

THE CHANGES THAT the industrial revolution made in the way people lived in Europe and American proliferated through the nineteenth century until by the start of the twentieth a whole new age seemed imminent. That impression was particularly forceful in Russia, where, within the first two decades of the fresh century, an argumentative gaggle of revolutionaries overthrew a formidably entrenched aristocracy to found an innovative social order. Communist Russia's utopian promise seemed as vast as the practical difficulties the country faced. How logical, then, that its artists would create an art that glamorized machinery— symbol of the new world and sine qua non for the solution of its problems. To glamorize machinery, of course, was also to glamorize work, aligning the Constructivists with the proletarian ideology of the regime, which wanted people to fall in love with their tractors. Even the abstractions were idealistic, aiming at an unlocalizable, internationally understandable language that would evoke the freedom of modern speed and the geometrical forms of industrial objects. It is disquieting, however, to think that in this brave new world, the tanks and war planes of number 3 would be considered decorative.

1.

2.

3.

SUPERGRAPHICS

1. "Jokeri," Finland, 1967, designed by Annika Rimala, SP cotton, AYG and HFYG, 21%
2. "Tarha," Finland, 1963, designed by Annika Rimala, SP cotton, AYG and HFYG, 27%
3. "Joonas," Finland, 1964, designed by Maija Isola, SP cotton, AYG and HFYG, 17%
4. "Lokki," Finland, 1961, designed by Maija Isola, SP cotton, AYG and HFYG, 17%

THE FINNISH DESIGN firm Marimekko, founded by Armi and Viljo Ratia in 1951, began to export its fabrics to the United States in the late 1950s, to immediate success and much imitation. The patterns were based on bold graphic shapes in flat bright colors that often clashed. Most of all, the motifs were outsized. This declarative style was not at all nostalgic; its clean lines were totally modern. Another bold 1960s statement, it came to be known as "supergraphics."

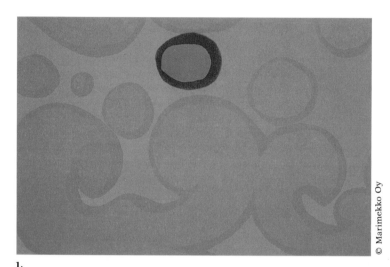

1.

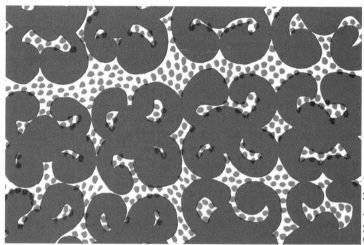

2.

© Marimekko Oy

3.

© Marimekko Oy

4.

WIENER WERKSTÄTTE

1. "Urwald," Austria, c. 1913, designed by L. H. Jungnickel, gouache on paper, 70%
2. "Wachau," Austria, 1910–12, designed by Gustav Kalhammer, BP linen, AYG, 90%
3. "Chypre," Austria, 1928, designed by Mathilde Flögl, BP or SP silk, AYG, 90%
4. "Clan," Austria, 1928, designed by Mathilde Flögl, BP or SP silk, AYG, 90%
5. "Konstantinopel," Austria, 1910–12, designed by Ugo Zovetti, BP linen, AYG, 90%

THE ARTS AND CRAFTS and Aesthetic movements' crusade to apply the highest standards of design to modern living was carried on in Austria by the Wiener Werkstätte (Vienna Workshops), founded in 1903 by Josef Hoffmann and Koloman Moser. Whereas the followers of William Morris had proposed design shops rather like the medieval guilds, the Wiener Werkstätte anticipated the Bauhaus's vision of the designer as a partner with twentieth-century industry. Its designs, too, were a bridge between the Arts and Crafts movement and the deliberately modern forms of Art Deco. The Weiner Werkstätte were indeed many workshops, producing not only metalwork, leatherwork, bookbinding, and cabinetry but eventually ceramics, carpets, wallpaper, fashion apparel, and woven, embroidered, and printed fabric. The Scottish architect and designer Charles Rennie Mackintosh was an important influence on the Wiener Werkstätte—he created a sympathetic logo for them, in fact—and the early output, following his example, was mostly quite spare and geometric. But the workshops' fabric designers soon came to relish other families of patterns, as the happily gamboling monkeys in number 1 and the typically abstract floral of number 5 attest. Though plagued by recurrent financial problems and the chaos wrought by World War I, the Wiener Werkstätte managed to stay in business until 1932.

1.

2.

3.

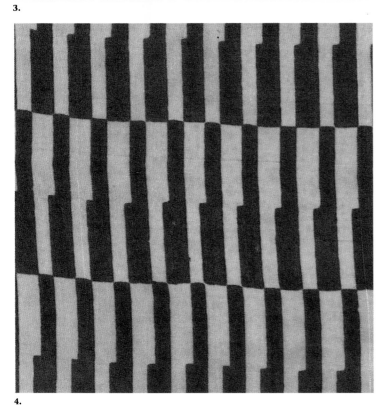

4.

5.

Bibliography

Achen, Sven Tito. *Symbols Around Us.* New York: Van Nostrand Reinhold, 1978.

Adburgham, Alison. *Liberty's: A Biography of a Shop.* London: George Allen and Unwin, 1975.

Affleck, Diane L. Fagan. *Just New from the Mills.* North Andover, Mass.: Museum of American Textile History, 1987.

Albrecht-Mathey, Elisabeth. *The Fabrics of Mulhouse and Alsace, 1750–1800.* Leigh-on-Sea: F. Lewis, 1968.

Ames, Frank. *The Kashmir Shawl.* Woodbridge, Suffolk: Antique Collectors' Club, 1986.

Aslin, Elisabeth. *The Aesthetic Movement: Prelude to Art Nouveau.* New York: Excalibur Books, 1981.

Battersby, Martin. *The Decorative Twenties.* London: Studio Vista, 1969.

Beer, Alice Baldwin. *Trade Goods.* Washington, D.C.: Smithsonian Institution Press, 1970.

Bindewald, Erwin, and Karl Kasper. *Fairy Fancy on Fabrics: The Wonderland of Calico Printing.* Braunschweig: Georg Westermann Verlag, 1951.

Bogdonoff, Nancy D. *Handwoven Textiles of Early New England.* Harrisburg, Pa.: Stackpole Books, 1975.

Brédif, Josette. *Printed French Fabrics: Toiles de Jouy.* New York: Rizzoli, 1989.

Campbell, Joseph. *The Power of Myth.* New York: Doubleday, 1988.

Cirlot, J. E. *Dictionary of Symbols.* New York: Philosophical Library, 1962.

Clouzot, Henri, and Frances Morris. *Painted and Printed Fabrics.* New York: Metropolitan Museum of Art, 1927.

Collins, Herbert Ridgeway. *Threads of History: Americana Recorded on Cloth, 1775 to the Present.* Washington, D.C.: Smithsonian Institution Press, 1979.

Crookes, William. *A Practical Handbook of Dyeing and Calico Printing.* London: Longmans, Green, 1874.

D'Allemagne, Henry-René. *La Toile Imprimée et les Indiennes de Traite.* Paris: Librairie Gründ, 1942.

Diehl, Gaston. *The Fauves.* New York: Harry N. Abrams, 1975.

Durant, Stuart. *Ornament.* London: MacDonald and Co., 1986.

Dyer, Rod, and Ron Spark. *Fit to Be Tied: Vintage Ties of the Forties and Early Fifties.* New York: Abbeville Press, 1987.

Flemming, Ernst. *An Encyclopedia of Textiles.* New York: E. Weyhe, 1927.

Forty, Adrian. *Objects of Desire: Design and Society, 1750–1980.* London: Thames and Hudson, 1986.

Fothergill, James, and Edmund Knecht. *The Principles and Practice of Textile Printing.* London: C. Griffin, 1924.

Gombrich, E. H. *The Sense of Order.* Ithaca, N.Y.: Cornell University Press, 1979.

Irwin, John. *The Kashmir Shawl.* London: Her Majesty's Stationery Office, 1973.

Irwin, John, and Katharine Brett. *Origins of Chintz.* London: Her Majesty's Stationery Office, 1970.

Jefferson, Louise E. *The Decorative Arts of Africa.* London: William Collins Sons, 1974.

Jones, Owen. *The Grammar of Ornament.* London: Day and Son, 1856.

The Journal of Design and Manufacturers. (London), 1–6: 1849–52.

Jung, Carl G. *Man and His Symbols.* London: Aldus Books, 1964.

Kallir, Jane. *Viennese Design and the Wiener Werkstätte.* London: Thames and Hudson, 1986.

Katzenberg, Dena S. *Blue Traditions: Indigo Dyed Textiles and Related Cobalt Glazed Ceramics from the 17th through the 19th Century.* Baltimore: Baltimore Museum of Art, 1973.

Larsen, Jack Lenor, with Alfred Bühler and Bronwen and Garrett Solyon. *The Dyer's Art: Ikat, Batik, Plangi.* New York: Van Nostrand Reinhold, 1976.

Lévi-Strauss, Monique. *The Cashmere Shawl.* London: Dryad Press, 1987; New York: Harry N. Abrams, 1988.

Milbank, Caroline Rennolds. *Couture: The Great Designers.* New York: Stewart, Tabori and Chang, 1985.

Montgomery, Florence M. *Printed Textiles: English and American Cottons and Linens, 1700–1850*. New York: Viking Press, 1970.

———. *Textiles in America, 1650–1870*. New York: W. W. Norton, 1984.

Noma, Seiroku. *Japanese Costume and Textile Arts*. New York: Weatherhill, 1974.

The Oxford Companion to the Decorative Arts. Edited by Harold Osborne. Oxford: Oxford University Press, 1985.

Parry, Linda. *Textiles of the Arts and Crafts Movement*. London: Thames and Hudson, 1988.

Peel, Lucy, and Polly Powell. *Fifties and Sixties Style*. Secaucus, N.J.: Chartwell Books, 1988.

Pettit, Florence H. *America's Indigo Blues*. New York: Hastings House, 1974.

Pettit, Florence H. *America's Printed and Painted Fabrics, 1600–1900*. New York: Hastings House, 1970.

Polo, Marco. *The Travels of Marco Polo (The Venetian)*. Edited by Manuel Kamroff. New York: Boni and Liveright, 1926.

Powell, Claire. *The Meaning of Flowers*. Boulder, Colo.: Shambhala Publications, 1979.

Racinet, Auguste. *L'Ornement Polychrome*. Paris: Firmin Didot Frères, 1869.

Radice, Barbara. *Memphis*. New York: Rizzoli, 1984.

Reilly, Valerie. *The Paisley Pattern*. Glasgow: Richard Drew, 1987.

Robinson, Stuart. *A History of Printed Textiles: Block, Roller, Screen, Design, Dyes, Fibres, Discharge, Resist, Further Sources for Research*. London: Studio Vista, 1969.

Rossbach, Ed. *The Art of Paisley*. New York: Van Nostrand Reinhold, 1980.

Schoeser, Mary, and Celia Rufey. *English and American Textiles, 1790–1990*. New York: Thames and Hudson, 1989.

Shirer, William L. *Gandhi: A Memoir*. New York: Simon and Schuster, 1979.

Spencer, Charles. *Leon Bakst*. New York: Rizzoli, 1973.

Steele, H. Thomas. *The Hawaiian Shirt: Its Art and History*. New York: Abbeville Press, 1984.

Storey, Joyce. *Textile Printing*. London: Thames and Hudson, 1974.

Tuchscherer, Jean-Michel. *The Fabrics of Mulhouse and Alsace, 1801–1850*. Leigh-on-Sea: F. Lewis, 1972.

Verneuil, M. P. *L'Animal dans la Décoration*. Introduction by Eugène Grasset. Paris: Librairie Centrale des Beaux-Arts, 1895.

Weber, Eva. *Art Deco in America*. New York: Exeter Books, 1985.

White, Palmer. *Poiret*. New York: Clarkson N. Potter, 1973.

Yasinskaya, I. *Revolutionary Textile Design: Russia in the 1920s and 1930s*. New York: Viking Press, 1983.

Index

Contents and Brief Introduction in French, German, Italian, Spanish, and Japanese

Table des matières

ABRÉVIATIONS

c.	(circa): environ
C	(century): siècle
BP	(block-printed): imprimé à la planche
CP	(copperplate-printed): imprimé à la planche de cuivre
PP	(perrotine-printed): imprimé à la perrotine
RP	(roller-printed): imprimé au rouleau
SP	(screen-printed): imprimé au cadre
A	(apparel): habillement
AYG	(apparel yard goods): pièces de tissu pour l'habillement
YG	(yard goods): pièces de tissu
HF	(home furnishings): ameublement
HFYG	(home-furnishing yard goods): pièces de tissu pour l'ameublement

Échelle: les dessins sont reproduits à un certain pourcentage de leur taille réelle.
Par exemple:
100%: même taille
110%: agrandi de 10%
90%: réduit de 10%

Certaines informations demeurent inconnues à ce jour, ce qui occasionne des lacunes dans quelques légendes.

Catégories de dessins

Les créateurs textile classent les dessins pour l'impression en quatre catégories: motifs floraux, motifs géométriques, motifs historiés (à un sujet ou à un thème) et dessins ethniques. A ceux-ci, nous avons ajouté une cinquième catégorie: les dessins inspirés par les tendances artistiques et les styles d'époque. Cette dernière catégorie n'en est pas vraiment une car elle n'a pas de motifs qui lui soient propres. Un motif de lis dans le style Arts and Crafts anglais de la fin du XIXᵉ est une version d'un dessin floral, et un motif de tracteur dans le genre constructiviste russe est un dessin à sujet. Mais les tendances artistiques et les styles d'époque sont tellement reconnaissables que nous leur avons donné une catégorie pour eux seuls.

Ces catégories de dessins créés pour l'impression se divisent en nombreux genres, selon un ou plusieurs des critères ci-dessous:

LE MOTIF PRINCIPAL: élément caractéristique du décor, il détermine la famille à laquelle le dessin appartient; c'est l'image de base (une rose, un carré, un clown, une palmette cachemire).

LA DISPOSITION DES MOTIFS: manière dont le motif principal est réparti sur le fond (semis régulier, jeté dans un désordre apparent ou formant des rayures).

LA COULEUR: certains dessins sont classés selon ce critère lorsqu'une teinture particulière (indigo, garance ou rouge Andrinople) apparaît comme l'élément dominant (prenant plus d'importance que le dessin).

LA TECHNIQUE D'IMPRESSION: l'ombré ou l'impression sur chaîne, parmi d'autres procédés d'impression, sont des techniques qui reproduisent un dessin en lui donnant un aspect particulier.

LA FABRICATION: le tissu sur lequel on imprime a aussi son importance. Certains d'entre eux sont étroitement associés à un style de dessin particulier. Le mot ››chintz‹‹ par exemple désigne le tissu c'est-à-dire une percale de coton glacée. Mais pour un dessinateur, cela implique un motif tout à fait précis.

Techniques d'impression

Les abréviations dans les légendes sont commentées dans la table des matières.

(BP) IMPRESSION À LA PLANCHE: déjà utilisée en Inde au IVᵉ siècle av. J.-C., c'est la plus ancienne technique d'impression. A la fin du Moyen Age, les étoffes imprimées selon ce procédé étaient régulièrement importées en Europe. Pour un même dessin, plusieurs planches de bois étaient gravées (une par couleur). La surface de la planche, gravée en relief, était appuyée sur un tamis saturé de colorant puis appliquée sur l'étoffe. Un coup de maillet sur l'envers de la planche facilitait la pénétration du colorant. L'imprimeur déplaçait ensuite la planche sur un endroit non encore imprimé de l'étoffe. Cette technique n'est plus guère employée sauf pour des tissus de luxe pour l'ameublement ou des foulards de soie, particulièrement en Angleterre.

(CP) IMPRESSION À LA PLANCHE DE CUIVRE: en Irlande et en Angleterre, Robert Jones, Francis Nixon et la fabrique de Bromley Hall ont régulièrement produit, dès 1765, des étoffes imprimées à la planche de cuivre. En France, Christophe-Philippe Oberkampf fut probablement le premier à faire marcher une presse pour imprimer à la planche de cuivre en 1770. Le dessin était gravé en creux sur une plaque de cuivre que l'on enduisait de colorant. La surface de la plaque était essuyée afin que le colorant ne restât que dans les creux de la gravure. On plaçait l'étoffe et la plaque sous une presse mécanique exerçant une très forte pression qui reportait le dessin sur l'étoffe. Les premières planches de cuivre étaient de grande dimension permettant de reproduire des dessins ayant un grand rapport. Ce nouveau procédé dit «taille douce» donna naissance à un style de tissu imprimé, les toiles à paysages ou à sujets dites «toiles de Jouy», qui reproduisaient des dessins créés par des artistes célèbres de l'époque.

(RP) IMPRESSION AU ROULEAU: l'Écossais Thomas Bell fut le premier à breveter en 1783 une machine à impression mécanique qui utilisait des rouleaux de cuivre. Un imprimeur au rouleau, avec une machine à six couleurs, produisait en une journée le travail de quarante imprimeurs à la main. Une machine française de la fabrique Oberkampf à Jouy-en-Josas pouvait en 1797 imprimer plus de 5 000 mètres par jour. La machine à imprimer au rouleau fait de l'impression sur étoffe la première industrie entièrement mécanisée et place cette industrie à l'avant-garde de la révolution industrielle; mais ce procédé est plus onéreux que l'impression au cadre qui l'a en grande partie remplacé.

(PP) IMPRESSION À LA PERROTINE: la machine dite Perrotine, inventée en 1832 par le Rouennais Louis Jérôme Perrot permettait d'imprimer mécaniquement à la planche de bois. Seule la gravure des planches était encore faite à la main. Un dessin imprimé à la Perrotine avait la précision d'une impression mécanique mais la gravure des planches à la main lui conférait un aspect «fait main».

(SP) IMPRESSION AU CADRE: l'impression au cadre plat (cadre de soie à l'origine, aujourd'hui remplacé par un voile synthétique) date des années 1920. Technique répandue en France, elle était pratique pour imprimer de petits métrages destinés à la mode (haute-couture). Actuellement la gravure se fait par procédés photographiques et l'impression au cadre rotatif allie ainsi la vitesse et la continuité de l'impression au rouleau à la qualité des aplats (couleurs vives et nettes) du cadre plat. Pour chaque couleur, il faut graver un cadre.

Musterfamilien

Textildesigner teilen Muster in vier »Familien« ein: Blumen-, geometrische, Genre- und ethnische Motive. Wir haben eine Kategorie hinzugefügt, die Kunstbewegungen und -epochen umfaßt. Diese fünf bilden die Kapitel des Buches.

Die letzte Kategorie stellt sicherlich im strengen Sinne keine Familie dar, da sie über keine eigenständigen Motive verfügt. So gehört ein »Arts and Crafts« -Lilienmotiv zur Familie der Blumenmuster, ebenso wie ein konstruktivistischer Traktor ein Genremotiv ist. Allerdings haben bestimmte Kunstbewegungen und -epochen derart eigenständige und typische Motive kreiert, daß wir uns entschlossen haben, sie in einem eigenen Kapitel vorzustellen.

Textile Designs gliedert die Musterfamilien in zahlreiche Unterkategorien, die sich an einem oder mehreren der folgenden Kriterien orientieren:

MOTIV: Dabei handelt es sich um das wichtigste Merkmal, da es bestimmt, welcher Familie ein Muster zugerechnet wird. Gemeint ist das Grundmotiv, zum Beispiel eine Rose, ein Quadrat, ein Clown oder eine Paisley-Zeichnung.

LAYOUT: Das Layout bestimmt die Anordnung des Motivs, ob es mit großen oder kleinen Zwischenräumen plaziert ist, in regelmäßiger oder gestreuter Form oder in Reihen, die Streifen bilden.

FARBE: Manche Stoffe sind nach Farben sortiert, wenn in ihnen ein bestimmter Ton das Erscheinungsbild beherrscht, so zum Beispiel Indigo, Madder oder Türkischrot.

DRUCKTECHNIK: Manche Drucktechniken ergeben ein Muster sowie ein spezifisches Aussehen, (z. B. Ombré- oder Kettdrucke).

GEWEBE: Die Struktur eines Stoffes beeinflußt das Aussehen eines aufgedruckten Motivs, und einige Gewebeformen werden automatisch mit bestimmten Mustern gleichgesetzt. So ist Chintz beispielsweise im strengen Sinne eine Gewebeart, aber Textildesigner verbinden mit dem Begriff eine Musterart.

Drucktechniken

Die verwendeten Abkürzungen finden sich im Anschluß an das Inhaltsverzeichnis.

(BP) BLOCKDRUCK: Dabei handelt es sich um das älteste Verfahren, das in Indien bereits im 4. Jh. nach Christus bekannt war. Im Spätmittelalter gehörte der Blockdruck in Europa zu den anerkannten Handwerken. Dabei werden für jede Farbe separate Druckstöcke geschnitzt, der Block mit dem erhabenen Muster wird auf ein farbgetränktes Wollsieb gedrückt und dann auf den Bedruckstoff aufgesetzt. Ein kräftiger Klüpfelschlag auf die Oberseite des Models überträgt das Muster. Nach jedem Schlag setzt man den Druckstock auf die nächste ungefärbte Stelle. Heute hat dieses Verfahren kaum noch kommerzielle Bedeutung. Es wird allerdings in kleinem Rahmen zur Herstellung von teuren Dekostoffen und Seidenfoulards, besonders in England, genutzt.

(CP) KUPFERPLATTENDRUCK: Bereits 1765 wurden Textilien in England und Irland von Robert Jones, Francis Nixon und der Firma Bromley Hall in großem Stil mit Hilfe gravierter Kupferplatten bedruckt. In Frankreich war Christophe-Philippe Oberkampf wohl der erste, der mit diesem Verfahren arbeitete, als er 1770 eine Plattendruckmaschine installierte. Das Muster wird dabei in eine Kupferplatte eingraviert, diese eingefärbt und hinterher sauber gewischt, so daß nur in den Vertiefungen Farbe verbleibt. Nun legt man den Stoff auf die Platte, und mit Hilfe einer mechanischen Presse wird das Muster übertragen. Die ersten Maschinen für dieses Verfahren waren sehr groß, damit großflächige Muster verarbeitet werden konnten. Die Technik ermöglichte den Aufstieg eines neuen Druckstils, des Toile-de-Jouy, bei dem von Künstlern entworfene, fein gravierte Genredarstellungen reproduziert wurden.

(RP) WALZENDRUCK: 1873 ließ der Schotte Thomas Bell die erste Stoffdruckmaschine, die mit gravierten Metallwalzen arbeitete, patentieren. Diese Sechs-Farben-Maschine produzierte pro Tag die gleiche Menge wie 40 Handblockdrucker. Ein französisches Modell in der Oberkampf-Manufaktur in Jouy-en-Josas brachte es auf fast 5000 Meter bedruckten Stoff pro Tag. Durch die Walzenmaschine wurde der Textildruck zum ersten voll mechanisierten Industriezweig und damit zu einem Vorreiter der industriellen Revolution. Allerdings ist das Verfahren teurer als der Filmdruck, der es heute fast vollständig ersetzt hat.

(PP) PERROTINDRUCK: Bei diesem 1834 von Louis-Jérôme Perrot aus Rouen entwickelten Verfahren handelt es sich um einen mechanisierten Handdruck, der wie der Blockdruck mit einem stempelartigen, von Hand geschnitzten Mustermodel vorgenommen wird. Diese Methode hat den Vorteil, daß sie handgearbeitete Motive mit der Präzision mechanisierter Herstellung kombiniert. Sie ist noch heute für Trachtenmuster gebräuchlich.

(SP) FILMDRUCK: Um 1920 begann man, den in Handarbeit ausgeführten Seidenfilmdruck kommerziell zu nutzen. In Frankreich erreichte das Verfahren die größte Beliebtheit, da es sich besonders für die Herstellung kleiner Mengen an Haute-Couture-Stoffen eignete. Heute werden die benötigten Schablonengitter meist fototechnisch hergestellt. Gedruckt wird mit einer Walze statt der traditionellen Rakel. So lassen sich die Vorteile des Walzendruckers (ununterbrochener Lauf, hohe Geschwindigkeit, Passergenauigkeit) mit den leuchtenden klaren Farben des drucklos arbeitenden Flachsiebs kombinieren. Für jede Farbe ist eine eigene Schablone erforderlich.

Inhalt

VERZEICHNIS DER ABKÜRZUNGEN

c.	(circa) circa
C	(century) Jahrhundert
BP	(block-printed) Blockdruck
CP	(copperplate-printed) Kupferplattendruck
PP	(perrotine-printed) Perrotindruck
RP	(roller-printed) Walzendruck
SP	(screen-printed) Filmdruck
A	(apparel) Kleidung
AYG	(apparel yard goods) Bekleidungsschnittware
YG	(yard goods) Schnittware
HF	(home furnishings) Dekostoffe
HFYG	(home-furnishing yard goods) Deko-Schnittware
Maßstab	In welchem Größenverhältnis die Reproduktion zum Original steht, ist in Prozent angegeben (z. B. 100% = Originalgröße; 110% = um 10% vergrößert; 90% = um 10% verkleinert).

Sofern einzelne Einträge fehlen, bedeutet dies, daß die Angaben nicht bekannt sind.

Indice

ABBREVIAZIONI

c.	(circa): circa	
C	(century): secolo	
BP	(block-printed): Stampa a impressione (con blocchi)	
CP	(copperplate-printed): Stampa a cilindro di rame	
PP	(perrotine-printed): Stampa Perrotine	
RP	(roller-printed): Stampa a cilindro	
SP	(screen-printed): Stampa a quadro	
A	(apparel): Abbigliamento	
AYG	(apparel yard goods): Tessuto per abbigliamento	
YG	(yard goods): Tessuto	
HF	(home furnishings): Arredamento	
HFYG	(home-furnishing yard goods): Tessuto per arredamento	
Scala	i disegni sono riprodotti in rapporto alla loro dimensione originale. Ad esempio: 100% = stessa dimensione 110% = ingrandito del 10% 90% = ridotto del 10%	

Nel caso in cui alcune informazioni
manchino nelle didascalie, si
deduca che i dettagli sono sconosciuti.

Famiglie di disegni

I disegnatori tessili riconoscono quattro famiglie di disegni: Floreale, Geometrico, Figurativo ed Etnico. A queste dobbiamo aggiungerne una quinta: movimenti d'arte e stili. Queste famiglie costituiscono i capitoli di questo libro. L'ultima categoria non è in realtà una famiglia in quanto non ha motivi suoi esclusivi. Ad esempio un disegno con gigli "Arts and Crafts" appartiene anche alla categoria del floreale, mentre un trattore costruttivista rientrerebbe anche nel genere figurativo. Ma movimenti d'arte e stili sono generi talmente distanti e riconosciuti che abbiamo dedicato loro un capitolo.

Textile Designs suddivide le famiglie in categorie basate su uno o più dei seguenti criteri:

IL MOTIVO: è il fattore più importante in qualsiasi disegno e determina la famiglia alla quale il disegno appartiene. Le immagini di base possono essere una rosa, un quadrato, un pagliaccio, un Cachemere.

DISPOSIZIONE: descrive la combinazione del motivo, se abbia molto o poco fondo, se sia in ordine preciso o a casaccio o in fili che formano strisce.

COLORE: i disegni sono così classificati quando una particolare tintura, indaco, robbia o rosso, ne determina l'aspetto predominante.

TECNICHE DI STAMPA: ombré o stampa chiné, tra alcuni dei processi, riproducono un disegno e vi impongono un certo stile visuale.

TESSUTO: anche un tessuto su cui viene stampato il disegno determina l'aspetto dello stesso ed alcuni tessuti sono diventati sinonimo di alcuni generi. Ad esempio il Chintz è in realtà un tessuto, ma un disegnatore pensa al Chintz come ad un genere specifico di disegno.

Tecniche di stampa

Una chiave per tutte le abbreviazioni delle didascalie è stampata nella pagina dei contenuti

(BP) STAMPA AD IMPRESSIONE CON BLOCCHI. La forma più antica di stampa su tessuto ovvero la stampa ad impressione con blocchi, veniva usata in India nel quarto secolo dopo Cristo. Durante il Medio Evo divenne oggetto di commercio ben affermato in Europa. Venivano incisi diversi blocchi di legno per ogni colore presente nel disegno. La parte del blocco col disegno inciso in rilievo veniva premuta contro un setaccio di lana imbevuto di colore e poi applicato sul tessuto. Un vigoroso colpo con un martello di legno alla parte posteriore del blocco trasferiva il disegno. Dopo ogni colpo di martello, lo stampatore spostava il blocco sullo spazio successivo, ancora non stampato, del tessuto. Al giorno d'oggi la stampa ad impressione con blocchi è obsoleta ma ancora usata, in alcuni casi, per tessuti d'arredamento molto costosi o per foulard di seta, soprattutto in Inghilterra.

(CP) STAMPA CON LAMINA DI RAME. In Irlanda ed in Inghilterra la stampa con lamina di rame era prodotta su larga scala nel 1765 da Robert Jones, Francis Nixon e dalla ditta Bromley Hall. In Francia Christophe-Philippe Oberkampf fu forse il primo ad installare macchine per la stampa con lamine di rame (1770). Il disegno veniva inciso su una lamina di rame piatta che veniva poi ben strofinata con il colorante per stampa; questo poi veniva tolto dalla superficie e rimaneva solo dentro le linee incise. Il tessuto veniva posto sulla lamina ed una forte pressione esercitata da presse meccaniche serviva a trasferire il disegno sul tessuto. Le prime lamine di rame erano piuttosto grandi e permettevano quindi al disegnatore di lavorare con disegni di grande dimensione. La nuova tecnica diede vita ad un nuovo stile di stampa, la tela scenica, che rappresentava immagini finemente incise, disegnate da artisti.

(RP) STAMPA A CILINDRO. La prima attrezzatura meccanizzata da stampa a cilindri di metallo incisi fu brevettata nel 1783 da uno scozzese, Thomas Bell. Si trattava di una stampante a cilindro a sei colori. Eseguiva quotidianamente il lavoro di circa quaranta stampatori ad impressione con blocchi; nel 1797 una macchina francese nella ditta di Oberkampf a Jouy en Josas riusciva a stampare quasi cinquemila metri di tessuto al giorno. La stampante a cilindro fece della stampa tessile la prima industria completamente meccanizzata e la mise in prima linea durante la rivoluzione industriale, ma il metodo è più costoso rispetto alla stampa a quadro che l'ha largamente sostituita.

(PP) LA STAMPA PERROTINE. La macchina per stampa Perrotine, inventata nel 1834 da Louis-Jerôme Perrot di Rouen, meccanizzò tutto quanto riguardava la stampa ad impressione, tranne i blocchi che dovevano ancora venire incisi a mano. Un disegno eseguito con stampa Perrotine ha la precisione di un prodotto fatto a macchina, mentre l'incisione dei blocchi introduce l'aspetto artigianale.

(SP) STAMPA A QUADRO. La stampa commerciale a quadro manuale si affermó negli anni venti. Popolarissima in Francia, era una tecnica utile per realizzare quantitativi ridotti di tessuti di alta moda. La maggior parte della stampa a quadro usa adesso un processo fotografico per incidere il disegno sul quadro ed una stampante a rotazione che unisce la registrazione a velocità elevata della stampante a cilindro al colore pulito, brillante ed uniforme del quadro piatto. Per ogni colore occorre un quadro separato.

Familias de diseños

Los diseñadores de telas reconocen cuatro familias de diseños: florales, geométricos, temáticos y étnicos. A éstas, nosotros hemos agregado una quinta familia, movimientos artísticos y estilos de época. Estos constituyen los capítulos del libro. La última categoría no es realmente una familia porque carece de motivos que le sean propios. Un diseño "Artes y artesanías" como lirio es, por ejemplo, la versión de un diseño floral y un tractor "Constructivista" es un diseño temático. Pero los movimientos artísticos y los estilos de época proveen unos "efectos" o tipos tan distintivos y reconocibles que les hemos dado un capítulo especial.

Los diseños textiles dividen las familias en numerosas categorías basadas en uno o más de los siguientes criterios:

MOTIVO: es el factor mas importante de cada diseño y determina la familia a la cual pertenece. El motivo es la imagen básica: una rosa, un cuadrado, un payaso, un "paisley".

COMPOSICIÓN: describe el arreglo del motivo—ya sea que aparezca, con respecto al fondo, ampliamente separado o densamente cerrado; en nítido orden o aparentemente al azar, o en filas que formen franjas.

COLOR: los diseños se clasifican por el color cuando un teñido particular, ya sea índigo, alizarina (madder) o rojo turco, produce el efecto predominante.

TÉCNICAS DE ESTAMPADO: el sombreado (ombré) o la impresión de urdimbre, entre otros métodos, reproducen un diseño que impone un cierto estilo visual.

FABRICACIÓN: la tela afecta también al aspecto del diseño y algunas aparecen asociadas a ciertas clases de diseños. Por ejemplo, el chintz (o calicó lustroso) estrictamente hablando, es una tela, pero un diseñador al pensar en el chintz tiene en mente un modelo específico.

Las técnicas de estampado

Una aclaración de todas las abreviaturas aparece en el índice del libro.

(BP) IMPRESIÓN CON TACOS DE MADERA. Es la forma más antigua de estampado textil y era usada en la India en el siglo cuarto, d.C.. Hacia la Edad Media era ya un oficio bien establecido en Europa. Para cada color de un diseño se tallaban diferentes tacos de madera. La cara del taco, con el dibujo tallado en relieve, era presionado contra un cedazo de lana saturado de tintura y luego aplicado a la tela. Con un fuerte golpe de maza de madera en la parte de atrás del taco se transfería el diseño. Después de cada golpe de maza, el impresor movía el taco hacia el próximo espacio del paño sin teñir. Este sistema es hoy prácticamente obsoleto, pero todavía se usa en escala limitada, en costosas telas para amueblamiento del hogar o en bufandas de seda, particularmente en Inglaterra.

(CP) IMPRESIÓN CON PLANCHA DE COBRE. Hacia 1765, los textiles estampados con planchas de cobre eran producidos regularmente en Irlanda e Inglaterra por Francis Nixon, Robert Jones y la firma de Bromley Hall. En 1770, Christophe-Philippe Oberkampf fue probablemente el primero en instalar una prensa de plancha de cobre en Francia. El diseño era grabado en una plancha plana de cobre, la cual era entonces bien frotada con la tintura de imprimir. A continuación, se limpiaba la tintura de la superficie, permaneciendo solamente en las líneas incisas. El paño era colocado sobre la plancha y, por medio de la prensa mecánica, se aplicaba una extremada presión transfiriéndose así el diseño a la tela. Las primeras planchas de cobre eran bien grandes, permitiéndole al diseñador trabajar en modelos de gran escala. La nueva técnica dio origen a un nuevo estilo de imprimir, la tela "escénica", que representaba imágenes finamente grabadas por maestros artistas.

(RP) IMPRESIÓN A RODILLO. La primera máquina que empleó el estampado mecánico de tela con rodillos de metal grabados fue patentada en 1783 por un escocés, Thomas Bell. Un rodillo impresor de seis colores hacía el trabajo diario de unos cuarenta impresores de tacos manuales, y en 1797 una maquina francesa en la tejeduría Oberkampf en Jouy-en-Josas podía estampar mas de 5,000 yardas de tela por día. El impresor a rodillo hizo del estampado textil la primera industria completamente mecanizada y la puso al frente de la revolución industrial, pero el método era más costoso que la impresión de pantalla de seda o serigrafia que en gran medida la reemplazó.

(PP) IMPRESIÓN PERROTINE. La prensa perrotine, inventada en 1834 por Louis-Jérôme Perrot de Rouen, mecanizó todo lo referente a la impresión con tacos de madera con excepción de éstos, que aun tenían que ser tallados a mano. Un diseño estampado con la perrotine tiene la precisión de la manufactura a máquina, mientras que el tallado de los tacos introduce el aspecto de la artesanía manual.

(SP) IMPRESIÓN SERIGRÁFICA — PANTALLA DE SEDA. El estampado serigráfico a mano comenzó en los años 20. Era el más popular en Francia, donde se utilizaba para estampar breves tiradas de telas de alta costura. En la mayoría de las impresiones serigráficas se usa hoy el procedimiento fotográfico para "grabar" el diseño en la pantalla (fotograbado) y una impresora de pantalla rotativa que combina la continua alta velocidad de registro de la impresión a rodillo y el color limpio, brillante, sin estrujar de la pantalla sin presión. Cada color requiere una pantalla separada.

Índice

ABREVIATURAS

c.	(circa): circa
C.	(century): siglo
BP	(block-printed): impreso con bloques o tacos de madera
CP	(copperplate-printed): impreso con plancha de cobre
PP	(perrotine-printed): impreso a la perrotine
RP	(roller-printed): impreso a rodillo
SP	(screen-printed): impreso con pantalla de seda o serigrafia
A	(apparel): ropa
AYG	(apparel yard goods): tela por metro para ropa
YG	(yard goods): telas por metro
HF	(home furnishings): amueblamiento para el hogar
HFYG	(home-furnishing yard goods): telas por metro para amueblamiento

escala: los diseños están reproducidos a un porcentaje de su tamaño original. Por ejemplo: 100% = el mismo tamaño 110% = ampliado un 10% 90% = reducido un 10%

Cuando falte información en una leyenda el lector debe asumir que esos detalles se desconocen.

目次

略語一覧

c.	(circa)	～頃
C	(century)	世紀
BP	(block-printed)	木版捺染
CP	(copperplate-printed)	銅版捺染
PP	(perrotine-printed)	ペロチン捺染
RP	(roller-printed)	ロール捺染
SP	(screen-printed)	スクリーン捺染
A	(apparel)	衣類用
AYG	(apparel yard goods)	衣類用ヤール巾の布
YG	(yard goods)	ヤール巾の布
HF	(home furnishings)	室内装飾用
HFYG	(home furnishing yard goods)	室内装飾用ヤール巾の布

比率：図版は原寸に対して下記のサイズで複製
　されている．
　　100％＝実物大
　　110％＝10％拡大
　　　90％＝10％縮少

キャプションで触れていない情報については，
読者にとって専門的にすぎる内容に関して，
これを省略している．

模様の種類

テキスタイル・デザイナーが認める模様の種類は，花模様，幾何学模様，風物の模様，民族的な模様の4種類があります．これに，私たちは5番目を付け加えることにしました．芸術運動や時代様式などを反映した模様です．本書の各章は，それぞれ以上の5種類によって構成されています．最後の5番目の模様は，それ自身を特徴づけるモティーフを何ら持っていないということで，正確には模様の種類としてひとつの範疇にまとめてしまうのは難しいでしょう．例えば，19世紀イギリスのアーツ・アンド・クラフツ運動のユリの模様は花模様のひとつですし，構成主義者たちのトラクターも風物の模様だといえるでしょう．しかし，そうはいうものの，芸術運動や時代様式を反映した模様は他のものとは違う，はっきりとこれだと分かる「見かけ」を持っているため，われわれは独立した1章を設けることにしました．

本書では，模様の種類を以下の基準に従って，数多くのカテゴリーに分類しています．

モティーフ：モティーフはどのようなデザインについても最も大きな要素です．モティーフによってその模様がどのカテゴリーに属するかが決定されます．つまりモティーフは模様の基本的なイメージを決定するものなのです．例えば，バラ，四角形，道化師，ペイズリーなどがそうです．

レイアウト：レイアウトとはモティーフの配置のことです．例えば，生地の上に模様を広く散らすか，隙間なく並べるか，また均一にするか，見るからにバラバラにするか，あるいは縞模様となるように一列に並べるかなどのことです．

色地：ぱっと見てある特定の染料，例えば，藍色，あかね色，トルコ赤などが最も目立つ要素として考えられる場合，その布地は色地というふうに分類されます．

捺染技術：様々な捺染技術の中でも，とくに捺染ボカシまたは捺染経絣は，布地の上に視覚的にひとつの様式となるような模様を作り出します．

布地構成：布地自体が模様になっているものは，もちろんその布地の外観にも影響を及ぼすわけで，そういった布地のいくつかは，ある特定のデザインと結びついています．例えば，チンツ（Chintz）更紗がそうです．厳密にいえば，チンツは布地の名称ですが，その名を聞けばデザイナーはある特定の模様のことを思い浮かべます．

キャプション中で用いられる捺染技術についての解説

キャプション中で用いられている略語は目次に一覧表があります．

〔BP〕BLOCK PRINTING　木版捺染

最も古くからある布地用捺染技術である木版捺染は，4世紀，インドで生まれ，中世の終わりには，ヨーロッパで既に商売として確固たる地位を築いていました．まず模様の色に応じてそれぞれ版木を彫ります．次に染料をたっぷり含ませた羊毛で作ったかたまりに，浮彫の施された版木の表面を押しつけてから布地にあてがいます．

そして，版木を裏側から木槌で思いっきりたたいてやると布地に模様が転写されるというわけです．木槌をひとふりするたびに，版木をまだ染められていない部分へと移動させてやります．この木版捺染は今日ではもうほとんどが時代遅れとなって使われていませんが，イギリスでは，高価な室内装飾用の布地や絹のフラー布など限られた範囲でまだ用いられています．

〔CP〕COPPERPLATE PRINTING　銅版捺染

アイルランドとイギリスでは，銅版捺染を用いた布はロバート・ジョーンズ，フランシス・ニクソン，そしてブロームリー・ホール商会によって1765年までにはもうコンスタントに生産されるようになっていました．一方フランスでは，1770年に，クリストフェ＝フィリッペ・オベルカンフがおそらく初めて銅版捺染を使ったと考えられます．まず平らな銅板の上に模様を彫り，その上に染料をこすりつけます．次に表面の染料をこすりとってやれば，彫られた部分にだけ染料が残ることになります．その上に布地を広げ，機械を使って大きな圧力を加えると，布地に模様が転写されます．初めのころは銅板が非常に大きな物であったため，デザイナーはもっぱら広範囲にわたる模様を扱っていました．その後新しい技術のおかげで，有名な芸術家たちによって彫られた模様をそのまま使ったシーニック・トワール（風景や情景の単色のクレトン更紗）と呼ばれる新しいスタイルのプリント模様が生まれています．

〔RP〕ROLLER PRINTING　ロール捺染

模様の彫られた金属製のローラーを使った最初の布地捺染用の機械は，スコットランド人トマス・ベルが1783年に特許を取得しています．6色刷のロール捺染機は1日に手刷りの捺染機40台分の仕事をします．フランスのジュイ＝アン＝ジョサにあるオベルカンフの工場では，1797年に，1日5000ヤード以上の布地に刷ることが可能でした．ロール捺染機によって布地の捺染は，初めて完全に機械化された工場で行われるようになり，一躍，産業革命の先頭におどり出したのです．しかし現在では，費用の点でその大部分がスクリーン捺染に取って代わられています．

〔PP〕PERROTINE PRINTING　ペロチン捺染

1834年，フランスのルーアンで，ルイ＝ジェローム・ペローによって発明されたペロチン捺染は，手で彫る以外に方法がなかった版木を除いて，木版捺染の全ての過程を機械化したものです．したがってペロチン捺染で刷られた模様の特徴は，機械によって作られたものがもつ正確さを持っていると同時に，手彫りの版木による手作り風の見かけをも持っていることです．

〔SP〕SCREEN PRINTING　スクリーン捺染

人間の手を使った商業的なスクリーン捺染が始められたのは1920年代のことです．この捺染方法が最も人気が高かったのはフランスで，短いサイクルで移り変わるファッション用の布地にとって便利な方法でした．今日使用されているスクリーン捺染のほとんどは，写真的なプロセスによってスクリーンの上に模様を「彫る」ロータリー・スクリーン捺染機と呼ばれるものです．この機械は，連続的にしかも速く枚数をこなせるロール捺染機の特徴と，圧力をかけなくても印刷ができる平版なスクリーンによる，明るく透明感のあるむらのない色彩とを兼ね備えています．1色につき1枚のスクリーンを必要とします．

テキスタイル・デザイン——ヨーロッパとアメリカのパターン200年　　　　　　　　　　　　　1991年10月25日第1版第1刷発行

著者―――――――スーザン・メラー／ヨースト・エルファーズ
発行者――――――今田　達
発行所――――――株式会社同朋舎出版
　　　　　　本　　　社／〒600 京都市下京区中堂寺鍵田町2　電話 075-343-0680
　　　　　　東京支社／〒101 東京都千代田区神田駿河台2-11-1　電話 03-3292-2021
　　　　　　郵便振替／京都5-22982
印刷・製本―――――凸版印刷株式会社

©1991, Printed in Japan
ISBN4-8104-0957-0 C0072